保险科技

基本原理与案例精选
（双语版）

主 编◎胡 斌

西南财经大学出版社
中国·成都

图书在版编目(CIP)数据

保险科技基本原理与案例精选:汉文、英文/ 胡斌
主编;胡艳萍等副主编.--成都:西南财经大学
出版社,2024.10. --ISBN 978-7-5504-6441-4

Ⅰ. F840.3

中国国家版本馆 CIP 数据核字第 2024B08F47 号

保险科技基本原理与案例精选(双语版)

BAOXIAN KEJI JIBEN YUANLI YU ANLI JINGXUAN(SHUANGYU BAN)

主　编　胡　斌
副主编　胡艳萍　王　鹏　陈　宏　金　静
　　　　周小菲　张　卫　唐瑜穗　张小兰

责任编辑:廖术涵
责任校对:周晓琬
封面设计:墨创文化
责任印制:朱曼丽

出版发行	西南财经大学出版社(四川省成都市光华村街55号)
网　　址	http://cbs.swufe.edu.cn
电子邮件	bookcj@swufe.edu.cn
邮政编码	610074
电　　话	028-87353785
照　　排	四川胜翔数码印务设计有限公司
印　　刷	郫县犀浦印刷厂
成品尺寸	185 mm×260 mm
印　　张	13.625
字　　数	389 千字
版　　次	2024 年 10 月第 1 版
印　　次	2024 年 10 月第 1 次印刷
书　　号	ISBN 978-7-5504-6441-4
定　　价	46.00 元

编委会

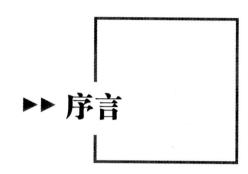

▶▶ 序言

　　保险科技是保险业主动拥抱新质生产力的智慧结晶，是金融科技的重要组成部分，正深刻地改变着世界保险业的发展方向。《保险科技基本原理与案例精选（双语版）》以习近平新时代中国特色社会主义思想为指导，以保险业与各种新质生产力的相互融合为主线，以中英文双语为文字载体，系统地介绍和讲述了保险科技的理论体系和应用场景，精选了一系列国内外最新案例呈现在读者面前，并契合每章主题系统嵌入了课程思政案例。

　　本教材共分为九章，每章由中文理论部分、中文国内案例、课程思政案例、英文理论部分、英文国外案例等几个部分构成，旨在系统介绍保险科技理论和相关国内外最新案例，进而激发学生开发保险科技应用场景和相关产品的兴趣。较之已有同类教材，本教材进一步归纳整理了保险科技的理论体系，全面更新了相关国内外案例，系统融入了课程思政元素，并为相关课程的中英文双语教学创造了条件。

　　本教材各章内容如下：第一章绪论，介绍保险科技的起源、现状、未来和保险科技公司以及相关案例；第二章大数据与保险业，介绍大数据与保险业相互结合的基本理论以及相关案例；第三章人工智能与保险业，介绍人工智能与保险业相互结合的基本理论以及相关案例；第四章云计算与保险业，介绍云计算与保险业相互结合的基本理论以及相关案例；第五章区块链与保险业，介绍区块链与保险业相互结合的基理论以及相关案例；第六章机器人与保险业，介绍机器人与保险业相互结合的基本理论以及相关案例；第七章生物科技与保险业，介绍生物科技与保险业相互结合的基本理论以及相关案例；第八章物联网与保险业，介绍物联网与保险业相互结合的基本理论以及相关案例；第九章保险科技监管，介绍保险科技监管基本理论以及相关案例。

　　本教材系西南民族大学四川省高等学校"双一流"建设贡嘎计划建设学科"应用经济学"、西南民族大学省级一流本科专业建设点"金融学"、西南民族大学2023年度人才培养综合改革项目"金融科技维舟微专业建设"的成果之一，是西南民族大学相关教师的集体智慧结晶。有关教材编写和出版的立项申请、框架设计、内容布局、章节提纲、思政主题、编写计划、组织协调和出版事宜等工作由经济学院胡斌老师完成；第一章的初稿编纂由经济学院胡斌老师完成；第二章的初稿编纂由经济学院陈宏老师完成；第三章的初稿编纂由经济学院陈宏老师完成；第四章的初稿编纂由经济学院王鹏老师完成；第五章的初稿编纂由经济学院张卫老师完成；第六章的初稿编纂由经济学院张卫老师完成；第七章的初稿编纂由经济学院周小菲老师完成；第八章的初稿编纂由经济学院唐瑜穗老师完成；第九章的初稿编纂由经济学院周小菲老师完成；本教材中文理论部分的初审由经济学院陈宏老师完成；本教材中文案例部分的初审由经济学院王鹏老师完成；本教材课程思政部分的初审由经济学院张小兰老师完成；本教材每章中文部分的复审和深度修改由经济学院胡斌老师完成；本教材英文部分的润笔、初审、修改、复审和再完善由外国语言文学学院胡艳萍老师、金静老师和经济学院胡斌老师完成；本教材整体格式的调整规范由经济学院张卫老师完成；本教材出版前的终审和校稿由经济学院胡斌老师、外国语言文学学院胡艳萍老师和经济学院张小兰老师完成。

同时，西南民族大学经济学院 2023 届保险学专业研究生林柏涛、崔志权、李心悦、缪克威、孟莉慧、席敏杰、薛诚信、王思恒、刘心如等同学参与了与本教材编写相关的素材查找、收集整理、校稿核对和资料传递等各种繁杂工作。

本教材全面贯彻"三全育人"的要求，有利于系统构建保险科技理论体系，有利于启发学生理清开发保险科技产品的思路，有利于引导学生形成正确的价值观。本教材不仅适用于金融保险类专业学生，而且适用于对保险科技有兴趣的理工科专业学生，还可作为保险科技界人士的参考用书。

本教材的编写及顺利出版受到西南民族大学相关职能部门、经济学院、外国语言文学学院的大力支持，得益于对有关保险科技的书籍、文献和新闻等资料的参考，得益于中国人寿保险股份有限公司成都市分公司教学实践基地李颖等基地导师对相关课程案例提出的宝贵意见，同时也离不开西南财经大学出版社相关工作人员的辛勤劳动，在此一并表示感谢！

诚然，由于编纂时间较紧以及相关知识的不断更新，该教材难免有疏漏之处，敬请广大读者批评指正！

胡 斌

2024 年 8 月 16 日

▶▶ 目录

25 / 2　大数据与保险业

35 / 2　Big Data and Insurance

目录

154/ 8　物联网与保险业

166/ 8　Internet of Things and Insurance

1

绪论

2021年,《中华人民共和国国民经济和社会发展第十四个五年规划和2035年远景目标纲要》(以下简称"十四五"规划)提出,要加快建设数字中国,并推动数字经济发展。这一战略方向的明确,保险科技行业随之兴起。

众所周知,保险是人类社会应对各种风险有效的管理方式。在科学技术飞速发展的新时代,保险业与现代科技力量融合越来越紧密,这正深刻地改变着传统保险业态,也给保险从业人员、科技从业人员带来了机遇和挑战。本章从保险科技的起源讲起,重点介绍了保险科技的现状、未来以及保险科技公司的发展,并为读者呈现了国内外的相关案例(包括1个课程思政案例),以期让读者能迅速地了解保险科技的概况,为后续章节的学习奠定基础。

1.1 保险科技的起源

随着人类科学技术的不断进步和人们对保险需求的不断变化,保险科技行业随之兴起。

1.1.1 传统保险业面临的困局

不论是在应对灾害事故、保障个人财产生命安全,还是维护社会稳定、促进经济发展等方面,保险都发挥着不可替代的作用。但保险业长期面临着较难突破的困局,阻碍着它的可持续发展。

1.1.1.1 信息不对称

信息不对称是指在参与经济交易的双方中,一方比另一方拥有更多或更准确的信息的情况。信息不对称会给保险业发展带来两大难题,一是逆向选择,二是道德风险。

一方面,在保险业中,信息不对称体现为保险人对保险标的所面临的风险状况不够了解。由于无法准确分辨被保险人的风险状况,加之被保险人可能为了降低保费支出而刻意隐瞒自身风险状况,保险人可能在风险定价方面出现偏差,无法客观、公正地确定保险费率,进而发生逆向选择。

另一方面，在保险业中，信息不对称还体现为投保人对保险产品及保险条款不够了解。相对于保险公司，投保人通常对保险产品仅有直观、肤浅和片面的了解，在购买保险产品的过程中，投保人往往处于信息劣势。同时，作为连接保险公司和客户的保险代理人可能会为了业绩做出主观隐瞒或欺骗客户的行为，这又会加剧交易双方的信息不对称。

此外，信息不对称也体现在保险理赔和保险监管过程中。有的险种因保险标的具有季节性或受损后标的易灭失等特点，不仅导致保险公司难以核实理赔资料的真实性，也加大了监管部门查实违规问题的难度。

1.1.1.2 运营成本高

保险业相较于其他行业，具有中介代理成本高昂的特征，根据原中国银保监会提供的数据，2019 年我国保险业保费收入为 4.3 万亿元，其中通过中介渠道实现收入 3.74 万亿元，占总保费的 86.98%。由此可见，保险中介仍然是保险销售的绝对渠道，保险公司每年都会为此付出高昂的代理佣金。高昂的代理佣金必然会抬高保险价格，降低人们对保险产品的需求，从而制约保险业的发展。

同时，算力建设、数据存储、客户管理、定损理赔、法律诉讼、争端解决、防范欺诈均需要耗费大量的人力、物力和财力。此外，由于保险业相关数据信息不能共享，保险公司在获取相关数据信息时也要付出额外的成本。

总之，高额的成本不仅会直接影响到保险公司的偿付能力，而且将降低保险公司的资产规模，减少保险公司在其他领域的投资。

1.1.1.3 运营效率不高

保险运营效率不高的问题主要发生在核保和理赔环节。以健康险核保为例，保险公司首先会了解客户的投保目的和动机、生活习惯、既往病史、家族病史、职业、工作环境、财务状况等基本信息，并进行初步审核。在初步审核无法做出核保判断的情况下，核保人员会进一步收集资料，如索要既往病症病历、近期体检结果、门诊病历记录、医保卡记录等，并根据资料开展调查。最终根据客户的实际情况以及保险合同的承保要求给出核保结论。在整个核保过程中大量重复、烦琐的审查工作主要依赖人力，会耗费大量资源。而在理赔环节，从客户报案到最后赔付需要经历漫长的理赔流程，其花费的时间少则几周，多则数月。如果保险公司与投保人之间因理赔条件、免责条款等发生分歧，可能还会有更多周折。如此耗时漫长、程序烦琐的理赔无疑会在一定程度上降低客户的体验感。

1.1.1.4 保险营销不精准

随着消费者保险意识的不断增强，广大消费者对保险产品及服务的需求也在不断增加，保险客户的信息也在变得越来越多、越来越繁杂琐碎。保险人和保险代理人在面对如此环境时，如何精准地对客户群体分门别类，如何通过适当的渠道从海量保险产品中将最合适的保险产品推荐给最需要它们的客户群体，从而在满足客户个性化需求的同时提升自己的业绩、实现自身和投保者的双赢也成为一大难题。

1.1.1.5 保险产品创新难

目前市场上存在的保险产品，同质化现象较为严重，各家保险公司推出的保险产品在保障范围、理赔条件、保费价格甚至在保险的营销渠道和方式等方面都几乎没有区别。同质化的产品使得多数保险公司缺乏核心竞争力，缺乏创新和差异化，不仅导致产品缺乏吸引力，而且难以满足客户多元化和个性化的保险需求。从市场营销学的角度来看，导致产品开发同质化的主要原因在于保险公司的产品设计研发与市场需求脱节。根据波特五力模型，企业要想在激烈的市场竞争中获得竞争优势，提供差异化的产品和服务是重要手段，而保险产品创新难这个问题，无疑制约了保险业的发展。

1.1.1.6　定价不准确

传统的保险定价方法通常是基于对整体人群风险的综合评估，计算出平均发生率和平均费用，以此来确定理赔成本。然而，这种方法往往忽视了个体风险的差异性，可能导致风险更高的个体只需支付平均费率就能获得保障，进而引发逆向选择问题。同时，基于过去对群体风险的度量，对于新投保个体的风险估计可能存在误差。

目前，保险行业积累了大量数据。保险数据具有复杂、多样和关联等特点，这些因素增加了数据处理的复杂性。随着数据量的迅速增长，数据的变化也提高了其对技术的要求。因此，传统的数据处理方法已经难以满足需求，传统的保险定价方法也显得相对复杂且缺乏效率。

1.1.1.7　防范保险欺诈较难

保险欺诈是指投保人或被保险人故意提供虚假信息或采取欺骗手段，以获取不应得到的保险赔偿或权益的行为。这种行为往往会对保险公司造成经济损失，同时也会影响整个保险市场的稳定和健康发展。传统的保险欺诈检测方法主要依靠人工审核和规则引擎，很难应对复杂多变的欺诈手段。由于缺乏先进的数据分析技术和人工智能技术，保险公司难以及时发现和防范欺诈行为。

1.1.1.8　面临的其他问题

除上述问题之外，传统的保险业还面临着诸如客户信息的泄露问题、保险公司盈利难、代理人流失率高、交易频率低、客户关系薄弱等诸多问题。

1.1.2　新质生产力与保险业

2023年9月，习近平总书记在黑龙江考察调研时首提"新质生产力"。2024年1月31日，习近平总书记在主持中共中央政治局第十一次集体学习时，对"新质生产力"进一步做了系统论述。习近平总书记强调："高质量发展需要新的生产力理论来指导，而新质生产力已经在实践中形成并展示出对高质量发展的强劲推动力、支撑力，需要我们从理论上进行总结、概括，用以指导新的发展实践。"新质生产力是推动我国经济高质量发展的重要动力。

法国经济学家萨伊认为经济增长的最终动力来源是三种基本生产要素，即劳动、土地、资本。而与之相对的，以创新为主导、摆脱传统经济增长方式、生产力发展路径，具有高科技、高效能、高质量特征、符合新发展理念的先进生产力质态被称为新质生产力。新质生产力的特点是创新、关键在质优、本质是先进生产力。它依靠科学技术、数据等新生产要素结合劳动、土地、资本等传统生产要素来推动经济增长。

在迈向社会主义现代化强国的道路上，保险作为"风险压舱石"与"社会稳定器"，责任重大。新质生产力能够助力传统保险业解决发展过程中面临的痛点和困境。一方面，新质生产力在保险业中的应用不仅可以提升保险行业的生产效率和服务质量，还可以促进保险市场的发展和创新，解决传统保险行业发展中的痛点问题，进而推动整个保险业的升级和转型。另一方面，保险业也能促进新质生产力的发展。科技企业在研发、生产和销售过程中面临多种风险，包括知识产权侵权、产品责任、网络安全和数据泄露等。保险公司可以为科技企业提供专门的科技保险，帮助科技企业有效管理这些风险，保障科技企业的可持续发展。另外，科技人员在工作中可能面临意外伤害、疾病等人身风险。保险公司可为技术人员提供意外伤害保险、重大疾病保险、医疗保险等，为他们和其家人提供全面的保障。这些保险产品不仅有助于科技企业吸引和留住优秀的科技人才，提升企业的竞争力和吸引力，还能帮助企业应对复杂的风险挑战，确保业务的稳健发展。

综上所述，新质生产力是助力保险业全面转型升级的必由之路；同时，保险业又能为新质生产力的发展提供全方位的保障服务。二者是相互关联、相互促进的关系。

1.1.3 保险科技的诞生

保险科技的起源可以追溯到 20 世纪 90 年代，随着互联网技术以及移动通信的发展，互联网保险逐步兴起，互联网的普及和数字化技术的发展为保险行业带来了新的机遇和挑战。学术界和业界普遍认为互联网保险是保险科技的起源。我国的保险科技起步略晚。直到 1997 年，随着国内某大型保险公司引进美国的 CBPS 寿险综合业务系统，我国保险业才初步实现了信息化和电子化。同年，中国保险学会和北京某股份有限公司共同成立的中国保险信息网，成为中国第一家保险网站，拉开了国内保险科技的序幕。该网站的成立为后续的数据分析和客户资源整合奠定了基础。

当前，全球范围内保险科技的发展势头令人振奋。CB Insight 数据显示，2011 年全球仅有 28 项保险科技投资，总额仅为 1.4 亿美元；到了 2012 年，保险科技投资数量增至 46 项，总额达 3.5 亿美元；2013 年共有 63 项保险科技投资，总额为 2.7 亿美元；2014 年有 28 项保险科技投资，总额飙升至 8.7 亿美元；而到了 2015 年，共有 122 项投资，总额高达 26.7 亿美元。在不同保险市场中，超过 60% 的美国保险科技投资集中在 A 轮阶段，投资规模逐年增长；相比之下，德国市场和美国不同，保险科技投资已进入中期阶段，即 B 轮阶段。2012—2016 年，德国保险科技融资总额达到 5 352 万欧元，目前已有不少于 5 家公司获得 B 轮融资。英国作为传统保险大国，2016 年欧洲地区最大规模的保险科技投资就发生在英国，超过了 1 500 万英镑。

尽管我国保险科技起步较晚，但发展却非常迅速。到了 2000 年，国内某寿险公司开通的"在线"网站，将我国保险业的发展推向了"互联网+保险"阶段，这可以视为保险科技的一种早期业态。"互联网+保险"主要通过互联网实现保险业务的线上操作，如销售、投保、核保等，旨在为客户提供更加及时和便利的服务。在此基础上，保险业与其他新兴科技进一步融合，通过科技创新赋能整个保险产业链，促进保险产业链的重塑和升级，引导"互联网+保险"从简单的规模扩张转向追求更高质量的发展。

1.2 保险科技的发展趋势

当今社会，在新质生产力的驱动下，保险业的革命已经拉开帷幕，无数新兴科技力量正在全面赋能新时代的保险行业。

1.2.1 保险科技的概念

保险是金融的一个细分领域，保险科技（InsurTech）自然也是金融科技（FinTech）的一个重要分支。保险科技既继承了金融科技的一些特性，也具有其自身的特点。

根据金融稳定理事会（Financial Stability Board）对金融科技的定义"通过技术创新引入的新的业务模式、应用、流程或产品，这些创新能够对金融市场、金融机构和提供金融服务的方式产生深远影响"，保险科技应是"科技+保险"的体现。

1.2.1.1 国际保险监督官协会（International Association of Insurance Supervisors，简称 IAIS）

保险科技是金融科技在保险领域的分支，是有潜力改变保险业务的各类新兴科技和创新商业模式的总和。

1.2.1.2 其他学者对保险科技的概述

完颜瑞云认为，目前社会各界对保险科技并无统一规范定义，但比较一致的是，都高度强调新兴科技在保险领域的运用和对整个保险业的影响。

1.2.1.3 改编自京东金融关于金融科技的定义

保险科技遵循保险本质，以数据为基础，以技术为手段，为保险行业服务，从而降低保险行业成本、提升行业效率。

综上所述，保险科技指的是通过将新质生产力包含的各种创新科技（如大数据、云计算、物联网、人工智能、区块链、机器人、生物技术等）与保险业深度融合创造出保险新模式、保险新应用和保险新产品的总和，即保险科技是新质生产力与保险业深度融合的产物。

1.2.2 保险科技在我国的发展现状

为了推动科技在金融领域，特别是在保险领域的发展，中央政府出台了一系列政策，这些政策在宏观层面上为我国保险科技的发展开辟了新的路径。2022 年 1 月，中国银保监会（现国家金融监督管理总局）发布了《关于银行业保险业数字化转型的指导意见》。这一指导意见涵盖了从鼓励保险服务全流程线上化到加快数字化、线上化、智能化转型的推进，设定到 2025 年银行保险业数字化转型取得明显成效的目标，为保险业的科技进步奠定了坚实基础。

在上述政策背景下，我国不断有保险公司尝试保险科技。2013 年，中国首家互联网保险公司——众安在线财产保险股份有限公司成立，标志着保险业务全面向互联网转型。该保险公司从成立之初就采纳了"保险+科技"的战略，致力于利用科技重塑保险全价值链。该保险公司在核心的核保环节引入了智能核保技术，推出了针对慢性病人群的个性化保障产品，为此前难以获得保障的用户群提供了解决方案。此外，该保险公司的健康险理赔流程的线上化率达到了96%，每9秒就能完成一个理赔结案，95%的案件实现了直通式理赔。

近年来，国内某大型保险公司及其他主要保险公司也通过数字化转型，基本实现了财产险销售端的线上化运营。客户从承保需求，到定价，再到销售出单，以及后续的各种增值服务和核心理赔服务，都能直接在线上一站式完成全部流程。同时，国内许多领先的保险公司的呼叫中心正在采用 RPA 机器人和人工智能技术替代传统的人工服务，显著提升了业务展开效率和降低了运营成本。此外，某些先进的保险公司已经完成从承保、保全服务、理赔到增值服务整个流程的数字化重构。围绕客户旅程为核心，一些保险公司已经实现数字化变革的全过程，标志着保险服务的质量和效率得到了显著提升。

国内某保险集团的副总裁表示，目前许多公司90%以上业务已经实现离柜化。国内某保险集团通过应用 ChatGPT 等技术，在服务、管理、销售三个方面实现了服务效率的显著提升，大幅度地替代了传统人工操作。同时，公司还与社会大数据平台合作，采用风险因子标注的方法，为每位客户实现了"一人一价"的个性化定价策略。在车险理赔领域，该保险集团通过结合数据分析和挖掘模型，以及引入图片自动定损和小额人伤自动定损技术，能够在几秒钟内处理小额的车辆损失案件。

与此同时，国内资本市场对保险科技的发展前景极为看好，每年都有大量资本流入保险科技领域，为其技术研发提供资金支持。2012—2019 年，国内对该领域的融资笔数已达 310 笔，总融资金额已超过 120 亿元，如图 1.1 所示。

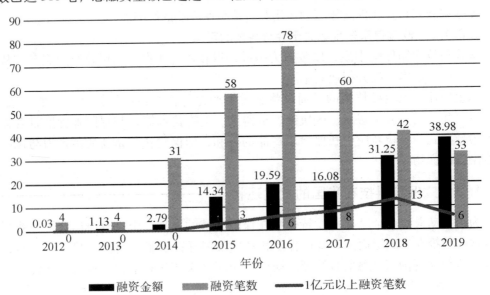

图 1.1　2012—2019 年中国保险科技投融资笔数及金额

数据来源：北京金融科技研究院发布的《2020 中国保险科技洞察报告》。

从 2015 年开始，我国保险科技市场的规模呈现出逐年递增的趋势。到 2020 年，我国保险科技的市场规模已超过 900 亿元，而且这几年的平均涨幅超过了 10%，如图 1.2 所示。目前，我国在保险科技融资领域已经成为仅次于欧美的热点地区，国内保险科技的发展稳定向好。

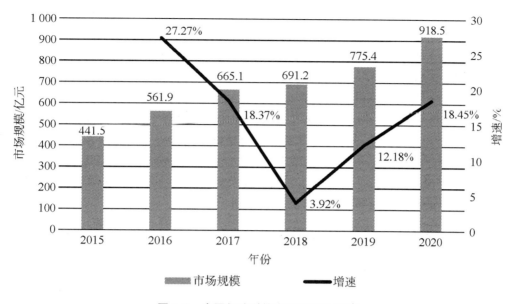

图 1.2　中国保险科技市场规模及增速

数据来源：徐忠镜. 保险科技行业分析报告［D］. 长沙：中南林业大学，2022.

1.2.3　保险科技的未来

基于前述介绍，保险科技的前景不言而喻。保险科技不仅将全面提升客户的保险体验，开拓更加广阔的保险市场，孕育更加精准的风险管理方式，也会引领保险监管的变革。

首先，保险科技将为保险业的发展带来协同效应，为保险公司带来巨大的业务增长，发挥出"1+1>2"的效应。例如，将传统车险与车联网技术结合，不仅可以进一步发展 UBI 车险，还可以全面提升客户的保险体验感。

其次，保险科技将理赔服务前移，不仅提高了保险公司与投保人之间的黏度，还能帮助投保人更好地进行事故预防，从而减少事故发生的概率及相应的损失和赔付，孕育出更加精准的风险管理方式。

最后，保险科技的发展还会催生监管科技和监管方式的升级换代，引领保险监管模式的全面变革。

相信未来，在科技创新的加持下，保险将不只是一种金融保障产品，而是一个能够帮助人们应对灾难和风险的新生态系统。

1.3　保险科技公司

随着科学技术的快速发展和保险需求的不断变化，基于大数据、人工智能、生物技术等新质生产力推出的保险产品和保险服务逐渐出现，保险科技公司应运而生。

1.3.1　保险科技公司的分类

当前，学术界和业界对保险科技公司尚无统一定义。参照本书对保险科技的定义，保险科技公司是指以新质生产力与保险业相互融合为业务基础，以各种保险产品创新和保险服务为主营业务实现利润最大化的公司。根据保险科技的发展深度不同，可将保险科技公司大致分为三类：专业保险科技公司、设立了保险科技部门的传统保险公司、涉足保险的科技公司。

（1）专业保险科技公司是指创立时间较短，由年轻的创业者组建的专门致力于保险科技领域的创业公司。该类公司专注于推动保险行业的数字化转型和创新发展。

（2）设立了保险科技部门的传统保险公司是指专门设立了从事科技研发和创新部门的传统保险公司，并且这些部门正在致力于推动本公司的数字化转型和技术升级。

（3）涉足保险的科技公司一方面指通过技术优势和海量数据开展保险业务的公司，另一方面指为保险行业提供专业服务的科技公司。

1.3.2　保险科技公司的运作模式

保险科技公司的运作模式十分多元化，大致能分为2A、2B、2C三类模式。

1.3.2.1　2A 模式

2A 模式主要体现为代理人平台形式，为保险代理人提供保险产品销售平台等服务，满足代理人远程设计保险产品规划和引导客户在线投保的业务需求，同时运用互联网技术手段提升代理人工作效率。当前2A 模式主要靠佣金收入支持。

1.3.2.2　2B 模式

2B 模式主要是保险 IT 公司、健康险服务商等保险科技公司，通过运用科技基础设施拓宽渠道、优化销售流程、降低理赔成本、提升客户端和中后台的运营效率，并利用技术进行一定的产品、服务创新，具体有车险风控、健康险风控、车险理赔等业务。具体来说，2B 模式参与者的来源更广，包括了保险公司、企业投保客户、保险中介机构、药厂、药店、医院、汽车生产企业等。

1.3.2.3　2C 模式

2C 模式下的保险产品直接面向个人客户，主要形式为在线保险市场、比价平台、KOL 代理人和互助平台，在线保险市场可以面对个人客户、保险代理人或经纪人、保险产品供应商。此类平台通常对个人客户是免费的，通过平台达成的保费合同，其所缴保费会以一定比例和平台分成，或者保险中介需要向平台支付一定比例的佣金或服务费用。该模式适用于在线保险市场的保险产品，产品针对特定场景或人群设计。

1.3.3　保险科技公司发展需要的营商环境

一个良好的营商环境可以为保险科技行业提供更多支持和有序的发展机会，并为行业吸引更多的投资和人才，提升行业的整体竞争力和可持续发展能力。相对于成熟行业，处于起步阶段的保险科技行业将面临更多的不确定性和更加激烈的竞争，需要社会为其可持续发展营造一个良好的营商环境，这至少涉及如下三个方面：

1.3.3.1　有利的政策环境

政策环境对于保险科技公司至关重要。政府在保险科技监管、税收和保险市场开放等方面的政策举措，都会对保险科技公司的发展产生深远影响。当前，各级政府高度重视优化营商环境，提出了新质生产力赋能保险业助力保险改革的政策方针，鼓励保险市场不断创新，为保险科技公司提供了多重支持政策。

1.3.3.2 完善的法律体系

保险科技涉及客户的数据应用及隐私保护等法律问题。健全的法律体系是保险科技可持续发展的前提条件，可以维护保险科技公司和客户的权益，保护投保双方的利益，为保险公司提供稳定的运营保障。当前，我国相关法律体系高度重视保险科技公司的监管和合规问题，但是相关法律条款亟待进一步完善。

1.3.3.3 有序的市场规则

保险市场是保险科技发展的主要场所。竞争有序的市场环境是保险科技公司可持续发展的前提。当前，保险科技市场尚处起步阶段，配套的相关市场规则和行业准则尚待建立健全，市场秩序急需进一步规范。

1.4 保险科技国内案例

案例题目：

保险科技引领传统保险产品转型：来自多家保险公司的成功实践

案例内容：

随着科技的迅速发展，YG 保险公司已研发出智能客服机器人，全面升级了客户的体验感，推动了传统保险行业数智化转型。智能客服机器人能够敏锐捕捉并精准响应客户的需求，实现高度拟人化的人机对话互动，在报案、咨询、批改、保全、客户回访等保险客服领域实现智能处理，咨询与办理场景智能化覆盖率实现 100%。尤其是通过智能技术对车险报案流程进行大胆变革，极大地简化了流程，降低了客户报案的复杂度，减少了报案花费的时间，提升了客户的体验感。

与此同时，随着 2022 年年末以 ChatGPT 为代表的生成式 AI 问世，国内保险企业也在积极布局生成式 AI 技术。2023 年，HN 保险公司完成大模型团队组建，积极探索和实践大模型在公司业务运营和经营管理等领域的落地，赋能审计合规、员工培训、智能运维等多个场景，并传承合作共建理念，推动建设保险大模型生态。

此外，ZY 人寿保险公司不断加速数字化布局，围绕数据资产聚焦服务场景，形成多方面产品矩阵，赢得了客户的广泛信赖，实现了以科技助力业务的发展模式。在数字化转型浪潮的驱动下，ZY 人寿保险公司自主研发了针对客户的 App、针对内部协调办公的 App 以及针对营销的 App，这三大 App 大大提升了客户体验感和办公效率，实现了公司内外运营的智能化及电子化。

案例评述：

这三家保险公司在新兴科学技术的引领下，不断推动保险行业的数字化转型和智能化升级。YG 保险公司通过智能客服机器人实现了客户需求的敏锐捕捉和高度个性化的服务，极大提升了客户体验，为保险行业的智能化发展树立了榜样。HN 保险公司不断推出多款在线化、数字化、智能化创新产品，并将 AI 技术与传统保险结合，为保险业务运营带来了全新的可能性。ZY 人寿保险公司在数字化布局方面也取得了突破，通过自主研发的多款 App 提升了客户的体验感和内部协调效率，形成了科技助力保险业务发展的成功范例。这些案例充分展现了保险科技产品在推动保险行业创新和发展方面的巨大潜力，为保险行业的未来发展指明了方向。

案例来源：

新华报业网.阳光保险：以新质生产力点亮保险业新升级.［EB/OL］.（2024-03-21）［2024-07-01］.https://www.xhby.net/content/s65fbc551e4b09dde337fd548.html.

1.5 课程思政案例

案例题目：

新质生产力赋能中国保险企业重塑核心竞争力

案例内容：

2024年1月31日，在中共中央政治局第十一次集体学习中，习近平总书记指出："新质生产力是创新起主导作用，摆脱传统经济增长方式、生产力发展路径，具有高科技、高效能、高质量特征，符合新发展理念的先进生产力质态。"

保险科技是新质生产力助力保险业转型升级的典型代表。

作为国有大型金融机构，ZG人寿保险公司充分发挥业务的功能作用和综合金融的优势，全力以科技来赋能推进保险企业升级、重塑保险企业竞争力、实现保险企业高质量发展。ZG人寿把环境、社会、治理要求全面嵌入公司经营管理流程和全面风险管理体系，将支持绿色金融列为战略资产配置的重点投资领域，并通过一系列举措，持续加大在节能环保、清洁能源、生态环境、基础设施绿色升级等领域的布局，并依托数据和技术优势加速构建数字金融生态，ZG人寿保险公司推出了一系列更加个性化、定制化的产品，提升了服务的普惠性。例如，在助力提升"三农"领域风险保障方面，推出面向农民群体的小额人身意外伤害保险、农业保险等产品。

同时，ZG人寿保险公司还积极促进数字技术和保险理赔服务深度融合，不断探索"互联网+保险"服务新模式。目前ZG人寿保险公司已通过与医保、第三方数据公司等单位的系统对接，实现医疗信息线上流转、全流程智能化作业、快速理算并支付。

此外，PA集团也充分利用平安人脸识别、云计算、大数据等创新科技手段，主打"智慧、便捷"，用"科技创新"和"服务速度"为用户提供智能化服务和极致化体验。未来，PA集团将会走向更加"智能化"和"平台化"的道路，并逐步构建社会化生态体系，最终实现真正意义上的"智慧财务"以及智能时代的财务腾跃。

案例评述：

随着科学技术的进步和保险需求的不断升级，保险业未来的高质量发展离不开新质生产力的推动。鉴于此，ZG人寿保险公司、PA集团等大型保险企业主动拥抱新质生产力，重塑保险企业核心竞争力，变革自身发展模式，创新保险产品体系，为社会发展提供更加精准而周到的保险服务，为广大保险企业高质量发展树立了榜样。

案例来源：

中国商务新闻网.中国人寿全力服务新质生产力发展.［EB/OL］.（2024-03-08）［2024-07-01］.https://www.comnews.cn/content/2024-03-08/content_38190.html.

1

Introduction

In 2021, the CPC Central Committee proposed to accelerate the construction of digital China and promote the development of the digital economy in the Outline of the 14th Five-Year Plan and the 2035 Vision Goals. With the clarity of this strategic direction, the InsurTech industry has emerged.

As we all know, insurance is an effective management method for human society to deal with various risks. With the rapid development of science and technology, the integration of insurance industry and modern scientific and technological forces are getting closer and closer, which is profoundly changing the traditional insurance industry, bringing opportunities as well as challenges to insurance practitioners and scientific and technological practitioners. This chapter starts from the origin of InsurTech, focuses on the current situation and future of InsurTech and the development of InsurTech companies, and presents readers with relevant cases at home and abroad (including a case for course ideological and political), so as to let readers quickly understand the general situation of InsurTech and lay the foundation for the study of the following chapters.

1. 1　The Origin of InsurTech

With the continuous progress of human science and technology and the constant change of people's demand for insurance, the insurance technology industry has emerged.

1. 1. 1　The Dilemma Faced by the Traditional Insurance Industry ├──

Insurance plays an irreplaceable role in dealing with disasters and accidents, protecting personal property and life safety, maintaining social stability and promoting economic development. However, the insurance industry has long faced the following insurmountable difficulties, which hinder its sustainable development.

1. 1. 1. 1　Information Asymmetry

Information asymmetry is a situation in which one of the two parties involved in an economic transaction has more accurate information than the other. Information asymmetry will bring two major problems to the development of insurance industry, one being adverse selection and the other, moral hazard.

On the one hand, in the insurance industry, information asymmetry is reflected in the insurer's lack of understanding of the risks the subject matter of insurance. Due to the inability to accurately distinguish the risk status of the insured, who may deliberately conceal its own risk status in order to reduce premium expenditure, the insurer may have a deviation in risk pricing, and cannot determine the insurance rate objectively and fairly, and then adverse selection will occur.

On the other hand, in the insurance industry, information asymmetry is also reflected in the lack of understanding of insurance products and insurance clauses. Compared with insurance companies, the insurance applicant usually has only an intuitive, superficial and one-sided understanding of the insurance products, and is often at an information disadvantage in the process of buying insurance products. At the same time, as an insurance agent connecting the insurance company and the customer, they may make subjective concealment or cheat the customer for the sake of performance, which will aggravate the information asymmetry between the two sides of the transaction.

In addition, information asymmetry is also reflected in the process of insurance claims and insurance supervision. Some types of insurance, due to the characteristics of the subject matter of insurance being seasonal or easy to lose after damage, not only lead to insurance companies difficult to verify the authenticity of claims, but also increase the difficulty of regulatory authorities to verify violations.

1. 1. 1. 2　High Operating Costs

Compared with other industries, the insurance industry has the characteristics of high intermediary agent costs. According to the data provided by the former China Banking and Insurance Regulatory Commission, the premium income of China's insurance industry in 2019 was 4. 3 trillion yuan, of which 3. 74 trillion yuan was achieved through intermediary channels, accounting for 86. 98% of the total premium. It can be seen that insurance intermediary is still the absolute channel of insurance sales, and insurance companies will pay high agency costs every year. High commission will inevitably increase the price of insurance, reduce people's demand for insurance products, and restrict the development of insurance industry.

At the same time, computing power construction, data storage, customer management, loss settlement, legal proceedings, dispute resolution, fraud prevention all require a lot of manpower, material resources and financial resources. In addition, because insurance related data information cannot be shared, insurance companies have to pay additional costs when obtaining relevant data information.

In short, the high cost will not only directly affect the solvency of insurance companies, but also reduce the asset scale of insurance companies and investment in other areas of insurance companies.

1. 1. 1. 3　Inefficient Operations

The problem of low efficiency of insurance operation mainly occurs in underwriting and claims settlement. Taking health insurance underwriting as an example, the insurance company will first understand the customer's insurance purpose and motivation, living habits, past medical history, family medical history, occupation, working environment, financial status and other basic information, and conduct a preliminary audit. In the case that the preliminary audit cannot make the underwriting judgment, the underwriting staff will further collect information, such as asking for medical records of previous illnesses, recent physical examination results, outpatient medical records, medical insurance card records, etc., and carry out investigations according to the data. Finally, the underwriting conclusion is given according to the actual situation of the customer and the underwriting requirements of the insurance contract. In the whole underwriting process, a large number of repetitive and cumbersome review work relies on manpower and consumes a lot of resources. In the claims process, from the customer report to the final payment needs to go through a lengthy claims process, which takes either a few weeks or a few months. If there is a disagreement between the insurance company and the policyholder due to the claim conditions, disclaimer clauses, etc., there may be more twists and turns. Such a time-consuming and cumbersome claim settlement undoubtedly degrades the user experience to some extent.

1. 1. 1. 4　Inaccurate Insurance Marketing

With the continuous enhancement of consumer insurance awareness, the demand for insurance products and services among consumers is also increasing. The information of insurance clients is becoming more and more extensive and complex. When facing such an environment, insurance professionals and agents need to accurately classify customer groups and recommend the most suitable insurance products to them through appropriate channels from a large number of insurance products. This not only meets the personalized needs of customers, but also improves their performance, achieving a win-win situation for both themselves and policyholders.

1. 1. 1. 5　Difficulty in Insurance Product Innovation

Looking at the existing insurance products in the market, the homogenization phenomenon is relatively serious, and the insurance products launched by various insurance companies are almost indistinguishable in terms of coverage, claim conditions, premium prices, even marketing channels and methods of insurance. Homogenized products make most insurance companies lack core competitiveness, innovation, and differentiation, which result in unattractive products and are difficult to meet the diversified and personalized insurance needs of customers. From the perspective of marketing, the main reason leading to the homogenization of product development is that the product design and development of insurance companies are disconnected from the market demand. According to Porter's Five Forces model, providing differentiated products and services is an important means for enterprises to gain competitive advantages in the fierce market competition, and the difficulty of insurance product innovation undoubtedly restricts the development of the insurance industry.

1.1.1.6　Inaccurate Pricing

Traditional insurance pricing methods are usually based on a comprehensive assessment of the risk of the whole population, and calculate the average incidence and average cost to determine the cost of claims. However, this method often ignores the difference of individual risks, which may lead to the protection of individuals with higher risks only by paying the average rate, which leads to the problem of adverse selection. At the same time, there may be errors in risk estimates for newly insured individuals based on measures of past group risk.

At present, the insurance industry continues to accumulate a large amount of data, insurance data with complex, diverse and related characteristics, these factors increase the complexity of data processing. As the volume of data grows rapidly, the changes in data also increase the requirements for technology. Therefore, the traditional data processing method has been difficult to meet the demand, and the traditional insurance pricing method is relatively complex and inefficient.

1.1.1.7　Difficulty in Preventing of Insurance Fraud

Insurance fraud refers to the behavior of the applicant or the insured to knowingly provide false information or take deceptive means to obtain the insurance compensation or rights that should not be obtained. This kind of behavior not only often causes economic losses to insurance companies, but also affects the stability and healthy development of the entire insurance market. Traditional insurance fraud detection methods mainly rely on manual audit and rule engine, which is difficult to deal with complex and changeable fraud methods. The lack of advanced data analysis technology and artificial intelligence technology makes it difficult for insurance companies to detect and prevent fraud in a timely manner.

1.1.1.8　Other Challenges Faced

In addition to the aforementioned issues, the traditional insurance industry also faces other challenges such as customer information leakage, profitability difficulties for insurance companies, high agent attrition rates, low transaction frequency, weak customer relationships, and more.

1.1.2　New Quality Productive Forces and Insurance

In September 2023, General Secretary Xi Jinping first proposed the concept of "new quality productivity" during his inspection and research in Heilongjiang Province. On January 31, 2024, while presiding over the 11th collective study session of the Political Bureau of the CPC Central Committee, president Xi Jinping further elaborated on the concept of "new quality productivity". President Xi Jinping emphasized, "High-quality development requires new productivity theories to guide it, and new quality productivity has already emerged in practice, demonstrating strong driving force and support for high-quality development. It requires us to summarize and generalize theoretically to guide new development practices." New quality productivity is an important driver for promoting high-quality economic development in China.

French economist Say believes that the ultimate driving force of economic growth comes from three basic production factors: labor, land, and capital. In contrast, advanced productivity characterized by innovation, leading away from traditional economic growth patterns and productivity development paths, with high technology, high efficiency, high quality features, and in line with new development concepts is termed as new quality productivity. The characteristics of new quality productivity are innovation, focusing on quality excellence, and essentially being advanced productivity. It relies on new production factors such as science, technology, and data combined with traditional production factors like labor, land, and capital to drive economic growth.

On the path towards building a socialist modernized strong country, insurance, as a "ballast stone of risk" and "stabilizer of society", bears significant responsibilities. New quality productive forces can help the traditional insurance industry solve the pain points and difficulties faced in the development process. The application of new quality productivity in the insurance industry can not only enhance the production efficiency and service quality of the insurance sector but also promote the development and innovation of the insurance market, address pain points in the traditional insurance industry development, and thereby drive the overall upgrade and transformation of the insurance industry.

Furthermore, the insurance industry can also promote the development of new quality productivity. Technology companies face various risks in the research, production, and sales processes, including intellectual property infringement, product liability, network security, and data breaches. Insurance companies can provide specialized technology insurance for technology companies to help them effectively manage these risks and ensure sustainable development. Additionally, technical personnel may face personal risks such as accidental injuries and illnesses in their work. Insurance companies can provide accident insurance, major illness insurance, medical insurance, etc., for technical personnel with comprehensive protection for them and their families. These insurance products not only help technology companies attract and retain excellent technical talents, enhance their competitiveness and attractiveness, but also help them address complex risk challenges and ensure the steady development of their business.

In conclusion, new quality productivity is an essential path to help the insurance industry comprehensively transform and upgrade; at the same time, the insurance industry can provide comprehensive protection services for the development of new quality productivity. The two are interrelated and mutually reinforcing.

1.1.3 The Birth of InsurTech

The origin of insurance technology can be traced back to the 1990s. With the development of Internet technology and mobile communication, Internet insurance has gradually emerged. The popularization of Internet and the development of digital technology have brought new opportunities and challenges to the insurance industry. The academic circles and the industry generally believe that Internet insurance is the origin of insurance technology. China's insurance technology started a little late, until 1997, with a large domestic insurance company introduced the United States CBPS life insurance integrated business system, China's insurance industry initially realized information and electronic. In the same year, the Insurance Society of China and a company in Beijing jointly established the China Insurance Information Network, which became the first insurance website in China and kicked off the prelude of domestic insurance technology. The establishment of the website laid the foundation for subsequent data analysis and customer resource integration.

At present, the development momentum of InsurTech in the world is exciting. According to CB Insight, there were only 28 InsurTech investments worldwide in 2011, totaling just $ 140 million. By 2012, the number of investments had increased to 46, totaling $ 350 million; In 2013, there were 63 investments totaling $ 270 million; There were 28 investments in 2014, with the total soaring to $ 870 million; In 2015, there were 122 investments totaling $ 2.67 billion. In different insurance markets, more than 60% of US InsurTech investment is concentrated in the series A stage, and the investment scale is growing year by year. In contrast, the German market, unlike the United States, has entered the medium stage of InsurTech investment, that is, the Series B stage. From 2012 to 2016, the total amount of German InsurTech financing reached 53.52 million euros, and no less than 5 companies have received Series B financing. As a traditional insurance country, the UK saw the largest investment in InsurTech in Europe in 2016, with more than £15 million.

Despite starting relatively late, China's insurance technology has developed rapidly. In 2000, the "online" website opened by a domestic life insurance company pushed the development of China's insurance industry to the stage of "Internet + Insurance", which can be regarded as an early form of insurance technology. "Internet + Insurance" mainly realizes the online operation of insurance business through the Internet, such as sales, insurance, underwriting, etc., aiming to provide customers with more timely and convenient services. On this basis, the insurance industry will further integrate with other emerging technologies, empower the entire insurance value chain through scientific and technological innovation, promote the reshaping and upgrading of the insurance industry chain, and guide the "Internet + Insurance" from simple scale expansion to the pursuit of higher quality development.

1.2 The Development Trend of InsurTech

In today's society, driven by the new quality productivity, the revolution of the insurance industry has begun, and countless emerging scientific and technological forces are comprehensively empowering the insurance industry in the new era.

1.2.1 The Concept of InsurTech

Insurance is a subfield of finance, and Insurance Technology (InsurTech) naturally falls under the umbrella of Financial Technology (FinTech) as an important branch. InsurTech inherits some characteristics of FinTech while also possessing its own unique features.

According to the Financial Stability Board's definition of financial technology as "new business models, applications, processes, or products introduced through technological innovation that have a profound impact on financial markets, financial institutions, and the provision of financial services", it is evident that InsurTech embodies the combination of technology and insurance. Furthermore, as InsurTech is still in its early stages of development, there are various interpretations of its definition, reflecting differing perspectives and insights.

1.2.1.1 International Association of Insurance Supervisors (IAIS)

InsurTech is the branch of Fintech in the insurance sector and is the sum of various emerging technologies and innovative business models that have the potential to transform the insurance business.

1.2.1.2 Introduction to Insurance Technology by the other scholars

There is currently no agreed definition of insurance technology across various sectors. However, there is a general consensus that emphasizes the significant role of emerging technologies in the insurance field and their impact on the entire insurance industry.

1.2.1.3 Adapted from Jingdong Finance's definition of Fintech

InsurTech follows the nature of insurance, takes data as the basis and technology as the means to serve the insurance industry, so as to reduce the cost of the insurance industry and improve the efficiency of the industry.

In summary, "insurance technology" refers to the integration of various innovative technologies containing new productive forces (such as Big Data, cloud computing, Internet of Things, artificial intelligence, Blockchain, robotics, biotechnology, etc.) with the insurance industry to create a sum of new insurance models, applications, and products. In other words, insurance technology is the product of the deep integration of new productive forces with the insurance industry.

1.2.2 The Current Situation of InsurTech ├───────────────

In order to promote the development of technology in the financial sector, particularly in the field of insurance technology, the central government has introduced a series of policies to facilitate this advancement. These policies have paved the way for the development of insurance technology in China at a macro level. In January 2022, the China Banking and Insurance Regulatory Commission (It has been restructured as China's National Financial Regulatory Administration) issued the "Guiding Opinions on the Digital Transformation of the Banking and Insurance Industries". This guidance covers initiatives ranging from encouraging full-process online insurance services to accelerating the digitalization, onlineization, and intelligence transformation, ultimately setting clear goals for the digital transformation of insurance by 2025, laying a solid foundation for technological progress in the insurance industry.

In the above policy background, China's insurance companies continue to test insurance technology. In 2013, China's first Internet insurance company was established, marking the beginning of a comprehensive transformation of insurance business to the Internet. Since its inception, the insurance company has adopted the strategy of "insurance + technology" and is committed to using technology to reshape the entire insurance value chain. The company has introduced intelligent underwriting technology in the core underwriting link, launched personalized protection products for people with three high and chronic diseases, and provided solutions for users who were previously difficult to obtain protection. In addition, the insurance company's health insurance claims process is 96% online, a claim settlement is completed every 9 seconds, and 95% of cases have achieved direct claims.

In recent years, a large domestic insurance company and other major insurance companies have basically realized the online operation of the property insurance sales end through digital transformation. From underwriting needs, to pricing, to sales orders, and subsequent value-added services and core claims services, users can complete the entire process directly online. At the same time, the call centers of many leading insurance companies in China are using RPA robots and artificial intelligence technology to replace traditional manual services, significantly improving the efficiency of business development and reducing operating costs. In addition, some advanced insurance companies have completed the digital restructuring of the entire process from underwriting, security services, claims to value-added services. With the customer journey at its core, some insurance companies have implemented the entire process of digital transformation, marking a significant improvement in the quality and efficiency of insurance services.

A vice president of a domestic insurance group said that at present, more than 90% of the business of many companies has achieved lock-out. Through the application of ChatGPT and other technologies, a domestic insurance group has achieved significant service efficiency improvement in three aspects of service, management and sales, and has significantly replaced traditional manual operations. At the same time, the company also cooperates with the social big data platform, adopts the method of risk factor labeling, and realizes the personalized pricing strategy of "one person, one price" for each customer. In the field of auto insurance claims, the insurance group is able to handle small vehicle loss cases in a matter of seconds by combining data analysis and mining models, as well as introducing picture automatic loss determination and small personal injury automatic loss determination technology.

Meanwhile, the domestic capital market is highly optimistic about the prospects of insurance technology development, with a substantial amount of capital flowing into the insurance technology sector each year to support its technological research and development. From 2012 to 2019, the number of financing transactions in this field in China has reached 300, with a total financing amount exceeding 12 billion yuan, as shown in Figure 1. 1.

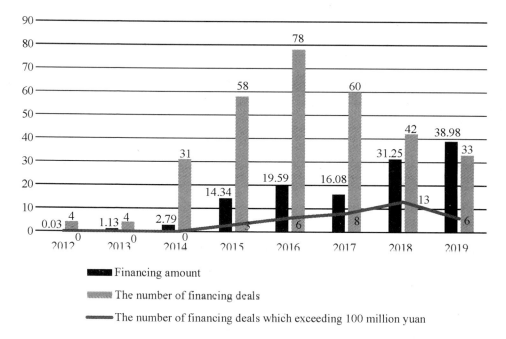

Financing amount

The number of financing deals

The number of financing deals which exceeding 100 million yuan

**Figure 1. 1　The number and amount of investment and financing
in InsurTech in China from 2012 to 2019**

Source: China Insurance Technology Insight Report 2020 released by Beijing Fintech Research Institute.

Since 2015, the scale of China's insurance technology market has shown an increasing trend year by year. By 2020, the market size of China's InsurTech has exceeded 90 billion yuan, and the average growth rate in recent years has exceeded 10%, as shown in Figure 1. 2. At present, China has become the hot spot of insurance technology financing after Europe and the United States, and the development of domestic insurance technology is stable and good.

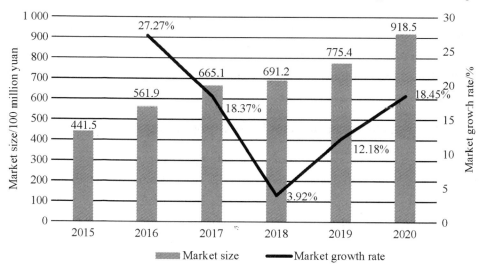

Market size　　Market growth rate

Figure 1. 2　Scale of China's InsurTech market and the growth rate

Source: Xu Zhongjing. Insurance technology industry analysis report [D]. Changsha: Central South Forestry University, 2022.)

1

Introduction

1. 2. 3　The Future of InsurTech

Based on the above introduction, the prospects of InsurTech are self-evident. Insurance technology will not only comprehensively improve customers' insurance experience, open up a broader insurance market, breed more accurate risk management methods, but also lead the reform of insurance supervision.

First of all, InsurTech will bring synergies to the development of the insurance industry, bring huge business growth to insurance companies, and play a $1+1>2$ effect. For example, combining traditional auto insurance with connected vehicle technology can not only further develop UBI auto insurance, but also comprehensively enhance the insurance experience of customers.

Secondly, insurance technology will move the claims service forward, not only improve the viscosity between insurance companies and policyholders, but also help policyholders better accident prevention, reduce the probability of accidents and the corresponding loss and compensation, and breed a more accurate risk management method.

Finally, the development of insurance technology will also promote the upgrading of regulatory technology and methods, leading to a comprehensive reform of the insurance regulatory model.

I believe that in the future, with the blessing of scientific and technological innovation, insurance will no longer be just a financial security product, but a new ecosystem that can help people cope with disasters and risks.

1. 3　InsurTech Companies

With the rapid development of science and technology and the constant changes of insurance demand, insurance products and insurance services based on new quality productivity such as Big Data, Artificial Intelligence and Biotechnology have gradually emerged, and insurance technology companies have emerged.

1. 3. 1　Classification of InsurTech Companies

At present, there is no agreed definition of InsurTech companies in academia and the industry. According to the definition of InsurTech in this book, InsurTech companies should refer to companies that are based on the integration of new quality productivity and insurance industry, and maximize profits with various innovative insurance products and insurance services as their main businesses. According to the development depth of InsurTech, InsurTech companies can be roughly divided into three categories: professional InsurTech companies, traditional insurance companies that have established InsurTech departments, and technology companies involved in insurance.

（1）Professional InsurTech startups refer to startups that have been established for a short period of time, usually by young entrepreneurs, and are dedicated to the field of InsurTech. Such companies focus on promoting the digital transformation and innovative development of the insurance industry.

(2) Traditional insurance companies that have established InsurTech departments refer to traditional insurance companies that have established departments specifically engaged in technology research and development and innovation, and these departments are working to promote the digital transformation and technology upgrading of the company.

(3) On the one hand, technology companies involved in insurance refer to companies that carry out insurance business through technological advantages and massive data; on the other hand, it refers to technology companies that provide professional services for the insurance industry.

1.3.2　The Operating Model of an InsurTech Company ┝────────

The operation mode of InsurTech companies is very diversified, which can be roughly divided into three categories 2A, 2B, 2C.

1.3.2.1　2A Mode

2A mode is mainly embodied in the form of agent platform, which provides insurance product sales platform and other services for insurance agents to meet the business needs of agents to design insurance product planning remotely and guide customers to apply online insurance. At the same time, Internet technology is used to improve the work efficiency of agents. The current profit model of 2A platform is mainly supported by commission income.

1.3.2.2　2B Mode

2B mode is mainly insurance IT companies, health insurance service providers and other insurance technology companies, through the use of technology infrastructure to expand channels, optimize sales and claims costs, improve the operating efficiency of the client and the middle and back office, and use technology to carry out certain product and service innovation, specific auto insurance risk control, health insurance risk control, auto insurance claims and other businesses. Specifically, 2B model participants come from a wider range of sources, including insurance companies, corporate insurance customers, insurance intermediaries, pharmaceutical factories, pharmacies, hospitals, automobile manufacturers, etc.

1.3.2.3　2C Mode

Under the 2C model, insurance products are directly oriented to individual customers, mainly in the form of online insurance market, price comparison platform, KOL agent and mutual aid platform. Online insurance market can face individual customers, insurance agents or brokers, and insurance product suppliers, and such platforms are usually free for individual customers. The premium paid through the premium contract reached through the platform will be shared with the platform in a certain proportion, or the insurance intermediary needs to pay a certain proportion of commission or service fees to the platform. This model is applicable to insurance products in the online insurance market, which are designed for specific scenarios or groups of people.

1.3.3 The Business Environment Needed for InsurTech Companies ├—

A good business environment can provide more support and orderly development opportunities for the insurance technology industry, attract more investment and talents for the industry, and enhance the overall competitiveness and sustainable development ability of the industry. Compared with the mature industry, the InsurTech industry in its initial stage will face more uncertainties and fiercer competition, which requires the society to create a good business environment for its sustainable development, which involves at least the following three aspects:

1.3.3.1 A Strong Policy Environment

The policy environment is critical for InsurTech companies. The government's policy initiatives in InsurTech regulation, tax policy and insurance market opening will have a profound impact on the development of InsurTech companies. At present, the Party Central Committee, The State Council, relevant ministries and governments at all levels attach great importance to optimizing the business environment, put forward the policy guidelines of new quality productivity enabling the insurance industry to help insurance reform, encourage continuous innovation in the insurance market, and provide multiple support policies for insurance technology companies.

1.3.3.2 Perfect Legal System

InsurTech involves legal issues such as data application and privacy protection of customers. A sound legal system is a prerequisite for the sustainable development of insurance technology, which can safeguard the rights and interests of insurance technology companies and customers, protect the interests of both insurers, and provide stable operation guarantee for insurance companies. At present, China's relevant legal system attaches great importance to the supervision and compliance of insurance technology companies, but the relevant legal provisions need to be further improved.

1.3.3.3 Orderly Market Rules

The insurance market is the main place for the development of insurance technology. An orderly competitive market environment is the prerequisite for the sustainable development of InsurTech companies. At present, the InsurTech market is still in its infancy. The relevant market rules and industry standards have yet to be established and improved, and the market order needs to be further standardized.

1.4   Foreign Cases

1.4.1   The First Case ├——————————————

Case Tile:
US InsurTech Market Analysis

Case Content:

The US InsurTech Market size is estimated at $ 49. 82 billion in 2024, and is expected to reach $ 66. 66 billion by 2029, growing at a CAGR of greater than 6% during the forecast period (2024–2029).

The United States is the largest insurance market globally, and it has been a hotbed for InsurTech companies. The market has experienced substantial growth in recent years, with investments pouring into InsurTech startups. InsurTech has attracted significant venture capital investment. InsurTech companies leverage various technologies such as artificial intelligence (AI), machine learning (ML), Big Data analytics, the Internet of Things (IoT), and Blockchain to streamline processes, enhance underwriting accuracy, automate claims handling, and personalize insurance products. InsurTech has facilitated the emergence of new insurance models, such as peer-to-peer (P2P) insurance, on-demand insurance, and usage-based insurance (UBI). These models offer more tailored coverage options and flexible pricing based on individual risk profiles. InsurTech companies in the United States focus on improving customer experience by offering user-friendly digital platforms, simplified policy purchasing processes, and faster claims settlement.

The post-COVID-19 scenario of the United States InsurTech market is experiencing significant growth. InsurTech companies are leveraging technology to provide innovative solutions and streamline insurance processes. Factors like increased digitization, rising customer expectations, and the need for personalized insurance offerings are driving the market.

Case Comments:

The growth of the US InsurTech market demonstrates the transformative impact of technology on the insurance industry. With a focus on leveraging AI, ML, Big Data analytics, IoT, and Blockchain, InsurTech companies are revolutionizing traditional insurance practices. The influx of investments into InsurTech startups shows the industry's recognition of the potential for technological advancements to drive efficiency and enhance customer experience. As InsurTech continues to reshape the insurance industry in the United States, we believe the insurance industry will experience further advancements in the US.

Case Source:

Mordor Intelligence Research & Advisory. US InsurTech Industry Size & Share Analysis–Growth Trends & Forecasts(2024–2029)[EB/OL].(2024–06–14)[2024–07–01].https://www.mordorintelligence.com/industry-reports/united-states-insurtech-market.

1. 4. 2　The Second Case

Case Tile:

The Development History of L

Case Content:

L has been rated the top InsurTech company in the US by numerous leading review sites.

According to independent reports, 94% of policyholders indicate they are likely to renew their policy, 96% would recommend their services to a friend and 97% have rated their claims experience positively. Such odds were unheard of in the InsurTech sector until now, as L continues to disrupt the market place.

We tracked their journey to success, pinpointing the company's milestone moments.

2015

L is born

L launches as a licenced carrier that sells its own products and services and in its first funding round in December 2015, raises \$ 13m through investors S Capital and Israeli VC A.

2016

Customer generation

Following it's official launch, L takes off with unprecedented success, signing up more than 14,000 customers within its first six months of operation. In the same period, Series A and B funding rounds generate a further \$ 48m in investments to expand the company. L also becomes one of the few insurance companies to receive B-Corporation certification.

2017

Kerching!

The money continues to roll in as investors fall over themselves to provide capital to the growing InsurTech. A company and SV company join up, as well as S bank-raising the investment total to \$ 180m.

2019-2020

Lift-off

L announces a further \$ 300m investment from S bank taking its investment capital total to \$ 480m. In April the company launches in the Netherlands. In July L becomes a public company, and in December, the InsurTech company wins its trademark dispute with T company over the use of pink on the logo.

Case Comments:

Overall, L's history is a testament to the power of science and technology in changing a traditional industry like insurance. As the InsurTech company continues to disrupt the marketplace and set new standards for the industry, its journey serves as an inspiration for aspiring entrepreneurs and businesses looking to make a significant impact in the world of insurance technology.

Case Source:

JOANNA. Timeline: the story of lemonade[EB/OL].(2021-05-06)[2024-07-01].https://InsurTechdigital.com/InsurTech/timeline-story-lemonade.

2

大数据与保险业

本章主要阐释大数据与保险业相互结合的基本思路与原理，并精选了相关国内外案例与学生分享，启发学生借助大数据开发保险科技应用场景和相关保险产品的思路。

2.1 大数据基本理论

21 世纪以来，随着计算机、互联网等电子信息技术的广泛应用，世界各地的美景、新闻、热点动态等基于互联网媒介，以数据的方式呈现在人们眼前。庞大的数据已经成为人们进行信息交融的重要途径。2008 年，《自然》杂志以大数据为封面推出专栏；2009 年，"大数据"成为热词，逐渐进入人们的视野。

2.1.1 大数据基本概念

数据（data）是事实或观察的结果，是对客观事物的逻辑归纳，是用于表示客观事物未经加工的原始素材。数据可以是连续的值，比如声音、图像，被称为模拟数据；也可以是离散的值，如符号、文字，被称为数字数据。能反映出自然界或人类社会的某种信息，也被称为数据。

大数据（big data），亦称巨量数据，是内容多、维度广、覆盖宽的信息数据的集合，是一种难以运用传统的数据处理工具进行提取、存储、共享及分析的新型生产要素。大数据技术犹如在浩瀚的垃圾场中搜寻有价值的东西。大数据技术处理以动态为主，实时产生大量的各类数据。

从数据到大数据，不仅是量的积累，更是质的飞跃。大数据将原本海量的、不同来源的、形式各异的单一数据整合起来，并系统地分析，从而挖掘出数据时代很难发现的新知识，为人类社会不断创造新价值。

2.1.2 大数据的特点

随着数字技术的崛起，大数据逐渐成为核心生产要素之一。相较于传统数据，大数据还呈现出以下五个不同特征：

2.1.2.1 数据量庞大

大数据本身承载的资料信息数量庞大。在大数据时代，数据的发展模式符合"摩尔定律"，互联网数据中心（Internet Data Center，IDC）预测数据将以每年50%的速度快速增长，这也意味着数据量每两年就会增长一倍。

2.1.2.2 高频

在信息化和全球化的时代，以数据为依托进行信息交流、资源互换的过程成本更低、速度更快、频次更高。相较于传统数据而言，大数据的传输与处理速度更呈现出指数级增长。

2.1.2.3 价值密度低

大数据虽然总体价值高，但其体量庞大，不可避免地会出现数据冗余、质量不佳、信息过载等问题，导致大数据集合中的有效信息所占比例相对较低，数据的利用效率较低，从而降低了数据的价值密度。

2.1.2.4 种类繁杂

数据可以划分为结构化数据、半结构化数据、非结构化数据三种。传统数据模式具有明确定义，易于储存、管理、集成，数据之间具有一致性，便于分析和挖掘，一般属于结构化与半结构化数据。而大数据获取渠道多样，并以文档、电子邮件、社交媒体帖子、图像、音频和视频等形式表现，个性化、定制化数据模式突出，难以运用传统方式进行处理和解读，从而出现数据量庞大但无序，呈现非结构化特征。

2.1.2.5 数据全量化

大数据的实质是"深度学习"，需要建立大规模训练数据集，依靠机器学习与训练建成服务决策的仿真环境和专家系统，最终通过这种数据量化分析对未来进行精准预测。大数据从"已知"推测"未知"和从"过去"预测"未来"的过程，被称为数据量化，贯穿大数据运用的整个过程。

2.1.3 大数据的发展现状与前景

2018年11月，希捷科技携手国际数据公司（IDC）以"世界的数字化由边缘到核心"为主题，发布了《数据时代2025》白皮书。白皮书预测全球数据量总和将在2025年达到175ZB（如图2.1所示），且将会有49%的全球已存储数据驻留在公共云环境中。

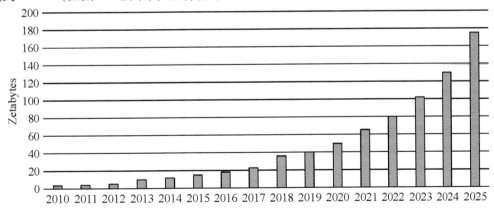

图2.1 全球数据圈的年度规模

数据来源：国际数据公司（IDC）《数据时代2025》。https://www.seagate.com/files/www-content/our
-story/trends/files/idc-seagate-dataage-chine-whitepaper.pdf。

从智能推送到智能搜索、从智能助理到智能家居、从无人驾驶到人形机器人，在信息共享、"万物互联"的时代，大数据极大地便捷了人类的生产与生活。随着各行各业的智能化转型、信息互联的不断深入，数据的增长速度与叠加数量将呈几何倍数增长，"全球数据圈"迅猛发展将推动全人类的数字化转型。

在未来，大数据的应用将带给人类社会无限的憧憬。随之而来的大数据治理必将成为人们关注的问题。科技变革推动了信息数据的爆炸性增长，人类世界正在经历数字化转型变革。运用大数据推动社会发展、完善社会治理、强化服务监管能力是未来大数据发展的重要趋势。

2.1.3.1 大数据的应用

从应用方面划分，大数据的实践可大致分为三个层次。虽然目前大数据的发展仍处于初级阶段，但大数据的三个层次的应用在现实中非常广泛。

第一个层次是描述性分析应用，指利用数据接入、数据存储、数据处理及可视化等技术，根据需求从数据库中精准定位目标数据或抽取相关信息。企业构建用户画像，了解商品销售情况等都属于这一层次的技术应用。

第二个层次是预测性分析应用，指基于以往大量数据发生的结果，构建数学模型剖析数据之间的联系，据此对事物发展状态与趋势做出预测。如微软公司纽约研究院研究员 David Rothschild 通过搜集和分析好莱坞证券交易所、社交媒体用户发布的帖子等大量公开数据，建立预测模型，对多届奥斯卡奖项的归属进行了预测。2014 年和 2015 年，其准确预测了 24 个奥斯卡奖项中的 21 个，准确率达 87.5%。

第三个层次是指导性分析应用，指在基于前两个层次的基础上，运用流计算、图数据库等技术，通过数据成像预测多个不同结果，对最终决策实现优化。如自动驾驶汽车通过多个传感器的实时感知数据，结合对地图与路况的精准定位，预判不同驾驶路径的后果，实现驾驶智能化。

在未来，随着数据应用领域的拓宽，数据共享平台的完善，大数据在以上三个层次的应用将迸发出更大的价值。以大数据为基础实现精准追踪、准确预测及自动判断，对人类的生产生活予以全智能化是未来大数据发展的重要方向。

2.1.3.2 大数据的治理

大数据能助力产业的智能转型升级，推动社会高质量发展，但也随之引发出对其的治理问题。一方面，大数据由于自身的非结构化特征，信息资源分散、流通无序，需要搭建共享开放统一的数据库平台，对数据资产进行集成化管理与规划；另一方面，大数据的数字平台搭建又可能会导致数据泄露以及隐私安全问题。因此，如何在数据互通的情况下保护个人隐私数据，是大数据治理的发展趋势。只有处理好数据共享与数据安全、隐私保护之间的关系，才能推动大数据应用的发展。

2.2 大数据与保险结合的应用场景

保险是进行风险管理的有效手段之一。随着人类社会的发展，风险也呈现出多样化、新型化、普遍化特征，保险要实现对风险的精准把控，更好地发挥其损失补偿、风险转嫁功能，就需要与以大数据为代表的新质生产力深度融合。

2.2.1 大数据与社会保险

2.2.1.1 大数据助推社会保险服务精细化

社会保障体系强调以人为本，服务核心是人民的需求。围绕人民的切实需求，直击社会痛点是社会保障体系数字化转型升级的目标。社会保障机构以大数据为技术手段，搭建技术中台、业务中台、AI 中台、数据中台，从优化缴费途径、拓宽社保类型、到简便投保方式等方面，以数据赋能贯穿社会保障全过程，切实推进社会保险服务精细化转型升级。

全国各地也在不断通过试点，探寻大数据与社会保险的融合。2021 年，江西省基于大数据，以生物识别手段打造"静默认证"，全省有 258 万老年居民享受到了"无感知免打扰"认证服务。"大数据精准定位+生物人脸识别"技术令录入对象无须做配合动作便可自动认证完成，使得在认证周期内的群众免于传统认证方式带来的不便，极大地为高龄、患病、失能群体提供了便利。

2.2.1.2 大数据提高社会保障效率

大数据的出现打破了以往社会保险体系运作的时空壁垒，以大数据为依托的社会保障模式更趋于多元化，同时居民可以享受到的社保资源也趋向普惠化。在数据平台的加持下，社会保障呈现多层次、多功能、跨地区、跨平台新特点，社会保障体系效率得到极大提高。

大数据平台推出后，居民可以通过"掌上 12333"或支付宝等 App 一键了解社会保险关系转移接续全流程，极大地节约了手续成本，同时促进了劳动力的流转。山东省青岛市基于大数据分析，打造"工伤保险智能一体化服务"，可以实现工伤远程取证、智能远程鉴定、职业病或工伤的远程同步认定，提供了跨地区、高效率的社会保险服务，解决了以往工伤认定久、取证难、赔付流程慢等一系列问题，全面提升了社会保障运行效率。

2.2.2 大数据与商业保险

2.2.2.1 定位需求，挖掘客户

大数据不仅可以帮助保险企业精准识别保险需求，还能激发客户的潜在保险需求。由于成本、人力、回报等问题，传统商业保险公司往往忽略了带病群体、老年群体、下沉市场的需求。这些群体较难有效参与保险。在大数据赋能下，保险公司可利用大数据为客户精准画像，准确定位客户需求，开展个性化保险定制服务。客户则可根据自身保险需求、经济状况在互联网平台实现灵活投保。在解决了传统保险服务成本高的问题的同时，又一定程度上增强了群众的保险意识，提高了保险的可获得性，进而

提高了保险覆盖率、丰富了保险保障层次。

2.2.2.2 开发险种，优化产品

大数据可以激发保险企业优化并创新保险产品体系。如在农业领域，借助大数据平台建立精细预测模型，突破以往农作物因病、因灾的受损不规律性，以及牲畜成长周期不定性等问题，解决巨灾快速理赔难题，通过保险科技拓宽承保风险类型，以保险的广覆盖助力乡村振兴。在气候变化应对方面，大量财产保险公司基于大数据精算模型，借助物联网、人工智能、遥感技术等，精准监控气候变化异常区域，对特定地区的极端天气进行预测，并推出预防措施，有效地防范了气候变化风险，实现了大数据背景下的"损失补偿"到"风险减量"的转型目标。

2.2.2.3 提高效率，降低成本

传统保险企业业务过程涉及推销、投保、核保、承保、定损、理赔等流程，由于代理人素质参差不齐、保险合同术语晦涩、被保险人真实情况难以了解等因素，传统保险经营具有成本高、耗时久、逆向选择与保险欺诈严重等弊端。

随着大数据的广泛应用，各家保险公司都加速推进自身数字化转型。App日益成为保险公司与用户形成消费关系、增进用户黏性的重要渠道。保险公司通过大数据分析客户的特征、习惯以及偏好，分析和预测客户需求，为寻找目标客户以及推出个性产品奠定重要基础。以大数据技术为依托的保险公司可以极大节约人力成本，略过代理人与转化客户层面实现保险公司与目标对象的连接，以最小成本取得最大效益。同时，通过大数据可以促进用户与保险公司的互惠互融。用户通过App可以一键式了解保险合同条款，保险公司也可以基于大数据、信用评级、机器学习等手段对用户真实信息做出判断。大数据将用户与保险公司串联起来，解决了以往的保险欺诈与逆向选择问题，有利于保险市场的绿色稳定发展。

2.2.2.4 精准定价，识别风险

目前，大数据在勘查定损、精准营销、差异化定价、动态保费厘定等方面已有运用。如某家美国的新兴健康险公司成立了专门的数据实验室，利用患者的个人数据、诊疗数据、健康数据等理赔大数据，整合形成临床资料库，通过大数据方式对就诊中的疾病化验、治疗、用药等数据进行深入分析，并将这套方法运用于健康保险中。通过患者的基本数据（比如年龄和性别、疾病数据、病理数据等），建立多维数理模型，用以区分个休的不同患病风险，利用风险系数来干预用户的行为，通过风险分析来进行产品设计，并据此给患者提供不同的保险服务，为差异化定价的推进提供技术支持。此外，大数据运用场景还出现在了快速理赔和反欺诈方面，借助图片识别技术，将被保险人所上传的照片等证明材料在庞大的数据库里面进行比对，再结合所培植的信用历史进行判断，可以在短时间内通过这些因素做出精准判断，并且在线完成索赔审核，在一定程度上帮助保险公司降低了骗保的行为和概率，大大降低了保险公司的承保风险。

2.3 "保险+大数据"国内案例

2.3.1 国内经典案例之一

案例题目：

大数据赋能保险运营"新生态"

案例内容：

随着数字化时代来临，客户已习惯在线上获取保险服务。为适应数字化和新媒体的快速发展趋势，国内 R 保险公司财险线上化团队将大数据技术、智能化技术应用在客户线上新媒体运营领域，开展客户线上运营数字化转型探索。

R 保险公司通过搭建数据共享平台，丰富触达客户的数字媒体，利用私域流量、电子实名支付等技术高效且低成本地进行线上获客，不断提高平台触达客户的能力。在公司已有的数据资产基础上，制作客户标签与画像，并将其与客户在线分层运营策略结合。项目团队将线上保险服务与线下资源相融合，不断延伸线上服务链条，为客户提供更优质的服务体验，在服务触达的同时开展数字化营销，最终实现客户转化的提升。R 保险公司运用大数据赋能保险运营链条主要有三种模式：

一是利用公众号、小程序、视频号、抖音等线上数字化媒体，最大化实现高效、低成本的获客目标。通过将线上数字载体的二维码技术、支付技术融入传统业务流程，推出了"二维码支付引流"工具、"私域流量获客"等线上工具，将获客流程与支付/服务流程合二为一，实现了线上低成本快速便捷地获客。通过各种数智化引流工具的建设，实现线上获客超过 5 000 万人；通过活动引流页面和深度链接的配置化，支持配置引流渠道超过 500 个，并及时监控媒体投放、营销活动推广及自媒体推广的运营成效。

二是数智化营销能力反向渗透线下服务，强化线上线下服务融合，形成了独有的优势与特色。将直播、视频类技术嵌入理赔、销售、保全流程，形成了视频查勘定损、人伤视频调解、视频保全、视频面签、直播销售等优质服务，提升了服务质量与效率。将线下服务资源与数智化平台整合，搭建了养车用车平台、汽车救援平台、智慧家居平台、健康服务平台，延伸了线上服务链条。微信小程序保险板块数字标签已支持 2 000 万客户按险种分类和应用场景等标签快速触达所需产品，同时提供在线直播方式为客户提供保险产品推荐、说明及销售服务。结合保险服务场景，深化小程序视频通信的应用，辅助业务开展、提升业务效率、降低业务成本，目前已实现保险视频理赔、视频批改、视频查勘、视频面签等功能，提供统一道路救援服务，现已服务百万客户。

三是使用企业微信、企业微信客服、微信公众号消息、订阅消息、视频号私信等技术，不断提高数智化线上触达能力，支持线上客户需求精准投放，在服务触达的同时开展数字化营销，最终实现客户转化率的提升。提升微信订阅消息和微信视频号私信消息等互联互通能力，快速推广企业微信"微信客服"功能，根据公众号、小程序、App、视频号等触达的快速入口，支持客户使用微信与专属客服团队的企业微信进行实时对话，服务客户超过 1 000 万人，日均收发消息量超过 100 万条。

案例评述：

R 保险公司基于大数据技术开辟了保险运营"新生态"，从低成本精准定位潜在客户，到以大数据赋能服务路径，再到目标导向的智能化、精准化，R 保险公司谱写了大数据赋能保险业的新篇章，为保险业实现转型升级，建设保险"新生态"提供了新思路。未来，大数据如何更好地与保险业结合，从而达到提振实体经济，实现全体人民共同富裕的目标，还需要保险全行业的共同探索与发力。

案例来源：

北京金融科技产业联盟. 中国人保：基于数字化媒体的线上运营模式［EB/OL］.（2023-08-09）［2024-07-01］. https：//www. bfia. org. cn/sites/home/MsgView. jsp？ msgId ＝29139.

2.3.2　国内经典案例之二

案例题目：

打造"数据阳光"，焕发保险行业新活力

案例内容：

"只有以科技创造出先进的武器，才有资格去参加未来的战斗"，Y 保险公司于 2015 年启动了"数据+算法"的数字化转型战略。2019 年，Y 保险公司启动组织变革，进行架构调整，成立了专门的科技中心。2021 年 5 月，中国企业数字化联盟和国内政企市场媒体企业网 DINet 联合发布《数字化转型白皮书（2021）》，全面开启数字化转型，并为此制定数据科技战略，强调要全面增强数据科技能力。Y 保险公司的数字化战略可以从需求端与供给端进行阐述。

从需求端来看，消费端多元化、整合式的需求开始呈现，并日益成为主流。"透过一扇窗"打开一条通向整体需求的路径，保险的多消费场景特点亦在凸显。保险不再是一个单点的服务需求，可能有财产保障、气候预测、健康管理、养老服务、理财服务、法律服务、医疗服务等覆盖人民生活方方面面的整体服务需求。

在气象灾害板块，Y 保险公司创新打造的"天眼风险地图平台"是基于位置智能、大数据技术的风险管理系统，融合灾害、地理、气象、保险等多学科，以暴雨、台风、地震、洪水、雪灾、大风、冰雹、雷电、风暴潮九种常见气象灾害为研究范围，建立的风险评估模型。该模型集成全国布设的物联网设备运行数据，通过中央监控大屏实时监测运行状态，并在设备发生预警时及时向企业安全负责人和 Y 保险公司的风控工程师同步信息，实现了企业的风险监控、快速预警和及时处置，也实现了自动化、线上化评估自然灾害风险与强风降水。据悉，2023 年，Y 保险公司累计通过短信、微信等平台方式，为客户精准推送百万余次气象灾害预警信息，在上一年汛期台风、暴雨等自然灾害高发期风险减量效果显著。如今，数字金融与实体经济已进一步融合，2023 年数据显示，Y 保险公司为 1.3 万个重要企业客户提供了科技减灾和专业风险咨询服务，向客户及社会公众等提供预警信息 80 万余次，以科技应用助力风险减量，服务实体经济。

在健康与养老板块，Y 保险公司正推进健康大数据工程，通过优化模型、建立智能风险量化实验室，深化人身险产品创新。Y 保险公司旗下的人寿子公司与医院进行合作，推出"融和直付"服务模式，帮助客户实现"免申请、零等待"的一站式全流程医疗费用理赔服务。依托 Y 保险公司打造的人伤医疗审核服务中心，汇集具有 5 年以上临床经验的医疗专家进行人伤医疗全国集中审核，打通伤情判断与费用最终审核的全流程专业管理堵点，搭建了人伤理赔服务平台。该平台曾荣获中国人民银行 2020 年金融科技发展奖三等奖。为助力第三支柱养老保险建设，Y 保险公司立足保险主业、多元发力布局，基于大数据技术，推出个性化产品与定制服务为客户提供全面的养老解决方案，先后推出"重度恶性肿瘤疾病保险""养老年金保险"等产品，为客户的老年生活提供保险保障。

从供给端来看，保险行业正直面全流程化的科技迭变。科技创新与技术应用在保险业务场景中不断渗透，正加快改变传统的保险经营流程。

在投保与核保方面，Y 保险公司创新性研发"懂你保险"。这是一款行业领先的人工智能保单检视工具，其运用大数据、影像识别、数据可视化等技术，实现客户需求梳理与智能解析、科学研判风险、精算保障缺口等操作，"极简、极快、极全、极智、极好"的专业化、定制服务赢得客户青睐。以拥有 10 张保单的一个家庭为例，通常人工检视保单所需时间最少需要四五个小时，"懂你保险"保单检视大多在 1 分钟内完成，大数据模型为千人千面实现适当保障奠定了技术基础。

在服务优化方面，2023 年，Y 保险公司旗下人寿子公司还创新升级推出"LX3.0"。该工具集中科技力量聚集于数据资源场景优化和客户服务体验升级，使得客户服务一次完成率大幅度提高，投诉率大大降低。"LX3.0"全新上线"随屏互动"功能，在客户办理业务遇到问题时，会根据客户的业务进度自动弹出，实时解答疑问并给予操作指导。为增进与客户的联动，"LX3.0"覆盖的"知识面"涵盖投保流程、产品咨询、理赔指引、销售预约、售后答疑等各个方面，而且以智能化、精准化服务实现了"懂你想问"。

案例评述：

Y 保险公司借助新质生产力不断焕发新活力，以大数据为依托实现公司业务的智能化转型升级。大数据技术和保险的融合顺应了时代发展的要求，保险全行业应主动拥抱大数据技术，围绕社会需求，加快推动保险由"风险存量保障"到"风险减量管理"的高质量转型。

案例来源：

中国网财经. 新质生产力焕发新动能［EB/OL］.（2024-03-21）［2024-07-01］.阳光保险以科技入新活力.https://finance.china.com.cn/roll/20240321/6095066.shtml#:~:text.

2.4　课程思政案例

案例题目：

大数据技术推动普惠保险发展

案例内容：

M 金服是一家新兴金融科技公司，核心业务是供应链金融和场景金融的搭建。

M 普惠保险云平台是 M 金服围绕保险行业搭建的金融服务场景。该平台运用金融科技手段为保险机构、保险经纪公司以及保险从业人员提供一站式全流程解决方案。

针对保险企业理赔流程烦琐、用户体验差，企业综合成本较高、盈利能力弱，代理人素质参差不齐、欺诈率高等多项痛点，M 普惠保险云平台联合多家金融机构深入保险行业，研发与产业特征相符的金融产品。针对传统保险业务痛点，利用平台技术优势赋能保险上下游，提升产业效率。利用大数据云计算能力赋能上游保险机构团队，搭建覆盖社保、医保及商业补充医疗保险结算平台解决理赔难理赔慢的普遍痛点，实现线上办理赔付，大大缩短理赔时效，提高理赔效率和保险行业的整体服务水平。同时，提供端到端、一站式服务，为下游保险代理人赋能，提升保险业务服务效率。以数据驱动，科技赋能，实现保险交易全流程线上无纸化操作，除降低人力物力的成本外，还将保险行业风险管控向数字化、立体化、前置化和智能化四个方向发展，进入全面智能风控时代。

M 金服结合 M 普惠保险云平台对业务推进，与各地政府开展保险园区合作，通过线上线下协同发展，助力保险行业健康发展。M 普惠保（普洱）就是 M 金服结合普惠保险的深刻地方实践。

M 普惠保（普洱）具有"普洱专属定制、全民统一定价、无投保门槛、保障强、性价比高、保障范围全"等惠民特点。M 普惠保（普洱）以互联网为平台，充分运用大数据技术，服务民生领域的重要指示精神。依托"医保+商业保险"直赔体系，配套专项定制的保险产品，该产品不设投保门槛。凡参与基本医疗保险的市民不受年龄、既往病史限制，均可投保。

"M 普惠保（普洱）"在保险科技的加持下简化了承保流程，精准了保费定价，提高了核保精确度，全方位优化了保险保障效率。具体有六大亮点：一是无投保门槛。凡是普洱市基本医疗保险缴费范围且为在保状态的参保人，不限年龄，全家老少都能参保，100 岁以上的老人也能买，老少同价，无须体检，有既往症也可投保。二是性价比高。一年只需 139 元，每天不到 0.4 元钱。三是保障范围全。医保范围内外保障全覆盖，医保外费用也可报销，包括特殊门诊费、住院费、手术费、药品费、检查费、床位费、治疗费。四是保额高。最高可享受 200 万元保障额度，包括 100 万元（基本医保范围内住院医疗费用）+100 万元（基本医保范围外住院医疗费用），且赔付比例高。本地就医的患者在医保报销范围内 90% 报销，在医保报销范围外 60% 报销。五是结算便捷。出院时，赔款自动结算，不用再为报销难、报销慢、少报销而烦心。六是操作简单。线上投保，缴费，生成保单。

案例评述：

普惠保险是普惠金融制度的重要组成部分，是保险业为广大人民群众提供的公平可得、保障适度、覆盖广泛的保险产品和服务。发展普惠保险，对完善我国多层次社会保障体系，提升人民群众总体保障水平，提振中小微企业信心，拓宽企业融资渠道，助力全面推进乡村振兴，实现共同富裕具有重要意义。

大数据技术的出现，一方面，为各大保险公司节约了经营成本，提高了承保收益；另一方面，也给民众带来了切切实实的好处。传统普惠保险依托各大保险公司开展，对承办主体而言，其无法精准识别投保群体的风险。因此，保险定价往往有失精度，服务也无法突出个性化差异，市场逆向选择较严重。对投保主体而言，虽然保费便宜，但其中有各种免责条款、限制条件，投保群体投保难、理赔慢的问题时有存在，普惠保险无法做到"惠普"。

大数据技术的应用让保险人可以实现精准定价、准确识别风险、筛选投保主体，解决了普惠保险以往的痛点、难点问题；同时，投保者还能借助大数据共享平台了解普惠保险各项条款，通过 App 实现一键式缴费投保与快速理赔。大数据的应用得以让普惠保险的惠普功能真正落到实处。

　　案例来源：

　　人民网. 人民金服正式推出人民普惠保险云，助力保险行业数字化转型升级［EB/OL］.（2020-05-20）［2024-07-01］.http://money.people.com.cn/n1/2020/0520/c42877-31716224.html.

2

Big Data and Insurance

This chapter mainly explains the basic ideas and principles of the combination of big data and insurance industry, and shares relevant domestic and foreign cases with students to inspire them to develop insurance technology application scenarios and related products with the help of big data.

2. 1　Basic Theory of Big Data

Since the 21st century, with the wide application of electronic information technology such as computer and Internet, beautiful scenery, news and hot trends around the world are stored and packaged in the form of data based on the Internet media. Huge data has become an important way for people to get information. In 2008, Nature magazine launched a column with Big Data as the cover title; In 2009, "big data" became a hot word and gradually came into people's view.

2. 1. 1　Basic Concepts of Big Data

Data is a fact or the result of observation, which is a logical inference of objective things, and is the unprocessed raw materials used to express objective things. Data can be continuous values, such as sound and images, referred to as analog data; or discrete values, such as symbols and text, referred to as digital data. If it can reflect information about nature or human society, it can be called data.

Big data, also known as mega data, is a collection of information data with abundant content, broad dimensions, and wide coverage. It is a new factor of production that is difficult to extract, store, share and analyze using traditional data processing tools. Big data technology is like searching for valuable things in a vast landfill. Big data technology mainly deals with various types of data generated dynamically and in real time.

From data to big data, it is not only the accumulation of quantity, but also a qualitative leap. Big data allows the original massive, different sources, different forms of single data integration, and can be systematically analyzed, so as to dig out new knowledge difficult to find in the era of small data, and constantly create new value for human society.

2. 1. 2　Characteristics of Big Data

With the rise of digital technology, big data has gradually become one of the core production factors. Compared with data, big data also presents at least the following different characteristics:

2. 1. 2. 1　Large Data Volume

Big data itself carries a huge amount of information. In the era of big data, the development model of data follows Moore's Law, and the Internet Data Center (IDC) predicts that data will grow at a rate of 50% per year, which also means that the amount of data will double every two years.

2. 1. 2. 2　High Frequency

In the era of informatization and globalization, the process of information exchange and resource exchange based on data is cheaper, faster and more frequent. Compared with traditional data, the transmission and processing speed of big data has shown exponential growth.

2. 1. 2. 3　Low Value Density

Big data, although it has high overall value, is inevitably plagued by problems such as data redundancy, poor quality, and information overload due to its huge volume, which leads to a relatively low proportion of effective information in the big data set and a lower utilization efficiency of data, thereby reducing the value density of data.

2. 1. 2. 4　Variety and Complexity

Data can be divided into structured data, semi-structured data, and unstructured data. Traditional data models have a clear definition, are easy to store, manage, and integrate, have consistency among data, and are easy to analyze and dig deep. They generally belong to structured and semi-structured data. Big data is obtained from various sources and is expressed in the form of documents, emails, social media posts, images, audio, and video. It has a personalized and customized data model that stands out and is difficult to process and interpret using traditional methods. The data volume is huge but disordered, showing unstructured characteristics.

2. 1. 2. 5　Full Quantization of Data

The essence of big data is "deep learning", which requires the establishment of large-scale training data sets and the use of machine learning to train artificial intelligence systems to build simulated environments and expert systems for decision-making. Ultimately, big data uses data quantitative analysis to make precise predictions about the future based on the "known" and the "past". The process of inferring the "unknown" from the "known" and predicting the "future" from the "past" is called data quantification, and it runs throughout the entire process of big data application.

2.1.3 Development Status and the Prospects of Big Data ┠──────

In November 2018, Seagate and International Data Corporation (IDC) released the white paper with the theme of "The digitization of the World by Edge to Core". The white paper predicts that the total amount of global data will reach 175ZB by 2025 (See Figure 2.1), and that 49% of the world's stored data will be located in public cloud environments.

From intelligent push to intelligent search, from intelligent assistants to smart homes, from autonomous driving to humanoid robots, in the era of information sharing and "interconnection of everything", big data has greatly facilitated human production and life. With the continuous deepening of intelligent transformation and information interconnection in various industries, the growth speed and accumulation numbers of data will grow exponentially, and the rapid development of the "global data ecosystem" will drive the digital transformation of all humanity.

In the future, the application of big data will bring unlimited prospects to human society. Consequently, big data governance will inevitably become a concern for people. The technological revolution has driven the explosive growth of information data, and human society is undergoing a digital transformation. Using big data to drive social development, improve social governance, and enhance service supervision capabilities is an important trend for the future development of big data.

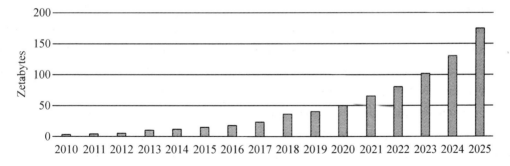

Figure 2.1　Annual Size of the Global Data Sphere

Source: Seagate and International Data Corporation (IDC) "Data Age 2025". https://www.seagate.com/files/www-content/our-story/trends/files/idc-seagate-dataage-chine-whitepaper.pdf

2.1.3.1 Big Data Practice Technology

In terms of application, the practice of big data can be roughly divided into three levels. Although the development of big data is still in its infancy, the three levels of big data application are very extensive in reality.

The first level is descriptive analytics application, which utilizes data access, data storage, data processing, and visualization technologies to precisely locate target data or extract relevant information from databases based on user needs. Building user profiles and understanding sales of goods are examples of the technical applications within this dimension.

The second level is predictive analysis application, which refers to the construction of mathematical models to analyze the relationship between data based on the results of previous large amounts of data, and accordingly predict the development status and trend of things. For example, David Rothschild, a researcher at Microsoft's New York Research Institute, established a prediction model by collecting and analyzing a large amount of public data such as the gambling market, the Hollywood Stock Exchange, and posts published by social media users, and predicted the attribution of many Oscar awards. In 2014 and 2015, it accurately predicted 21 of the 24 Oscar awards, with an accuracy rate of 87.5%.

The third level is guiding analysis application, which is based on the first two levels, using flow computing, graph database and other technologies to predict multiple different results through data imaging, and optimize the final decision. For example, autonomous vehicles can predict the consequences of different driving paths through real-time perception data from multiple sensors, combined with accurate positioning of maps and road conditions, and realize intelligent driving.

In the future, with the expansion of data application fields and the improvement of data sharing platforms, the application of big data at the above three levels will burst out greater value. It is an important direction for the future development of big data to realize accurate tracking, accurate prediction and automatic judgment on the basis of big data, and make production and life fully intelligent.

2.1.3.2 Big Data Governance

Big data can help the intelligent transformation and upgrading of the industry and promote the overall high-quality development of society, but it also causes governance problems. On the one hand, due to the unstructured characteristics of big data, information resources are scattered and disorderly, so it is necessary to establish a shared, open and unified database platform to conduct integrated management and planning of data assets. On the other hand, the construction of digital platforms based on big data may lead to data leakage and privacy security issues. Therefore, how to protect personal privacy data in the case of data interoperability is the development trend of big data governance. Only by handling the relationship between data sharing, data security and privacy protection can we promote the development of big data applications.

2.2 Application Scenarios Combining Big Data and Insurance

Insurance is one of the effective means of risk management. With the development of human society, risks are also diversified, new and universal. In order to achieve accurate risk control and better play the functions of loss compensation and risk transfer, insurance needs to deeply integrate with the new quality productivity represented by big data.

2.2.1 Big Data and Social Insurance

2.2.1.1 Big Data Helps Refine Social Security Services

The social security system emphasizes people-oriented, and the core of service is the needs of the people. Focusing on the practical needs of the people, hitting the social pain points is the goal of the digital transformation and upgrading of the social security system. Social security institutions take big data as a technical means to build a technology center, a business center, an AI center, and a data center, and use data empowerment to run through the whole process of social security from the aspects of optimizing payment channels, expanding social security types, and simple insurance methods, to effectively promote the refined transformation and upgrading of social security services.

The country are making experiments constantly to explore the integration of big data and social insurance through pilots. In 2021, Jiangxi Province built "silent authentication" based on big data and biometric identification, and 2. 58 million elderly residents in the province enjoyed the "no perception, no disturb" authentication service. The "big data accurate positioning + biological face recognition" technology enables the input object to be automatically authenticated without cooperating with the action, which makes the masses in the certification cycle free from the inconvenience brought by the traditional authentication method, and greatly facilitates the elderly, sick, and disabled groups.

2. 2. 1. 2　Big Data Improves the Efficiency of Social Security

The emergence of big data has broken the temporal and spatial barriers of the operation of the social security system in the past, and the social security model based on big data is more diversified, while the social security resources that residents can enjoy are also tending to be inclusive. With the blessing of the data platform, social security has shown new characteristics of multi-level, multi-functional, cross-regional and cross-platform, and the efficiency of the social security system has been greatly improved.

After the launch of the big data platform, residents can understand the whole process of social security relationship transfer and follow-up through apps such as "Palm 12333" or Alipay with one click, which greatly saves the procedure cost and promotes the flow of labor. Qingdao, Shandong Province, based on big data analysis, to create "industrial injury insurance intelligent integrated service", can achieve remote identification of industrial injury, intelligent remote identification, occupational disease or industrial injury remote synchronous identification, to achieve cross-regional, efficient social security services, to solve the past industrial injury identification, evidence difficulties, slow compensation process and a series of problems, comprehensively improve the efficiency of social security operation.

2. 2. 2　Big Data and Commercial Insurance

2. 2. 2. 1　Locate Needs and Tap Customers

Big data can not only help insurance companies accurately identify insurance needs, but also stimulate customers' potential insurance needs. Due to the costs, manpower, return and other problems, traditional commercial insurance companies often ignore the sick group, the elderly group, the sinking market, and the group in demand is difficult to effectively participate in insurance. Under the power of big data, insurance companies can use big data to accurately depict customers, accurately locate customer needs, and carry out personalized insurance customization services. Customers can realize flexible insurance on the Internet platform according to their own insurance needs and economic conditions, which not only overcomes the high cost of traditional insurance services, but also promotes the insurance awareness of the masses to a certain extent, improves the availability of insurance, and then improves the insurance coverage rate and enriches the insurance protection level.

2.2.2.2　Develop Diverse Types of Insurance and Optimize Products

Big data can stimulate insurance companies to optimize and innovate insurance product systems. For example, in the field of agriculture, the use of big data platform to establish a fine prediction model, break through the past crop diseases, disaster due to irregular damage, livestock growth cycle uncertainty and other problems, overcome the problem of rapid disaster claims, through insurance technology to expand the types of insured risks, with the wide coverage of insurance to help rural revitalization. In terms of coping with climate change, a large number of property insurance companies, based on big data actuarial models, use the Internet of Things, artificial intelligence, remote sensing technology, etc., to accurately monitor abnormal areas of climate change, predict extreme weather in specific areas, and introduce preventive measures to effectively prevent climate change risks. The transformation goal of "loss compensation" to "risk reduction" under the background of big data has been realized.

2.2.2.3　Improve Efficiency and Reduce Costs

The traditional insurance business process involves marketing, insure, underwriting, approve, loss assessment, claims and other processes. Due to the uneven quality of agents, obscure insurance contract terms, difficult to understand the real situation of the insured and other factors, the traditional insurance business has disadvantages such as high costs, long time, adverse selection and serious insurance fraud.

With the wide application of big data, various insurance companies are accelerating their own digital transformation. App has increasingly become an important channel for insurance companies to form a consumption relationship with users and enhance user stickiness. Insurance companies use big data to analyze customer characteristics, habits and preferences, analyze and predict customer needs, and lay an important foundation for finding target customers and launching personalized products. Insurance companies based on big data technology can greatly save labor costs, skip the agent and customer conversion level to realize the connection between insurance companies and target objects, and achieve the maximum benefit at the minimum cost. At the same time, the mutual benefit between users and insurance companies can be promoted through big data. Users can understand the terms of the insurance contract with one click through the app; Insurance companies can make judgments on users' real information based on big data, credit ratings, machine learning and other means. Big data connects users with insurance companies, solves the problems of insurance fraud and adverse selection in the past, and promotes the stable development of the insurance market.

2.2.2.4　Accurate Pricing and Risk Identification

At present, big data has been used in exploration and loss determination, precision marketing, differentiated pricing, dynamic premium determination and so on. For example, Clover Health, an emerging health insurance company in the United States, has set up a special data lab to integrate and form a clinical database by utilizing big data such as patients' personal data, diagnosis and treatment data and health data to conduct in-depth analysis on the data of disease testing, treatment and medication during treatment. This method is applied to health insurance. Through the basic data of patients, such as age and gender, disease data, pathological data, etc., a multidimensional mathematical model is established to distinguish different disease risks of individuals, intervene users' behavior through risk coefficient, design products through risk analysis, and provide different insurance services to patients accordingly. Provide technical support for the promotion of differentiated pricing. In addition, the application scenario of big data also appears in the rapid claims and anti-fraud, with the help of image recognition technology, the photos uploaded by the insured and other proof materials are compared in a huge database, and then combined with the cultivated credit history to judge, make accurate judgments through these factors in a short time, and complete the claim review online. To a certain extent, it helps insurance companies reduce the behavior and probability of insurance fraud, and greatly reduces the underwriting risk of insurance companies.

2.3   Foreign Cases of "Insurance + Big Data"

2.3.1   The First Case

Case Tile:

Using Data to Guarantee Health

Case Content:

The "Health and Wellness" consumer category is going through lots of changes. According to a recent Forbes report from The A Group, consumers are more aware of the connection between health, wellness, food, energy, than ever before. For example, "more so than any other generation, B looks to exercise as a way to treat or prevent illness, and it is particularly relevant for emotional and stress-related issues".

At the same time, the rise of wearable tech, like FitBit and Apple Watch, gives users the ability to collect and monitor their own data. Whether people were competing over how many steps they could take a day, or how many hours they slept, users had an unprecedented level of ease in tracking their every move.

C company, an insurance provider, created a program called "Vitality" to capture value from this change in behavior. Modeled on successful programs from other countries, C realized that they could benefit from the positive and proactive attitude towards preventative health (exercise, diet) and rising levels of comfort with wearable technology that collects data. They created the program "Vitality", which is novel in that it can monitor the data of consumer's health habits and reward consumers for good behavior. Participants in the Vitality program are provided with a free Fitbit to track their movements. The consumers can win "vitality points" by making healthy decisions about exercise, which the healthcare provider can then see through the Fitbit data. This can translate into real savings.

"The higher your Vitality Status, the more you can save on your life insurance premiums-up to 10% a year. You can also earn up to $600 in annual savings on your healthy food purchases, as well Apple Watch Ⓒ Series 2 for just $25, simply by exercising regularly."

Instead of a static relationship between healthcare provider and provide, and offline data collection that relies on truthful information, consumers are incentivized to make better decisions about their healthcare and able to improve their deductibles and/or premiums through their healthy choices.

Cis incentivizingthe consumers to make healthier choices benefits the insurance company in several ways. First, it is widely accepted that prevention is better than the cure. The companies are saving themselves money down the road by creating a generation of healthier customers who are motivated to keep themselves healthy. Second, insurance companies can better manage their claims and forecasts with more accurate data and dynamic pricing-they can better service their customers with a better snapshot. Third, insurance companies can start communicating much more data with doctors and physicians, which will not only cut down on administration costs but help both doctor and patient make more informed and accurate choices as opposed to sometimes misleading self-reporting.

C is giving consumers the option to "give out private data for discount in insurance". For consumers ready to share their data and stay healthy to spend less, C captures a great market.

Case Comments:

"The health data trend + insurance companies" is capturing the richness of the data. We can imagine this partnership would be super valuable for basically all health insurance companies. The modern technologies can add value to even such an established business like insurance. Furthermore, this is a perfect economic incentive for people to live healthier lives.

Case Source:

BRODY C. Health insurance remained: John Hancock's vitality[EB/OL]. (2017-04-06)[2024-07-01].https://d3.harvard.edu/platform-digit/submission/health-insurance-reimagined-john-hancocks-vitality-using-data-to-promote-health.

2.3.2 The Second Case

Case Tile:

Insurance Company Cleverly Utilizes Data Science

Case Content:

Ever since the phrase "Big Data" was coined in the 1990s, the benefits of leveraging large amounts of data in business have been clear. Yet in 2021, only a quarter of executives described their companies as being data-driven. A insurance company is among the minority that fully embraces data science. How does data science help enhance its predictive capabilities? The concrete ways are as follows:

Firstly, using data to optimize credit management.

Data science can seem a bit like a crystal ball. But it's actually a combination of machine learning, programming skills and statistical analysis. Using these techniques and tools, A identify patterns in historical data to create models that predict what could happen in the future.

These data-driven models are tailored to meet specific business needs. They can be trained to identify the warning signs of customer dissatisfaction, and on the flip side, find potential new customers. They also play an integral role in risk management, detecting fraud and providing early warning signals of potential financial difficulty among buyers.

Secondly, beyond Excel: predicting bankruptcy risk with machine learning.

While data science is a relatively new field, insurance companies have always worked with actuaries who use similar statistical techniques to predict risks. But what puts data science in a league of its own is that it can comprehensively analyze so much data. Much more than a simple Excel spreadsheet ever could.

Machine learning can gather information from millions of companies, analyzing key factors like debt, liquidity, and country and sector risks. With this information, A is able to highlight which companies may be at risk of non payment, or even filing for bankruptcy.

However, they also rely on "human power". They update and adapt the models constantly with the help of risk analysts who review company financials daily and check the model for accuracy. So, while their advice is informed by large volumes of high-quality data, human analysis is the key. Thanks to this powerful combination, A can help their clients make safe, confident decisions and protect themselves against risk.

Thirdly, driving innovation in credit management.

As the insurance industry move further into the digital age, the power of data-driven decision-making is becoming undeniable. At A Trade, they are taking full advantage of this opportunity. They are using data science to improve their predictive capabilities and gain efficiencies by detecting weak signals across a large range of subjects, from fraud detection to debt collection.

But they are not stopping there. As the field of data science evolves, so too do A. A stay at the forefront of the latest technologies and techniques to continuously improve their models, enhance the complement of data science and their expert analysis, and provide clients with the best possible service. The future of data science in trade credit insurance is bright, "we're excited to be leading the way", the leader of the A trade said that.

Case Comments:

A empowers the company's operational chain with big data technology, utilizing data science and technology to accurately predict credit risk, financial risk, customer churn risk, and other risks in the company's business process. A is a pioneer in the application of big data technology in the insurance industry, which has also given some inspiration to insurance companies in the industry: big data technology can not only be used for specific products, but can also be combined with the company's own construction, providing important protection for internal governance and risk prevention.

Case Source：

TRADE A. How Allianz Trade uses data science to enhance predictive capabilities［EB/OL］.（2023－03－21）［2024－07－01］. https：//www. allianz－trade. com/en＿global/news－insights/business－tips－and－trade－advice/How－Allianz－Trade－uses－data－science－to－enhance－predictive－capabilities.html.〉

3

人工智能与保险业

本章主要阐释人工智能与保险业相互结合的基本思路与原理，并精选相关国内外案例与学生分享，启发学生借助人工智能开发保险科技应用场景和相关保险产品的思路。

3.1 人工智能基本理论

3.1.1 人工智能的基本概念

人工智能（Artificial Intelligence，简称 AI）是新一轮科技革命和产业变革的重要驱动力量。人工智能是指利用计算机科学模拟人的一些智能行为，使得机器能够和人类一样学习、处理和解决问题。它是被研究、开发用于模拟、延伸和扩展人的智能的理论、方法、技术及应用系统的一门新的技术科学。人工智能包括机器人、语言识别、图像识别、自然语言处理、专家系统、机器学习、计算机视觉等，是智能学科重要的组成部分。并生产出一种新的能以人类智能相似的方式做出反应的智能机器。人工智能可以分为以下几种类型：

3.1.1.1 弱人工智能

弱人工智能（Artificial Narrow Intelligence，简称 ANI）是指不能真正实现推理和解决问题的智能机器，这些机器表面看像是智能的，但是并不真正拥有智能，也不会有自主意识。

3.1.1.2 强人工智能

强人工智能（Artificial General Intelligence，简称 AGI）是指真正能思维的智能机器，并且认为这样的机器是有知觉的和自我意识的。这类机器可分为类人（机器的思考和推理类似人的思维）与非类人（机器产生了和人完全不一样的知觉和意识，使用和人完全不一样的推理方式）两大类。

3.1.1.3 超强人工智能

超强人工智能（Artificial Super Intelligence，简称 ASI）。科学家把超强人工智能定义为在几乎所有领域都比最聪明的人类大脑聪明很多，包括科学创新、通识和社交技能。

3.1.2 人工智能的发展历程

3.1.2.1 人工智能发展的孕育期

1946 年，电子计算机的发明变革了信息存储与处理技术，随着计算机理论的发展，产生了计算机科学，这为后来人工智能的产生做了铺垫。1950 年，艾伦·麦席森·图灵提出了机器思维的想法"I propose to consider the question,'Can machines think?'This should begin with definitions of the meaning of the terms'machine'and'think'"，并于 1950 年 10 月发表了《机器能思考吗》的文章，由此奠定了他"人工智能之父"的地位。从本质上来看，人工智能是计算机技术的一种延伸。

3.1.2.2 人工智能的元年

1956 年夏季，以麦卡赛、明斯基、罗切斯特和申农等为首的年轻科学家，共同研究和探讨关于机器模拟智能的一系列有关问题，并首次提出了"人工智能"这一术语，标志着"人工智能"这门新兴学科的正式诞生。从这之后，人工智能也迎来了它发展的元年。

3.1.2.3 人工智能的第一次发展高潮

在 1956 年首次提出"人工智能"之后，人工智能迎来了它的第一次发展高潮。在这段长达十余年的时间里，计算机被广泛应用于数学和自然语言领域，用来解决代数、几何和英语问题。1956 年，塞缪尔成功研制的西洋跳棋程序，战胜了当时的西洋棋大师罗伯特尼赖。1968 年，美国斯坦福研究所（SRI）研发了首台智能机器人 Shakey，它拥有类似人的感觉，如触觉、听觉等。这让很多研究者看到了机器向人工智能发展的希望。

3.1.2.4 人工智能的第一次低潮

20 世纪 70 年代，人工智能的发展进入了一段痛苦而艰难岁月。科研人员在人工智能的研究中对项目难度预估不足，不仅导致与美国国防高级研究计划署的合作计划失败，还让大家对人工智能的前景蒙上了一层阴影。在这段时间里，舆论对人工智能的态度也开始发生了变化，大量的科研经费都被分流到了其他领域。

3.1.2.5 人工智能的第二次发展高潮

卡内基梅隆大学于 1980 年研制出一种"专家系统"，被称为 XCON。这是一个使用了人工智能的系统，通俗地说就是"知识库+推理引擎"的结合体。1981 年，日本经济产业省拨款八亿五千万美元支持第五代计算机项目。到 1986 年，这个系统每年为公司节约 4 000 多美元。

3.1.2.6 人工智能的第二次低潮

20 世纪 80 年代末，由于维护成本高，升级难度大等，XCON 出现了各种各样的问题。到 1987 年，Apple 和 IBM 公司生产的台式机性能都超过了 Symbolics 等厂商生产的通用计算机，XCON 走向没落。而日本的第五代计算机项目的目标也没能实现，人工智能的发展再次陷入低谷。

3.1.2.7 人工智能发展的平稳期

自 20 世纪 90 年代中期以来，随着人工智能特别是神经网络技术的逐渐成熟，人类对人工智能的认识也越来越客观和理性，人工智能逐渐步入了一个稳定的发展阶段。"深蓝"于 1997 年击败世界棋王卡斯帕罗夫，再次在公共领域掀起一场关于人工智能的热潮。这是人工智能发展史上的一大里程碑。2006 年，Hinton 在神经网络上的研究取得了突破性进展，使人们再一次期待机器追赶上人类。2011 年，由 IBM 研发的名为"沃森"的人工智能项目在一个智力竞赛中击败了两个人类冠军，取得了胜利。

3.1.2.8 人工智能的蓬勃发展期

自 2012 年以来，人工智能的研究和发展逐步由专业领域深入社会生活的各个方面，在图像识别、语音识别等方面都有了长足的进步，促进了人工智能技术的普及。由此，出现了"人工智能+金融""人工智能+医疗""人工智能+保险"等全新的场景。此外，当前的人工智能研究正逐步向基于深度学习的人工智能领域发展，例如，自然语言处理、计算机视觉、语音识别、增强学习等。深度学习技术的兴起与发展，为人工智能的应用与发展带来了新的推动力与发展方向。

3.1.3 人工智能的特点

随着人工智能的不断发展，呈现出了以下五个特点：

3.1.3.1 智能

人工智能最大的特点就是智能。从本质上来说，对于机器，用人类写出来的程序来提升自己的数据处理能力，这就是机器学习。在这个过程中，没有任何的自主意识，神经网络算法逐渐完善，这就是深度学习，是表征学习数据法的一种。

3.1.3.2 自主

人工智能是可以创作的，具有自主性。人有自己的意识，这一点是任何一个人工智能都没有的。而对人工智能来说，人类只是对设计过程进行了控制，在识别和获得了数据后，本体可以在没有人干涉和控制的情况下进行学习、推理和决策，具备了一定的自主能力。

3.1.3.3 专用

专用性指的是目前一种人工智能应用通常仅能用于一个领域，无法实现通用的人工智能。面向特定任务（比如下围棋）的专用人工智能系统由于任务单一、需求明确、应用边界清晰等形成了人工智能领域的单点突破。

3.1.3.4 专业

专业性指的是人工智能具有了等同甚至超越人类专业水平的能力。随着深度学习等技术的成熟，人工智能已不仅能够进行简单的重复性工作，还能够完成专业化程度很高的任务。

3.1.3.5 普惠

普惠性指的是人工智能技术能够与不同的产业相结合产生新的应用，对各行各业都产生了普惠效应。

3.1.4 人工智能的发展现状和前景

在新科技革命和产业变革的大背景下，人工智能与产业深度融合，为加快战略新兴产业发展，构筑综合竞争优势注入活力。人工智能技术的各种产品在各个领域代替人类从事简单重复的体力或脑力劳动，大大提升了生产效率和生活质量，也促进了各个行业的发展和变革。目前，人工智能技术已在金融、医疗、安防、教育、交通、制造、零售等多个领域实现技术落地，且应用场景也愈来愈丰富。

如图 3.1 所示，近年来，中国人工智能产业处于高速发展阶段，核心产业规模呈现爆发式增长，涌现出了大量的人工智能企业。中国人工智能产业逐渐趋于稳定，产业模式探索已基本完成，产业焦点从技术研发转向各行业多元化场景应用落地。未来随着新兴技术逐渐成熟应用并形成协同效应，更多的创新应用将成为可能，中国人工智能产业将迎来新一轮的增长点。预计到 2025 年，中国人工智能产业规模将达到 3 369.3亿元，较 2022 年增长 63.85%。未来人工智能的发展呈现出如下趋势。

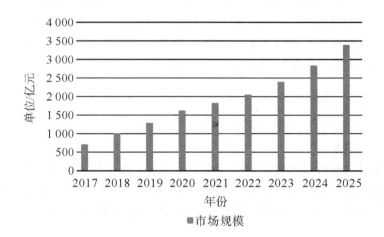

图 3.1　中国人工智能产业规模及预测

图片来源：https://baijiahao.baidu.com/s？id＝1764476198217525291&wfr＝spider&for＝pc.

第一，智能化与自动化。未来人工智能的发展趋势主要是智能化与自动化。智能化是指让计算机具备类似人类的智能能力，可以通过学习和推理来完成各种任务。自动化是指让计算机能够自主地感知、决策和执行任务，减少人类的干预，提高工作效率和质量。

第二，多模态融合。未来人工智能的发展趋势还包括多模态融合。多模态融合是指将多种感知模态（如图像、语音、文本等）结合起来，进行更全面和准确的信息处理和分析。多模态融合将成为人工智能技术在自然语言处理、计算机视觉等领域的重要方向。

第三，人机协作。未来人工智能的发展趋势还包括人机协作。人机协作是指让计算机与人类进行更紧密的合作和交互，发挥各自的优势，提高工作效率和质量。人机协作将成为人工智能技术在生产制造、医疗等领域的重要应用方向。

第四，个性化。未来人工智能的发展趋势还包括个性化。个性化是指根据用户的个性和需求，为用户提供个性化的服务和体验。

第五，场景化。场景化是指将人工智能技术应用于特定的场景和领域，如智能家居、智能医疗等，计算机的决策过程也会更加可靠和可信，减少出错的风险，提高人们对人工智能技术的信任感和接受度。

3.2 人工智能与保险结合的应用场景

在保险业，人工智能已逐步被应用于前端销售、定损理赔、风控减损等领域。目前，我国保险领域人工智能技术的应用，仍以理解式为主。但从行业发展态势来看，人工智能大模型与保险业的结合很可能在不久的未来实现迭代升级，重塑保险行业的生态。

3.2.1 智能客服

智能客服是人工智能在保险行业运用最为广泛的场景之一。智能客服能够综合应用语音识别、语义理解、语音合成、光学字符识别、人脸识别、电子签名、数字员工等多项人工智能技术，为客户提供咨询、外呼及回访等众多咨询和业务服务。比如 PA 的智能客服"小惠"，能随时为客户提供产品咨询、业务办理。T 寿保险公司的智能客服机器人"小麦"，能实时解答客户的问题。YG 保险公司也在去年上线了人工智能机器人，提供文本对话交互功能。此外，瑞士的一家保险公司，不久前成为世界上第一家推出基于 ChatGPT 技术的直接客户联系服务的上市保险公司。该公司将 ChatGPT 与其已有的 AI 助理 Clara 结合，可以向客户提供有关保险、养老金和房屋所有权的智能咨询。

3.2.2 保险营销

基于大模型技术构建智能保险产品推荐机器人，通过分析客户的背景、需求、偏好、风险承受能力等信息，结合保险领域大模型丰富的保险产品知识，应用自然语言交互技术，为客户提供个性化、全天候在线的保险产品推荐和配置方案建议，回答客户关于保险产品的各种问题，包括保险种类、保险责任、保险期限、投保条件、保险条款、保费等，提高了保险的销售效率和客户的体验感。例如，R 公司将创新的 AI 技术和深入的业务流程解决方案应用于保险销售，帮助实现了销售效率和业绩的提升。上述应用已经服务于中国 RM 保险、ZA 保险等。

3.2.3 保险理赔和防欺诈

保险理赔一直以来都是消费者和保险监管比较关注的保险服务关键节点，也是人工智能应用的重要场景。传统保险理赔方式存在理赔流程环节冗长、理赔资料审核复杂、过度依赖经验判断等痛点。随着人工智能的发展与应用，智能定损、智能理赔、风险预警、风险反欺诈等各个环节，都有人工智能施展的空间，从而提高了理赔的效率、降低了理赔成本、提高了客户的体验感。ZA 健康险的理赔速度在人工智能赋能下持续提升。通过 ZA 保险"智能理赔"系统，每 42 秒就有一个理赔结案。截至 2021 年上半年，ZA 健康险已实现 94% 的线上理赔申请，客户获赔等待时长同比减少 55%。ZA 保险还为万元及以下理赔案件建立了专属通道——"1 日赔"，符合标准的理赔案件中99% 都实现了 24 小时快速理赔，极大地提升了理赔效率。

3.3 "保险+AI" 国内案例

3.3.1 国内经典案例之一 ┤

案例题目:

MY 保上线行业首个 AI 保险规划师"省心配"

案例内容:

近年来，AI 技术正不断推动保险业数字化转型，MY 保推出的 AI 客服、AI 理赔等创新服务模式，不仅给消费者带来了更好的体验感，还为保险公司实现了降本增效。

在众多保险产品中挑出适合的产品并不容易。保险产品类型多怕买错，对保额需求了解不足怕买多，这些难题长期困扰着保险产品需求者。

为了解决这些难题，2023 年 4 月 12 日，MY 保再度重磅发布智能保险配置工具"省心配"。省心配团队基于保险精算理论，结合传统金融学的马科维茨理论及经济学中帕累托最优算法独创了"HRAAM 保险配置模型"，用户输入年龄、地区等基本信息后，该模型便会通过风险分析、保障评估、产品匹配三个步骤进行配置，从为用户模拟匹配的几万种保险配置方案中，推荐最匹配用户需求的一组方案。这一工具能根据用户的年龄、地区、预算、保险需求等综合分析，通过智能模型为用户量身打造省钱、省时、省心的保险配置方案。据悉，这也是业内首个 AI 保险规划师。通过"省心配"，用户可以避免买错保险、重复购买同类保险等问题，能节省 30% 的预算。另外，"省心配"生成方案只需 30 秒，节省了用户选保险的时间。

同时，"省心配"还会根据结果为用户推荐适合的产品。目前，MY 保已与约 90 家保险公司建立合作，且与保险公司共同打造了"金选"系列产品，为客户提供丰富的产品选择，从配置方案到决策购买，全流程体验流畅。

此外，"省心配"本着客观、公正的原则，根据用户的个人情况和实际需求来推荐配置，完全不受产品热度、销售佣金等其他因素的影响，也不会向用户和保险公司收取费用。

值得一提的是，继"金选""安心赔"后，MY 保推出的"省心配"是其服务上的又一重大突破，借助 AI 实现了保险产品在"选品、配置、理赔"三个环节的高品质服务的全覆盖。

案例评述:

通常来说，保险服务的核心环节包括选品、配置和理赔。然而，由于保险产品的专业性，认知门槛比市场上的其他商品要高。鉴于此，优化这三个环节的服务就显得至关重要。传统保险规划师通常服务于高知人群，而 AI 保险规划师"省心配"能让大众免费获得专业的保险配置服务，满足工薪阶层的需求，为共同推动大众对于保险保障的认知和实践水平的提升注入新的力量。

总之，人工智能在保险业的应用不但能极大节省消费者的决策精力和成本，满足人们的保险需求，也有助于保险行业提升消费者满意度和推动保险产业高质量发展。

案例来源：

贝壳财经. 破解保险配置难题，蚂蚁保上线行业首个 AI 保险规划师"省心配"〔EB/OL〕.（2023-04-12）〔2024-07-01〕.https://finance.sina.com.cn/jjxw/2023-04-12/doc-imyqcprh3925857.shtml.

3.3.2　国内经典案例之二

案例题目：

PA 人寿保险公司"智能理赔"打造"三省"服务新体验

案例内容：

随着技术的快速发展和数字化进程的推进，保险行业面临着提高效率和优化用户体验的迫切需求。传统理赔申请流程存在一些痛点，如理赔流程复杂、手动输入繁琐、材料上传不便捷等，给用户业务办理及保司审核带来了时间成本及人力成本的压力。

对于保险客户，理赔最关键的触点环节在报案、申请和审核。在传统理赔业务模式下，由于报案需要提供的字段多，对于部分人群来说，操作相对复杂。在理赔申请环节，用户线下前往客服中心申请费时费力，线上申请易发生漏传、错传等情况，导致申请失败。进入理赔审核环节时，对用户而言，若材料提交不合格，审核时效滞后，导致多次提交影响理赔体验。对保险公司而言，理赔审核字段、理赔影像材料、理赔责任、理赔金额均需人工逐一录入和核对，理赔审核效率低、时间长、差错风险高。

PA 人寿保险公司持续践行保险为民，为充分贯彻落实《关于促进"互联网+医疗健康"发展的意见》《健康保险管理办法》等文件精神，积极借助信息技术手段，简化理赔流程，提升服务效率。2023 年，PA 人寿保险公司推出全新"AI 智能理赔"服务流程，利用人工智能技术，搭建一个从理赔申请到理赔审核全程智能化、高效率的系统，为用户带来便捷和准确的服务体验，缩短理赔申请时间并提高用户的满意度，让用户理赔省心省时又省钱。

该流程通过虚拟数字真人形象，与用户面对面沟通，指导用户用一句话语音理赔报案，再通过图像类型识别、质量判断、信息核验、合规检测四大功能模块，实现信息自动识别，完成理赔申请填报，最大限度地减少用户理赔报案和申请操作。同时，在用户提交理赔申请后，AI 后台实现审核字段智能录入、理赔资料自动审核、责任风险主动识别、赔付金额自动计算，从而实现快速理赔，让用户零等待，让用户理赔省心省时又省钱。

智能理赔流程已于 2023 年 6 月在广东、甘肃、大连等省市的多家机构试点上线。上线后用户理赔报案平均时间 2 分钟，较传统报案流程大幅提效，最快仅需 20 秒即可完成报案。理赔申请平均只要 10 分钟，较传统流程提效显著。

综上，PA 人寿保险公司打造了以智能报案、智能申请、智能审核为中心的智能理赔流程，有效解决了传统理赔流程的诸多痛点问题，树立了保险理赔智能化数字化改造的行业标杆，颠覆性地完成理赔流程重构，给用户带来省心、省时、省钱的"三省"服务体验。

案例评述：

PA 人寿保险公司借助 AI 全新打造的智能理赔流程，从用户的角度出发，解决了长期以来用户在理赔报案、申请、审核环节的痛点问题，实现了用户触点体验再升级、审核自动化、用户零等待及运营服务能力再提升，真正做到把复杂问题留给自己，把简单和便捷带给用户，让用户省心、省时、省钱。

总之，PA 人寿保险公司秉持以人民为中心，以用户需求为导向，用 AI 等科技赋能提升理赔服务水平，坚持专业让生活更简单的文化理念，为客户提供有温度、有速度的保险理赔服务。

案例来源：

中国银行保险报. 平安人寿"智能理赔"打造"三省"服务新体验｜2023 保险业数字化转型案例展示［EB/OL］.（2023－11－30）［2024－07－01］. https://baijiahao. baidu. com/s？id=1783975447274268025&wfr=spider&for=pc.

3.4 课程思政案例

案例题目：

Z 人寿财险利用 AI 探索创新"绿色保险"，助力绿色发展

案例内容：

习近平总书记强调，"中国式现代化是人与自然和谐共生的现代化"。党的二十大报告指出，"要加快发展方式绿色转型，实施全面节约战略，发展绿色低碳产业，倡导绿色消费，推动形成绿色低碳的生产方式和生活方式"。2023 年中央金融工作会议指出，要做好科技金融、绿色金融、普惠金融、养老金融、数字金融五篇大文章。绿色金融已成为撬动绿色发展的重要力量。

"十四五"规划伊始，Z 人寿财险已将"绿色"理念融入自身重大战略决策，积极部署、有力落实，逐步探索绿色发展新路径，推进金融保险业务和绿色发展相融合。

丰富的绿色保险产品，离不开坚实的技术保障和持续的科技创新。Z 人寿财险利用科技赋能绿色保险，从绿色销售、绿色运营、绿色办公等方面找准发力点，加强线上化、智能化、自动化应用，全力推动公司发展绿色转型。

在移动端，Z 人寿财险全新打造集招募、获客、学习、营销、商圈、管理于一体的 Z 寿天财（安心版），平台注册用户数突破 10 万人，实现车险线上化出单量占比超 75%、非车险移动出单量占比超 30%；上线"车 e 销"车险极速报价出单工具，利用 OCR、人脸识别等人工智能技术，支持敏捷信息采集和快速电子出单，出单时长缩短 49%；上线"非车 e 销"非车险配置方案，基于销售场景实现产品责任灵活配置、快速审批、快速上线，实现投保全链条无纸化、线上化、智能化。

在理赔端，Z 人寿财险通过 AI 图片智能定损、人脸识别、轮胎破损分类识别等技术有效地降低理赔运营成本的同时，探寻汽车"低碳修复"技术，助力建设可持续发展与节约型社会。

低碳保值维修理念持续深化，明确低碳保值维修企业准入管理和理赔操作细则，推动事故受损原件修复替代更换。目前，低碳修复配件累计超 64 万件，涉及金额超 28 亿元。Z 人寿财险新疆分公司积极搭建低碳修复合作平台，与低碳修复第三方公司及汽车凹陷无痕修复公司建立合作关系，采用专业设备和专业恢复技术，将传统汽车维修过程中易损塑料件、铝制件、灯具、轮辋等配件，通过专业设备和技术手段进行

修复，使修复后的配件与汽车原有性能及外观相同，有效减少更换配件的整车维修模式，助力减损降赔和绿色低碳发展。

此外，Z 人寿财险大力推广 RPA 流程机器人应用，当前累计已上线超 400 个自动化流程，累计节省人工操作时间近 50 万个小时；将 AI 技术与流程机器人 RPA 有机结合，致力打造流程机器人与业务场景的深度融合，全新推出了"AI+RPA"和企业级流程机器人。持续推进短信降本增效专项治理，引入 AIM 短信，进一步丰富短信发送内容。

目前，新型绿色保险逐渐深入全产业链的各个环节，以满足生产经营过程中的不同保险需求。人工智能技术的赋能，为绿色保险创新提供了更多可能。

案例评述：

站在实现中华民族可持续发展的战略高度，习近平总书记提出"绿水青山就是金山银山"的科学论断。绿色发展是以效率、和谐、持续为目标的经济增长和社会发展方式。绿色发展既是对可持续发展的继承，也是可持续发展中国化的理论创新，符合历史潮流的演进规律。这一重要的发展理念，也是推进现代化建设的重大原则。新发展阶段，推进"双碳"工作是破解资源环境约束突出问题、实现可持续发展的迫切需要，是我国经济从要素数量驱动向要素质量与创新驱动转化的内在要求。

在人工智能的赋能下推动绿色发展，助力高质量发展，保险公司责无旁贷。Z 人寿财险牢固树立和践行"绿水青山就是金山银山"的理念，努力践行金融央企责任担当，发挥保险保障服务功能，助力"双碳"经济，为经济高质量发展不断注入绿色发展新动能。

案例来源：

中国银行保险报. 中国人寿财险探索创新"绿色保险"着力书写绿色金融文章 [EB/OL].（2023–12–12）[2024–07–01].http://www.xinhuanct.com/money/20231212/c823d5c02efe425d87dad3dde0bbb8ef/c.html.

3 | Artificial Intelligence and Insurance

This chapter mainly explains the basic ideas and principles of the combination of artificial intelligence and insurance industry, and shares relevant domestic and foreign cases with students to inspire them to develop insurance technology application scenarios and related insurance products with the help of artificial intelligence.

3. 1 Basic Theory of Artificial Intelligence

3. 1. 1 The Basic Concept of Artificial Intelligence

Artificial Intelligence (AI) is an important driving force for a new round of scientific and technological revolution and industrial change. Artificial intelligence refers to the use of computer science to simulate some intelligent human behaviors, so that machines can learn, process and solve problems like humans. It is a new technical science to study and develop the theory, method, technology and application system for simulating, extending and expanding human intelligence. Artificial intelligence is a very broad science, including robotics, language recognition, image recognition, natural language processing, expert systems, machine learning, computer vision, etc. Artificial intelligence is an important part of the discipline of intelligence and has produced a new class of intelligent machines that can react in a similar way to human intelligence. Artificial intelligence can be divided into the following types:

3. 1. 1. 1 Weak Artificial Intelligence

Artificial Narrow Intelligence (ANI) is an intelligent machine that cannot actually reason and solve problems, which appears to be intelligent, but does not have real intelligence and does not have autonomous consciousness.

3. 1. 1. 2 Strong Artificial Intelligence

Artificial General Intelligence (AGI) refers to intelligent machines that can actually think and believe that such machines are sentient and self-aware. Such machines can be divided into two categories: humanoid (machines that think and reason like people do) and non-humanoid (machines that produce completely different perceptions and consciousness and use completely different ways of reasoning than those of people).

3.1.1.3 Super Artificial Intelligence

Artificial Super Intelligence (ASI). Scientists define super AI as being significantly smarter than the smartest human brain in almost every area, including scientific innovation, general knowledge, and social skills.

3.1.2 Development History of Artificial Intelligence

3.1.2.1 The Gestation Period of Artificial Intelligence Development

In 1946, the invention of electronic computers revolutionized information storage and processing, and with the development of computer theory, computer science was produced, which paved the way for the later production of artificial intelligence. In 1950, Alan Matheson Turing proposed the idea of machine thinking. "Can Machines Think?" published in October 1950 has ever since established his status as the "father of artificial intelligence". In essence, artificial intelligence is an extension of computer technology.

3.1.2.2 First Year of Artificial Intelligence

In the summer of 1956, young scientists led by Mc Cassey, Minsky, Rochester and Shennon jointly studied and discussed a series of issues related to simulating intelligence with machines, and proposed the term "artificial intelligence" for the first time, marking the official birth of the emerging discipline of "artificial intelligence". Since then, artificial intelligence has ushered in its first year of development.

3.1.2.3 The First Artificial Intelligence Spring

After it was first proposed in 1956, artificial intelligence ushered in its first upsurge of development. For more than a decade, computers were widely used in mathematics and natural languages to solve problems in algebra, geometry, and English. In the same year, Samuel developed a successful checkers program, defeating the then chess master Robert Nilay. In 1968, the Stanford Research Institute (SRI) in the United States developed the first intelligent robot Shakey, which has human-like feelings, such as touch, hearing and so on. This has led many researchers to see confidence in the development of machines to artificial intelligence.

3.1.2.4 The First Artificial Intelligence Winter

In the 1970s, artificial intelligence entered a painful and difficult period. The insufficient prediction of project difficulty by researchers in artificial intelligence research not only led to the failure of the cooperation plan with the U.S. Defense Advanced Research Projects Agency, but also cast a shadow on the prospect of artificial intelligence. During this time, the attitude of public opinion toward artificial intelligence has also begun to change, and a large amount of research funding has been diverted to other topics.

3.1.2.5 The Second Artificial Intelligence Spring

Carnegie Mellon University developed an "expert system" called XCON in 1980. This is a system that uses artificial intelligence, which is a combination of "knowledge base + inference engine". In 1981, the Japanese Ministry of Economy, Trade and Industry allocated $ 850 million to support the fifth-generation computer project. By 1986, the system was saving the company more than $ 4,000 a year.

3.1.2.6 The Second Artificial Intelligence Winter

In the late 1980s, due to the high maintenance cost, the difficulty of upgrading and other reasons, the "expert system" encountered a variety of problems. By 1987, desktop computers produced by Apple and IBM outperformed general-purpose computers like Symbolics, and expert systems declined. The goal of Japan's fifth-generation computer project has not been achieved, and the development of artificial intelligence has once again fallen into a trough.

3.1.2.7 Stable Period of Artificial Intelligence Development

Since the mid-1990s, with the gradual maturity of artificial intelligence, especially neural network technology, human understanding of artificial intelligence has become more and more objective and rational, and artificial intelligence has gradually entered a stable stage of development. "Deep Blue" defeated the world chess champion Garry Kasparov in 1997, once again setting off a wave of artificial intelligence in the public sphere. This is a major milestone in the history of artificial intelligence. In 2006, Hinton's research on neural networks made a breakthrough that once again led to expectations that machines would catch up with humans. In 2011, an artificial intelligence project called "Watson", developed by IBM, beat two human champions in a quiz.

3.1.2.8 Period of Vigorous Development of Artificial Intelligence

Since 2012, the research and development of artificial intelligence has gradually penetrated from the professional field to all aspects of social life, and great progress has been made in image recognition, speech recognition and other aspects, which has promoted the popularity of artificial intelligence technology. As a result, new scenarios such as "artificial intelligence + finance" "artificial intelligence + medical" and "artificial intelligence + insurance" have emerged. In addition, the current artificial intelligence research is gradually developing into artificial intelligence fields based on deep learning, such as natural language processing, computer vision, speech recognition, reinforcement learning, and so on. The rise and development of deep learning technology has brought new impetus and development direction for the application and development of artificial intelligence.

3.1.3 Characteristics of Artificial Intelligence

With the continuous development of artificial intelligence, the following characteristics have emerged:

3. 1. 3. 1　Artiflcial Intelligence is Intelligent

The biggest feature of artificial intelligence is intelligence, in essence, for machines, using human-written programs to improve their data processing capabilities, which is machine learning. In this process, there is no autonomous consciousness, and the neural network algorithm is gradually improved, which is deep learning, a kind of representation learning data method.

3. 1. 3. 2　Artiflcial Intelligence Has Autonomy

Artificial intelligence is creative and autonomous. Humans have consciousness, which any artificial intelligence doesn't possess. For artificial intelligence, humans only control the design process, and after identifying and obtaining the data, AI in itself can learn, reason and make decisions, and has a certain autonomy without human interference and control.

3. 1. 3. 3　Artificial Intelligence is Specific

Specificity refers to the fact that at present, an AI application can usually only be used in one field, and cannot achieve general artificial intelligence. Dedicated artificial intelligence systems for specific tasks (such as playing Go) have formed a single breakthrough in the field of artificial intelligence because of the single task, clear requirements, and clear application boundaries.

3. 1. 3. 4　Artificial Intelligence is Professional

Professionalism refers to the ability of artificial intelligence to equal or exceed human expertise. With the maturity of technologies such as deep learning, artificial intelligence is not only able to carry out simple repetitive work, but also complete tasks with a high degree of professionalism.

3. 1. 3. 5　Artiflcial Intelligence is Inclusive

Inclusive means that artificial intelligence technology can be combined with different industries to produce new applications, and have a beneficial effect on all walks of life.

3. 1. 4　Development Status and Prospects of Artificial Intelligence

In the context of the new scientific and technological revolution and industrial transformation, the deep integration of artificial intelligence and industry has injected vitality into the development of strategic emerging industries and the construction of comprehensive competitive advantages. Various products based on artificial intelligence technology replace human beings in various fields to engage in simple and repetitive physical or mental labor, which greatly improves production efficiency and quality of life, and also promotes the development and change of various industries. At present, artificial intelligence technology has achieved technology landing in many fields such as finance, medical care, security, education, transportation, manufacturing, retail, and application scenarios are becoming more and more abundant.

As shown in Figure 3. 2, in recent years, China's artificial intelligence industry is in a stage of rapid development, the scale of core industries has shown explosive growth, and a large number of artificial intelligence enterprises have emerged. China's artificial intelligence industry is gradually stabilizing, the exploration of industrial models has been basically completed, and the industrial focus has shifted from technology research and development to diversified application scenarios in various industries. In the future, as emerging technologies gradually mature and form synergies, more innovative applications will become possible, and China's artificial intelligence industry will usher in a new round of growth. It is estimated that by 2025, the scale of China's artificial intelligence industry will reach 336.93 billion yuan, an increase of 63.85% over 2022. The development of artificial intelligence in the future shows the following trends:

First, intelligence and automation. The development trend of artificial intelligence in the future is mainly intelligence and automation. Intelligence refers to the ability of computers to have human-like intelligence, which can complete various tasks through learning and reasoning. Automation refers to enabling computers to perceive, decide and perform tasks autonomously, reducing human intervention and improving work efficiency and quality.

Second, multi-modal fusion. The future development trend of artificial intelligence also includes multi-modal fusion. Multimodal fusion refers to the combination of multiple perceptual modes (such as images, speech, text, etc.) for more comprehensive and accurate information processing and analysis. Multimodal fusion will become an important direction of artificial intelligence technology in natural language processing, computer vision and other fields.

Third, man-machine collaboration. Future AI trends also include human-machine collaboration. Man-machine collaboration refers to making computers and humans cooperate and interact more closely, giving play to their respective advantages, and improving work efficiency and quality. Man-machine collaboration will become an important application direction of artificial intelligence technology in manufacturing, medical and other fields.

Fourth, personalization. The future development trend of artificial intelligence also includes personalization and scenarialization. Personalization refers to providing users with personalized services and experiences according to the user's personality and needs, and at the same time, the computer's decision-making process is more transparent and interpretable, so that users can understand the computer's decision-making logic and basis.

Fifth, scene. Scenarioization refers to the application of artificial intelligence technology to specific scenarios and fields, such as smart home, smart medical treatment, etc., and the decision-making process of the computer will be more reliable and credible, reduce the risk of error, and improve people's trust and acceptance of artificial intelligence technology. Forecast of China's AI industry scale see Figure 3.1.

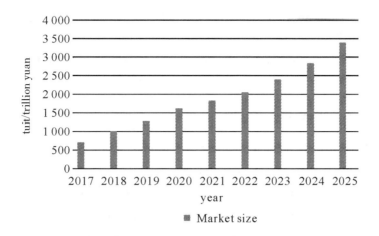

Figure 3. 1　**Forecast of China's AI Industry Scale**

Photo credit: Sadie Consultants https://baijiahao. baidu. com/s? id = 1764476198217525291&wfr = spider&for = pc.

3. 2　Application Scenarios Combining Artificial Intelligence and Insurance

Artificial intelligence technology has been widely used in front-end sales, loss settlement, risk control loss reduction and other fields. At present, the application of artificial intelligence technology in the insurance field in China is still dominated by understanding. However, from the current situation of the industry, it is speculated that although the combination of large model and insurance industry is still in the stage of theoretical exploration, it is likely to achieve iterative upgrading in the near future and reshape the industry ecology. Here are a few application scenarios for the combination of artificial intelligence and insurance.

3. 2. 1　Intelligent Customer Service

Intelligent customer service is one of the most widely used scenarios of artificial intelligence in the insurance industry. Intelligent customer service can comprehensively apply a number of artificial intelligence technologies such as speech recognition, semantic understanding, speech synthesis, OCR, face recognition, electronic signature, digital employee, etc., to provide customers with many consulting and business services such as consulting, outbound call and return visit. For example, Ping An's intelligent customer service " Xiaohui" can provide customers with product consultation and business management at any time. The intelligent customer service robot "Wheat" of Pacific Life Insurance can answer customers' questions in real time. Sunshine Insurance also launched an artificial intelligence robot last year to provide text conversation interaction. In addition, Swiss insurance company Helvetia recently became the first listed insurance company in the world to launch a direct customer contact service based on ChatGPT technology. The company combines ChatGPT with its existing AI assistant Clara, which can provide customers with intelligent advice on insurance, pensions and home ownership.

3.2.2 Insurance Marketing

Based on large model technology, intelligent insurance product recommendation robot is built. By analyzing customers' background, needs, preferences, risk tolerance and other information, combined with the rich insurance product knowledge of large models in the insurance field, natural language interaction technology is applied to provide customers with personalized, all-weather online insurance product recommendation and configuration scheme suggestions. Answer customers' questions about insurance products, including insurance types, insurance liability, insurance term, insurance conditions, insurance terms, premiums, etc., to improve the sales efficiency of insurance and customer experience. Recurrent AI, for example, has applied innovative AI technology and in-depth business process solutions to insurance sales, helping insurance companies achieve sales efficiency and growth, and it now serves People's Insurance of China, Zhongan Insurance and Water Tideland.

3.2.3 Insurance Claims and Fraud Prevention

Insurance claims has always been a key node of insurance services that consumers and insurance regulators pay more attention to, and it is also an important scenario for artificial intelligence applications. The traditional insurance claims settlement method has some pain points, such as lengthy claims process, complicated claims data review and over-reliance on experience judgment. With the development and application of artificial intelligence, intelligent loss determination, intelligent claims, risk warning, risk anti-fraud and other links have room for artificial intelligence to display, thereby improving the efficiency of claims, reducing claims costs, and improving customer experience. Zhongan Health insurance's claims speed continues to improve under the ability of artificial intelligence. Through Zhongan Insurance's "intelligent claims" system, a claim is settled every 42 seconds. As of the first half of 2021, Zhongan Health Insurance has achieved 94% of claims online applications, and the waiting time for customers to receive claims has decreased by 55% year-on-year. Zhongan Insurance has also established an exclusive channel for claims of 10,000 yuan and below— "1-day claims", and 99% of claims that meet the standard have reached a 24-hour rapid claim limitation, greatly improving the efficiency of claims.

3.3　Foreign Cases of "Insurance + AI"

3.3.1　The First Case

Case Tile:

"AI + Insurance" Drives the Experience of Insurance Company Customers

Case Content:

K (a company) assisted a large insurance company to develop a customer contact solution. By utilizing a variety of AI techniques to reduce the number of calls from customers, the organization aims to improve customer satisfaction and increase the efficiency of agents. Using a Natural Language Processing (NLP) and a classification algorithm, K helped the client to analyze and then categorize calls to the support center. Many were insurance policy-related questions that represent quick wins. For example, queries about policy dates and whether children are covered. Overall, the analysis showed that many of the queries could be handled more effectively through a self-service solution. K professionals are working closely with the insurance business to consider how an AI-based solution will enable customers to simply ask a virtual assistant question like "what is my life insurance coverage?" and "is my family covered?" to get answers quickly and conveniently. This provides a cost-effective way to answer queries the first time, while reducing call volumes and improving customer satisfaction. Waiting times for queries that require human input will likely be reduced and customer service agents can focus on customer queries that require human input.

Increasing customer convenience and engagement are key to loyalty in an industry where personalized experiences are most valued. But how AI will ultimately enhance productivity and performance, and deliver the benefits and ROI are still being understood.

Some of the unknowns include an equally game-changing emerging technology: quantum computing is the next frontier. This could revolutionize data processing and analytics. Matching its unlimited processing power with Generative AI learning could see insurers make complex calculations, solve problems, analyze data, assess risks and personalize products in real time.

Some insurers are even deferring investment as they believe AI might leap again in less than a year. It's a dynamic picture and K has a measured approach to technology investment that focuses on gaining momentum: think big, start small, scale quickly. As James Henderson, Customer Insurance Director, K in the UK, explains, "We help clients strike the balance between imagining the enterprise-wide possibilities and not biting off more than they can chew. Setting clear KPIs and success metrics up front are critical steps to get the most out of each AI use case — seeing the potential and pitfalls up front".

Case Comments:

The case study highlights the successful application of artificial intelligence (AI) technology in the insurance industry, specifically focusing on improving customer experience and operational efficiency and also demonstrates how AI technology can help insurance company stay competitive in a rapidly evolving market.

Case Source:

KPMG official website. How AI could transform the insurance industry[EB/OL].(2023-12-06)[2024-07-01].https://kpmg.com/au/en/home/insights/2024/03/ai-transform-insurance-industry.html.

3.3.2 The Second Case

Case Tile:

"Computer Vision + AI" Helps Insurance Companies Reduce Car Crash Fraud

Case Content:

Taking advantage of the confluence of edge computing and AI, an Italian startup has been granted a patent to record the front visual panorama of a moving vehicle, identify the driver's driving style, and certify the accident by recording its dynamics.

When the engine starts, the device begins recording the video and simultaneously transmits it to the cloud using proprietary technology that allows secure transmission of encrypted video snippets. Once in the cloud, the video snippets are reassembled and processed using computer vision algorithms that anonymise the personal data collected during the recordings (such as people's faces and car license plates) to comply with data privacy regulation (e. g., GDPR).

The anonymised video can then be used as evidence of accident dynamics and to extract key data to identify driving styles and the ability to classify driver risk.

The system has received funding from the Italian government to develop part of the project.

These are a few examples of data-driven AI models that have been successfully deployed. However, at SR (an insurance company) and across the industry, many AI projects are also internally driven and address core processes, for example, using natural language understanding to help ingest and classify unstructured data into decision-making processes or to better understand the exposure in contracts and the overall portfolio.

Through the various entry points, AI has the potential to impact and add value to the entire insurance value chain and bring significant benefits to customers. However, with wider access to these powerful tools, it is also crucial to be on top of their risks and challenges. Data and responsible AI literacy are key for companies to ensure that humans remain in control of the decision-making process.

There are many new risks associated with the use of AI at scale that policymakers, big tech companies and insurance companies need to consider working on now so that AI adds value to society and that we can still effectively protect against the new risks associated with it. And, of course, as many of us ponder the potential for AI to enhance our own lifestyles, we'd love it if AI could free up more time for some of life's enjoyable activities!

Case Comments:

This case exemplifies the potential of AI to drive positive societal impact while emphasizing the importance of ethical considerations and responsible AI practices in its deployment.

The author holds that as the use of AI continues to evolve, policymakers, tech companies, and insurers must work together to address emerging challenges and ensure the ethical and responsible use of AI technologies. By fostering transparency, human oversight, and a proactive approach to risk mitigation, companies can maximize the benefits of AI while safeguarding against potential pitfalls.

Case Source:

PRAVINA LADVA. Benefits and use cases of AI in insurance[EB/OL].(2023-04-17) [2024-07-01].https://www.swissre.com/risk-knowledge/advancing-societal-benefits-digitalisation/opportunities-ai-insurance.html.

4

云计算与保险业

本章主要阐释云计算与保险业相互结合的基本思路与原理，并精选了国内外相关案例与学生分享，启发学生借助云计算开发保险科技应用场景和相关保险产品的思路。

4.1　云计算基本理论

4.1.1　云计算是什么

Amazon 公司于 2006 年 3 月推出弹性计算云（elastic compute cloud）服务。在 2006 年 8 月 9 日，Google 首席执行官埃里克·施密特（Eric Schmidt）在搜索引擎大会（SES San Jose 2006）首次提出云计算（cloud computing）的概念，这是云计算概念第一次出现在公众视野中。2013 年 12 月，IBM 首次宣布将其顶级计算基础结构服务引入我国，随后 Amazon 公司也将 Amazon 的公有云计算服务引入我国。虽然云计算产生的历史并不长（如图 4.1 所示），但对其定义有多种说法。

4.1.1.1　厂商角度

云计算的"云"是存在于互联网服务器集群上的资源，它包括硬件资源［如中央处理器（CPU）、内存储器、外存储器、显卡、网络设备、输入输出设备等］和软件资源（如操作系统、数据库、集成开发环境等），所有的计算都在云计算服务提供商所提供的计算机集群上完成。

4.1.1.2　用户角度

云计算是指技术开发者或者企业用户以免费或按需租用的方式，利用云计算服务提供商基于分布式计算和虚拟化技术搭建的计算中心或超级计算机，使用数据存储、分析以及科学计算等服务。

4.1.1.3　抽象角度

云计算是指一种商业计算模型。它将计算任务分布在由大量计算机构成的资源池上，使各种应用系统能够根据需要获取计算力、存储空间和信息服务。

4.1.1.4 美国国家标准与技术研究院的定义

云计算是一种按使用量付费的模式，这种模式提供可用的、便捷的、按需的网络访问，进入可配置的计算资源共享池（资源包括网络、服务器、存储、应用软件、服务），只需投入很少的管理工作，或与服务供应商进行很少的交互，这些资源就能够被快速提供。云计算的发展阶段如图 4.1 所示。

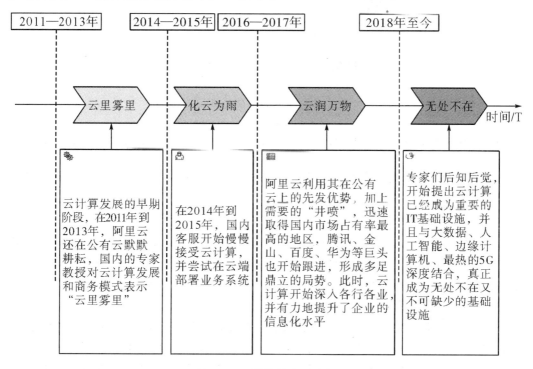

图 4.1 云计算的发展阶段

综上所述，云计算可以更一般地被定义为一种基于互联网的计算模式，通过将计算资源、存储资源和应用程序提供给用户，实现按需使用和灵活扩展的服务。

4.1.2 云计算的原理

云计算的原理是将计算任务分布在大量的分布式计算机上，而不是在本地计算机或远程服务器上，其核心思想是通过互联网提供便捷、按需的网络服务。在"云"中，庞大的运算程序被分割为多个小程序，然后送到计算资源共享池中进行搜索、计算和分析，最后返回到使用者手中。云计算将网络两端连接起来，通过云端获取存储、数据库、服务器、应用软件和网络等所需的计算资源，从而极大地减少了使用成本（如图 4.2 所示）。

图 4.2　云计算的原理

4.1.3　云计算的分类

云计算可以为用户提供满足不同算力和存储需求的解决方案。从部署云计算方式的角度出发，云计算可分为四类。

4.1.3.1　公有云

公有云也称外部云，通常是指云计算服务提供商为公众提供的能够使用的云计算平台。公有云建立在一个或多个数据中心上，由云计算服务提供商操作和管理，通过公共的基础设施给多个用户提供服务。

4.1.3.2　社区云

社区云在一定的地域范围内，由云计算服务提供商统一提供计算资源、网络资源、软件和服务能力所形成的云计算平台。社区云基于社区内的网络和技术易于整合等特点，结合社区内用户需求的共性，通过对区域内各种计算能力进行服务模式的整合统一，实现面向区域用户需求的云计算服务模式。社区云建立在一个特定小组里的多个目标相似的成员之间，他们共享一套基础设施，所产生的成本由社区云成员共同承担，能节约一定的成本。社区云的成员都可以登录社区云中获取信息和使用应用程序。

4.1.3.3　私有云

私有云也称内部云，是一种只供单个用户或者企业使用的云计算平台，这样就可以对数据安全，以及服务质量进行最有效的控制。采用私有云计算的企业掌握了基础架构，并且能够控制将应用部署到该基础架构上。与私有云相关的网络、计算以及存储等基础设施都是企业用户独有的，并不与其他的企业用户共享。

4.1.3.4　混合云

混合云是由两个或两个以上不同类型各自独立的云（私有云、社区云、公有云）组成。混合云使用不同的标准或专有的技术将不同的类型进行云整合，这些技术能实现云之间数据和应用程序的平滑流转。将公有云和私有云两种不同的部署模式相结合是目前最流行的混合云。出于安全性和管理方面的考虑，企业不会将所有数据都放在公有云中，因此，已经采用了云计算的大多数公司都将采用混合云模型。

4.1.4 云计算的特点

通过查阅相关资料和适当的归纳总结,云计算至少存在以下五个特点:

4.1.4.1 可扩展性

在云计算下,物理或者虚拟资源可以在横向上迅速伸缩,并具备较强的恢复能力,通过自动化供应,实现资源的快速增减。云计算用户可以在任何时间、任何地点,通过互联网获取大量的实体或虚拟资源。通过云计算,用户只要有需求,就能轻松、快速地获得新的、无限的资源。用户不必为存储资源和计算能力而烦恼。

4.1.4.2 超大规模

云计算中心是一个非常庞大的"市场",许多提供云计算服务的企业都拥有几十万甚至上百万台服务器。而那些采用私有云计算的公司通常都会有数百甚至数千台服务器。云计算可以将大量的电脑集合在一起,给用户带来规模空前的储存空间与运算能力。

4.1.4.3 运维成本低

当用户通过各个终端从云计算获得应用服务时,用户无须了解特定的运行地点和参与的服务器的数目。这样,可以大大节省使用者花费在 IT 资源上的人力、物力、财力。云计算通过对流程进行抽象简化,从而避免了对用户的复杂处理复杂。对于用户而言,他们只了解到服务正在运行,而不了解资源的使用情况。资源池把一些本来应该由用户来做的工作,比如维护,交给了提供商。

4.1.4.4 按需服务

在不增加任何人工干预或全部硬件投资的情况下,用户可以在任何时间、任何地点得到所需的服务。这就好比客户去吃一顿自助餐,不需要自己准备食物,只需要拿自己喜欢的东西就行了。

4.1.4.5 高可靠性

一方面,云计算具有巨大的资源优势,能够方便地解决资源冗余问题;另一方面,建立云计算能够在硬件出现故障的情况下,实现资源的有效迁移和恢复。同时,云计算环境下的部署、监测、安全等方面的成熟技术为保障网络的稳定提供了有力的保障。

4.1.5 云计算的发展现状

云计算是实现数据挖掘和人工智能创新科技手段的基础。当前,云计算的发展呈现出四个发展特征。

4.1.5.1 增长快速

云计算市场持续增长。中国信息通信研究院发布的《云计算白皮书(2023 年)》显示,2022 年全球云计算市场规模约为 3.5 万亿元,增速达 19%,预计在大模型、算力等需求刺激下,市场仍将保持稳定增长,到 2026 年全球云计算市场将突破约十万亿元。我国云计算市场规模在 2022 年达到 4 550 亿元,较 2021 年增长 40.91%,相较于全球 19% 的增速,我国云计算市场仍处于快速发展期。预计 2025 年我国云计算整体市场规模将超万亿元。

4.1.5.2 服务多样化

云计算提供了多种服务模式,包括软件即服务(Software-as-a-Service,SaaS)、平台即服务（Platform-as-a-Service，PaaS）和基础设施即服务（Infrastructure-as-a-Service，IaaS）三种服务模型。用户可以根据需求选择适合的服务模式。

4.1.5.3 大规模应用

云计算已广泛应用于各个行业和领域，包括企业级应用、移动应用、大数据分析等。许多企业和组织已经将部分或全部的 IT 基础设施迁移到云计算平台上。

4.1.5.4 创新不断

云计算领域不断涌现出新的技术和解决方案，如容器技术、无服务器计算、人工智能等。这些技术的发展推动了云计算的进一步演进。

4.1.6 云计算的发展前景

随着市场不断扩大，云计算具有广阔的发展前景。

4.1.6.1 增长潜力巨大

随着数字化转型的推进和数据量的不断增长，在未来云计算将迎来更加广阔的前景。越来越多的企业和组织将采用云计算来提高效率、降低成本和实现创新。

4.1.6.2 智能化发展

人工智能和机器学习等技术与云计算的结合将推动智能化应用的发展。云计算提供了强大的计算和存储能力，为智能化应用提供了基础设施和支持。

4.1.6.3 边缘计算日渐兴起

随着物联网的快速发展，边缘计算作为云计算的延伸，将在未来得到更广泛的应用。边缘计算可以将计算和存储资源更靠近终端设备，提供更低延迟和更高效的服务。

4.1.6.4 重视安全与隐私

随着云计算的普及，安全和隐私问题也日益受到关注。在未来云计算将加强数据安全和隐私保护措施，提供更可靠的服务。

4.2 云计算与保险业的融合

在科技重构保险业态的当下，发展云计算是保险机构实现数字化升级和科技驱动的第一步。基于云计算能力搭建保险业务平台，具有算力弹性扩展、系统运行稳定、客户体验良好等优点。基于云计算技术的保险消费者服务平台功能架构见图 4.3。

4.2.1 云计算与保险结合的应用场景

基于云计算技术的保险消费者服务平台功能架构如图 4.3 所示。

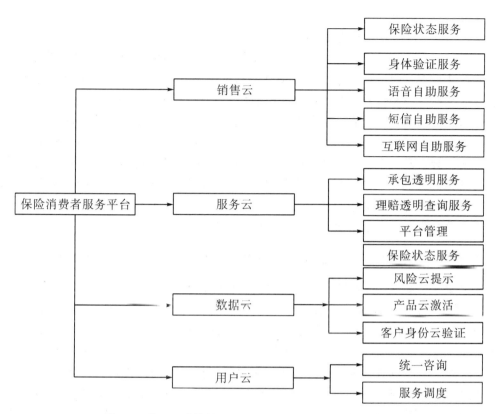

图 4.3　基于云计算技术的保险消费者服务平台功能架构

随着社会对保险需求的日益增长，以及云计算的快速发展，云计算与保险业可以在以下场景中相互融合。

4.2.1.1　优化保险企业 IT 资源，降低保险企业运维成本

传统保险企业需要自行搭建 IT 平台，这样会花费大量的人力、物力和财力。云计算技术不仅能使保险企业享受到更多的 IT 资源，还会增加保险机构在业务高峰期的算力和存储空间，保证承保理赔的高效率，降低保险企业的 IT 资源运维成本。

4.2.1.2　保险数据分析与风险评估

云计算为保险业提供了强大的计算与存储能力，有助于保险业者更好地处理海量的保单信息，如客户资料、理赔记录、市场动向等。在云计算平台上，保险业者通过机器学习、数据挖掘等方法，对海量数据进行深度挖掘，进而实现对风险的精确评估，并设计出更加合理的保障方案。

4.2.1.3　在线保险销售与服务

云计算为保险业提供了高可用、灵活的网络架构，帮助企业建立稳定、可信的线上营销、客服体系。利用云计算技术可以实现网上投保、网上理赔等业务，提升客户的体验感，提升业务效率。

4.2.1.4　保险智能化与自动化

云计算技术为保险业提供了一种新的技术手段，为保险业的发展提供了新的思路。比如，利用人工智能、机器学习等方法建立智能理赔系统，实现对理赔的自动审核与处理。同时，云计算技术也能帮助企业完成保单管理、保费核算等业务过程的自动化，

提升工作效率，降低人为误差。

4.2.1.5　数据安全与隐私保护

云计算平台往往具有先进的安全性和数据加密机制，能够有效地保护用户的隐私。通过在云中储存资料，保险企业可以降低资料遗失与泄漏的风险，更能应对网络攻击和抵御针对资料安全性的威胁。许多公司都要从头做起，购买网络和服务器等 IT 设备，然后在此之上搭建自己的企业应用程序。但是，当企业的业务不断扩大时，IT 操作员将会面对各种各样的 IT 遗留问题，例如，老的系统无法完全替代，数据的移植很容易产生问题。要启动一个新的系统，就得花很多钱，不仅要重新训练，还要克服费用的压力。越来越多的保险公司之所以想要用云计算替代他们的传统 IT 系统，是因为云计算技术可以避开保险企业中 IT 扩张所产生的问题，允许保险企业将精力集中在业务拓展上，从而使保险企业能够更迅速地适应市场的需要。

4.2.2　云计算在保险业中应用举例

4.2.2.1　某一小型财产保险公司的保险的云实践

ZA 在线财产保险股份有限公司（简称"ZA 保险"）是国内第一家核心业务上云的公司。早在 2014 年，为满足当时业务高速发展的需求，ZA 保险就决定在云端搭建保险核心系统——"无界山 1.0"；2019 年，ZA 保险对无界山进行全面升级，"无界山2.0"正式上线。ZA 保险基于阿里云平台和分布式体系架构，建立了新核心业务系统。此系统不仅支持外部用户通过多种途径访问保险前端系统，也向外部开放平台提供接口网关及行业解决方案，并通过大数据手段来挖掘新的社会需求以及实时对接保监会审查。

此外，ZA 保险基于云计算建立了"两地三中心"灾备体系，实现数据库秒级灾备切换，单机房灾难应用不受影响，双机房灾难数据丢失时间少于 30 秒。为保证 ZA 保险云上业务平稳运行，阿里云平台为 ZA 保险配备了专属技术服务经理（TAM）。TAM一方面通过钉钉群提供 7×24 小时日常问题快速响应，另一方面也会定期与 ZA 保险团队进行交流，跟进日常需求与重大项目。阿里云平台对 ZA 保险保驾护航。

（资料来源：https://www.docin.com/p-2018656733.html.）

4.2.2.2　TP 保险的云实践

2017 年，TP 集团成功部署集团私有云平台——TP 云，完成了多地域、多数据中心资源的统一管理，并为全集团提供统一、快捷、按需申请的基础设施服务。TP 云建设规划一期落地，实现了"TP 云"平台的五个子目标（具体为：为集团各单位提供统一、快捷、按需申请的基础设施分配服务；面向应用开发能够提供开箱即用的开发平台、应用支持、安全防护等 PaaS 服务；统一管理的多地域、多数据的中心资源；提供多租户方式下的调度管理和服务计费功能；满足现有对虚拟化的资源需求，支持未来灵活的需求），TP 集团拥有了一个在架构和功能上都较完整、先进的，真正意义上的私有云。

经过前期在云平台、存储和网络等 IT 基础设施建设上的积累，中国 TP 积极谋划建设创新的云平台，进一步提升 IT 基础架构的可用性和可靠性，满足业务创新发展需要。从推动包括存储、网络等在内的 IT 基础设施转型，到全面升级到高性价比、更加稳固、功能更加丰富的云平台，中国 TP 正在构建起一个更加坚实的数字底座，不仅可以为集团数字化转型提供有力支撑，还可以加速数字化转型。

（资料来源：https://www.163.com/dy/article/GTCKC1TU051182SL.html.）

4.2.2.3 某大型人寿保险公司的云实践

某大型人寿保险公司紧抓云计算发展机遇，践行集团"科技国寿"战略，以加快建立更加先进高效、动态灵活的云数据中心为目标，全力打造具有国寿特色的混合云，建成了国内行业首个混合云平台，实现了"云化之路"的重要突破。2012年，这个人寿保险公司基于云计算理念前瞻规划并落地"大后台+小前端"IT布局，建成业界领先的国寿混合云。自2017年年底TP云发布以来，经过持续迭代升级，目前ZGRS混合云已面向全集团提供云服务，有力保障了集团及成员公司IT系统的安全稳定高效运行。

ZGRS混合云一方面发挥公有云资源快速部署、弹性扩展、成本低廉优势，另一方面通过将前端应用快速部署在公有云上，后台数据安全存放在私有云中的方式，有效满足了监管机构以及企业自身对于数据安全、核心技术自主掌控的要求。通过统一的管理平台，实现各类资源的统一纳管、统一运维、统一运营、统一云服务。ZGRS混合云随需应变，实现了迅捷高效的云端服务，如云端服务应对大流量直播访问挑战、解决高并发线上销售场景、快速满足智能销售训练需要等。依托云计算提供的强大算力，智能世界为人们提供了丰富的应用，也产生了海量的数据，大幅节约了运营成本，还智能提升了运营质量。

（资料来源：https://baijiahao.baidu.com/s?id=1670830141284909627.）

4.3　"保险+云计算"国内案例

4.3.1　国内经典案例之一

案例题目：

"保险+云"赋能五大生态圈

案例内容：

PA云诞生于2013年，2014年正式上线投入商用，经过多年的成长积累，目前是金融行业应用最为广泛的云平台之一。PA云不仅为PA集团旗下95%的业务公司提供支持，支撑它们80%的业务系统，同时还在为500多家客户提供云服务。

第一，作为PA服务的综合输出平台。PA云最初的目的是满足PA集团内部的业务需求，支持PA集团的战略转型。PA云从诞生到发展，PA集团也完成了向全渠道商业模式转型，转型过程中包括智能认知、人工智能、区块链、信息安全在内的五大核心科技发挥了关键性作用，而PA云为这五大核心科技提供了重要支撑。更可贵的是，PA云很好地支持了PA集团的转型战略，并以金融为起点，将业务拓展至更广泛的医疗健康和智慧城市等领域。

第二，PA云的三大核心价值。PA云已经具备提供IaaS、PaaS到SaaS的全栈云服务能力，业务涵盖内部云、公有云、专有云以及私有云解决方案；同时还提供众多行业领先的AI解决方案，包括人脸识别、声纹识别、微表情、客服机器人、OCR识别等都已经在云端开放；还有金融、医疗、房产等多个行业的解决方案上线。而除这些方面具有独特优势外，安全合规、稳定可靠和专业服务是作为 PA 云的核心竞争力之一，也是其三大价值主张。

第三，与生态伙伴合作，共创云端未来。PA 云重点围绕金融、医疗、汽车、房产、智慧城市构建五大生态圈。在金融生态圈建设中将通过金融壹账通赋能金融科技；在医疗生态圈建设中将构建"PPP"开放平台、全面整合医疗健康数据、技术和服务资源；而汽车生态圈将以云平台、AI 为核心，赋能商家（包括汽车主机商、经销商、二手车商）打造闭环；房产生态圈则以政府、企业和中小企业为战略重点，助力房产生态建设；智慧城市生态圈的目标是将打造一套完整、科学的、解决实际问题的智慧城市管理体系。PA 云以积极姿态与各种合作伙伴合作，包括硬件供应商合作伙伴、SaaS 合作伙伴、技术合作伙伴、行业合作伙伴、云服务商伙伴和渠道合作伙伴，一起做大五大生态圈，共同开创 PA 云的美好未来。

案例评述：

PA 云是一个开放的平台，可以通过自身巨大的数据、渠道和先进的技术来帮助合作伙伴达成多样化、开放的合作。在时代趋势下，以竞合代替竞争，求同存异，最大化地实现合作价值，以深度合作伙伴（硬件供应商合作伙伴、SaaS 合作伙伴、技术合作伙伴、行业合作伙伴、云服务商伙伴和渠道合作伙伴）的内部开源为基础，打造一个全球范围内的合作伙伴生态圈，从而推动伙伴乃至各个垂直领域实现突破发展，共同开创 PA 云的美好未来。

案例来源：

邹大斌. 平安云正式发布，赋能五大生态圈［EB/OL］.（2018-10-22）［2024-07-01］.http://cloud.zhiding.cn/2018/1022/3112276.shtml.

4.3.2　国内经典案例之二

案例题目：

HW 云助力 YA 保险打造保险行业新生态

案例内容：

随着"云+5G+AI+IOT"新一代信息技术的发展，数字化转型已经成为数字中国、智慧社会建设的重要动能。得益于数字技术和国家政策的助力，保险行业也在数字化转型中表现出强大的张力。YA 保险作为全国财产险排名前列的保险公司，积极拥抱云计算、大数据、移动互联网技术、云数据库等，积极为未来打造高可靠、高安全、高扩展、及时响应业务需求的基础设施。携手 HW 云进行云上业务改造，更是大幅提升了销售、承保、理赔等环节的效率，实现从内部运营到外部销售全业务链条的云化。基于保险业务的安全诉求、多元融合以及金融监管的要求，HW 云数据库团队对 YA 业务系统进行了精准评估与分析，快速制定出一套高安全、高可靠、高可用、高性能的数据库迁移方案，实现了主流商业数据库的安全切换，大幅提升了业务运转效率。

第一，重新搭建核心金融云平台，创新"云端保险"服务。HW 云重新搭建了分布式金融云平台和数据库，成功助力 YA 保险将意外险和健康险两套业务系统迁移上云，实现 RPO（Recovery Point Objective）等于 0，也即实现数据零丢失；RTO（Recovery Time Objective）秒级，即在出现灾难后实现了以秒为单位即可恢复。

第二，全新分布式架构部署，数据上云更安全稳定。HW 云根据 YA 意外险和健康险两个业务系统的特点及要求，聚焦新业务服务架构优化调整，基于 HW 云服务一体化、高可靠、高可用的分布式金融云平台架构部署，重构核心系统并实现主流商业数据库切换。HW 云平台有效应对流量高峰场景下可靠性和性能的问题，确保系统在高访问场景下数据不丢失，同时降低了运维压力，实现 RPO＝0、RTO 秒级，不仅满足了金融监管要求，而且整体资源投入节省了 25%，为未来数字化转型打下了坚实的云上核心分布式架构和数据底座基础。

第三，超高性能，海量访问无压力。YA 保险的保单数据量巨大，很可能会达到几十TB，会对数据库造成很高的并发压力，对性能要求极高。YA 保险通过部署 HW 云 GaussDB（for MySQL）数据库，实现了 7 倍性能的提升，海量访问无压力。而且 Gauss-DB（for MySQL）支持 1 写 15 读，128TB 海量数据存储，分钟级扩容，可以承受线上大型保险代理平台带来的巨大压力，高并发场景下仍可以保持超高性能，极大地满足了YA 保险对高性能数据库的诉求。

第四，业务不中断，数据平滑迁移。针对 YA 保险复杂的数据迁移需求，HW 云数据复制服务（Data Replication Service，DRS）通过单库拆分迁移，为系统后台提供分库分表和微服务的能力，满足客户特殊需求。同时提供数据对比功能，快速实现行数对比，给客户直观展示迁移过程中源库和目标库的数据一致性情况，确保数据 0 丢失。此外，在异构数据库迁移方面，HW 云数据库提供了完整的改造迁移方案，包含对象改造、SQL 优化、割接方案等，确保业务平稳割接，整个过程业务无须停机，做到了对客户最大程度的平滑无感迁移，让客户在迁移时对业务安心、使用省心、割接有信心。

案例评述

得益于数字技术和国家政策的助力，保险行业也在数字化转型中表现出强大的张力。YA 保险作为全国财产险排名前列的保险公司，积极拥抱云计算、大数据、移动互联网技术、云数据库等，积极为未来打造高可靠、高安全、高扩展、及时响应业务需求的基础设施。YA 保险经过此次对主流商业数据库的上云切换，其业务系统实现了较大幅度的效率提升，业务可靠性和安全性得到极大增强，企业资源投入成本降低 25%。未来 HW 云会持续助力 YA 保险进一步业务创新，提升客户服务、承保和理赔创新服务能力，为保险业务提供更多可能性。

案例来源：

技术火炬手."云端保险"正当时，华为云如何赋能永安保险数字化转型？［EB/OL］.（2020-11-04）［2024-07-01］.https://bbs.huaweicloud.com/blogs/205541.

4.4　课程思政案例

案例题目：

"保险＋云计算"为铸牢中华民族共同体意识贡献力量

案例内容：

近年来，原中国银保监会（现国家金融监督管理总局）为落实习近平总书记在党的十九大报告中提出的乡村振兴战略，围绕"三农"问题，仅在金融保险领域就发布了多项政策：2021 年 5 月 27 日，中国银保监会召开专题会议，贯彻落实中央第七次西藏工作座谈会精神，研究部署银行业保险业支持新时代西藏和四省涉藏州县的主要工作，并提出坚持以人民为中心，积极服务民生领域建设，做好巩固拓展脱贫攻坚成果同乡村振兴有效衔接的金融服务工作。2021 年 10 月 11 日，新时代银保监会发布《关于 2021 年银行业保险业高质量服务乡村振兴的通知》，从八个方面提出了 2021 年银行业保险业高质量服务乡村振兴工作要求，包括优化金融服务供给体系和服务机制、提升县域金融服务质效、发挥保险保障作用、创新金融产品和服务等，共涉及 23 项具体内容。

一直以来，智保云秉承助力保险行业高质量发展的初心，坚定自身技术服务和系统提供商的品牌定位，在中介机构与代理人党支部的督促下，不断加强技术科研实力的同时，对全国各地的行业发展情况，以及对地方发展现状和政策要求保持密切关注。

2022 年 1 月，《保险中介机构信息化工作监管办法》正式发布，保险行业发展从蓬勃发展转向规范发展，全国各地的保险中介机构也正式开展信息化合规建设的相关工作。而对于绝大多数保险中介机构，信息化建设成本巨大、技术能力不足等问题，为智保云的发展创造了机遇，也让智保云笃定了为保险行业做好技术服务的决心。

为此，智保云通过自身技术优势，积极响应国家号召，于 2022 年 6 月发布了支持藏语等多种少数民族语言的系统版本，通过与西藏地区的保险机构的通力协作，落实国家政策，做好金融保险相关的援藏工作。经过数月努力，智保云在西藏地区的服务有了重大进展。在中介机构与代理人党支部的领导下，智保云与西藏 XDF 保险代理有限公司、西藏 XYZC 保险代理有限公司等西藏范围内所有专业中介法人机构相继完成了信息化系统签约，正式启用智保云系统开展保险业务。

至此，智保云也实现了西藏范围内所有专业中介法人机构信息化系统服务全覆盖。未来，智保云会竭诚服务好西藏范围内的所有客户，并积极开展该地区汽车经销商、旅行社、银行等兼业代理的相关服务工作，全方位发扬建党精神，助力西藏地区保险行业高质量发展。

2021 年，新疆保险行业协会正式发布"保险云"数据共享小程序。据介绍，"保险云"数据共享小程序是统计信息平台移动端的可视化展示，界面以柱状图、条形图、环形图、旋风图等图表充分展示了行业关注的地区、公司、险种维度保费人力及各指标的增速、占比等数据，通过后台分析，所属保险机构根据专属账号和密码，就可以清楚地看到"行业整体+公司"的数据分布，帮助管理人员迅速找到反映区域内保险行业运营情况的当前或历史数据信息，并从复杂的信息中迅速找到数据信息之间的关系，获得多维度统计结果和分析判断。

据了解，2020 年新疆保险行业协会数据统计信息平台全面改版升级，"保险云"数据共享小程序则是移动端的充分展示。在改版升级过程中，就报表类型、报送管理、统计管理、查询功能、移动及 PC 端共享呈现等模块进行重点优化，实现会员公司通过平台上传数据，系统校验、数据修改、数据汇总、数据呈现等功能，满足协会、会员公司数据分析需求，实现数据统一管理。

新疆保险行业协会相关负责人表示，当今是数字经济时代，信息技术创新日新月异，协会也紧跟时代发展，依托大数据、云服务等技术手段，完善行业基础设施建设，通过整合行业需求，采取成熟一个上线一个的策略，致力于打造涵盖数据统计、诚信体系管理等综合性的行业数据服务中心，进一步提升行业大数据应用能力和信息化服务水平，建立行业基础数据标准化管理流程，为新疆保险业健康发展提供决策参考和依据。

案例评述：

铸牢中华民族共同体意识是新时代党的民族工作的主线，也是民族地区各项工作的主线。保险业为响应政府与银保监的号召，以高度的政治责任感和使命感细化落实措施。一方面，智保云为中介机构与代理人党支部提供党建栏目、在线学习、党费交纳，服务数万党员代理人。智保云支持多数少数民族语言，包括保险产品介绍、计划书、投保环节，服务民族同胞。农村银行保险业务信息化方案，服务村镇银行。另一方面，新疆保险行业协会以数据智能赋能业务发展，帮助监管机构、协会、会员公司从深度广度挖掘数据价值，为新疆保险业健康发展提供决策参考和依据。在为行业为用户创造价值的同时，还积极培育民族地区保险市场，不断丰富保险产品，拓宽保险服务领域，履行企业公民责任，不忘初心，为民族区域提供高质量保险服务，为社会创造价值，铸牢中华民族共同体意识，加强了民族团结。

案例来源：

中国保险业协会. 新疆保险业"保险云"数据共享小程序正式发布[EB/OL]. (2021-10-22)[2024-07-01]. http://www.iachina.cn/art/2021/10/22/art_23_105563.html.

4

Cloud Computing and Insurance Technology

This chapter mainly explains the basic ideas and principles of the combination of cloud computing and insurance industry, and shares relevant domestic and foreign cases with students to inspire them to develop insurance technology application scenarios and related insurance products with the help of cloud computing.

4. 1　Basic Theory of Cloud Computing

4. 1. 1　What is Cloud Computing

Amazon launched its Elastic Compute Cloud service in March 2006. On August 9, 2006, Google CEO Eric Schmidt introduced the concept of Cloud Computing at the Search Engine Conference (SES San Jose 2006). This is the first time the concept of cloud computing has appeared in the public eye. In December 2013, IBM announced for the first time that its top computing infrastructure services were introduced in China, and Amazon introduced Amazon's public cloud computing services in China. Although the history of Cloud Computing is not long (See Figure 4. 1), there are many definitions of it.

4. 1. 1. 1　Manufacturer's Perspective

The "cloud" of cloud computing is the resource existing on the Internet server cluster, which includes hardware resources [such as central processing unit (CPU), internal memory, external memory, graphics card, network equipment, input and output devices, etc.] and software resources (such as operating system, database, integrated development environment, etc.). All computing is done on a cluster of computers provided by the cloud computing service provider.

4. 1. 1. 2　User Perspective

Cloud computing refers to technology developers or enterprise users who rent computing centers or supercomputers based on distributed computing and virtualization technologies by cloud computing service providers for free or on demand to use data storage, analysis and scientific computing services.

4.1.1.3　Abstract Angle

Cloud computing refers to a business computing model, which distributes computing tasks on a resource pool composed of a large number of computers, so that various application systems can obtain computing power, storage space and information services as needed.

4.1.1.4　The Definition of the National Institute of Standards and Technology

Cloud computing is a pay-per-use model that provides available, convenient, on-demand network access to a configurable shared pool of computing resources (including networks, servers, storage, applications, services) that can be quickly provided with little administrative effort or minimal interaction with service providers. Stages of Cloud Computing see Figure 4.1.

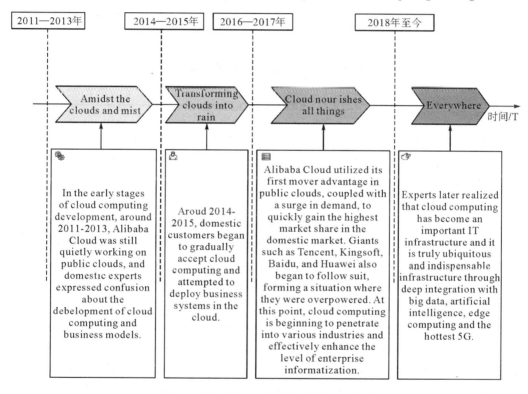

Figure 4.1　**Stages of Cloud Computing**

To sum up, cloud computing can be more generally defined as an Internet-based computing model that provides computing resources, storage resources and applications to users to achieve on-demand use and flexible expansion of services.

4.1.2　Principle of Cloud Computing

The principle of cloud computing is to distribute computing tasks on a large number of distributed computers, rather than on local computers or remote servers, and its core idea is to provide convenient and on-demand network services through the Internet. In the "cloud", a huge computing program is divided into several small programs, and then sent to the computing resource sharing pool for search, calculation and analysis, and finally returned to the hands of the user. Cloud computing connects the two ends of the network and obtains computing resources such as storage, database, server, application software and network through the cloud, thus greatly reducing the cost of use (See Figure 4.2).

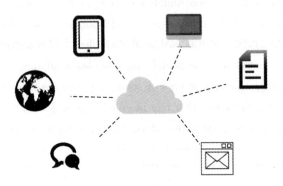

Figure 4.2 **Principles of cloud computing**

4.1.3 Classification of Cloud Computing

Cloud computing can provide users with solutions to meet different computing power and storage needs. From the perspective of deploying cloud computing methods, cloud computing can be divided into the following four categories.

4.1.3.1 Public Cloud

Also known as the external cloud, it usually refers to the cloud computing platform provided by the cloud computing service provider for the public to use. Public clouds are built on one or more data centers, operated and managed by cloud computing service providers, and provide services to multiple users through a common infrastructure.

4.1.3.2 Community Cloud

In a certain geographical scope, cloud computing platform formed by cloud computing service providers to provide computing resources, network resources, software and service capabilities. Community cloud is based on the characteristics of easy integration of network and technology in the community, combined with the common needs of users in the community, through the integration and unification of various computing capabilities in the region, to achieve a cloud computing service model that meets the needs of regional users. The community cloud is built among multiple members with similar goals in a specific team, who share a set of infrastructure, and the costs incurred are shared by the community cloud members, which can save some costs. Members of the community cloud can log into the cloud to access information and use applications.

4.1.3.3 Private Cloud

Also known as the internal cloud, it is a type of cloud computing that is only used by a single user or enterprise, so that data security and quality of service can be most effectively controlled. Enterprises that adopt private cloud computing have control over the infrastructure and can control how applications are deployed on that infrastructure. The network, compute, and storage infrastructure associated with a private cloud is unique to the enterprise and is not shared with other enterprise users.

4. 1. 3. 4 Hybrid Cloud

It is composed of two or more different types of independent clouds (private cloud, community cloud, public cloud). Hybrid clouds integrate different types of clouds using standard or proprietary technologies that enable the smooth flow of data and applications between clouds. Combining two different deployment models, public and private, is the most popular hybrid cloud today. For security and management reasons, companies don't put all their data in the public cloud. As a result, most companies that have already adopted cloud computing will adopt a hybrid cloud model.

4. 1. 4 Cloud Computing Features

After consulting relevant information and appropriate summary, cloud computing has at least the following characteristics.

4. 1. 4. 1 Scalability

Under cloud computing, physical or virtual resources can be rapidly scaled horizontally, and have strong resilience. Through automated supply, resources can be rapidly increased or decreased. Cloud computing users can access a large number of physical or virtual resources through the Internet at any time and anywhere. With cloud computing, users can easily and quickly access new, unlimited resources whenever they need them. Users don't have to worry about storage resources and computing power.

4. 1. 4. 2 Very Large Scale

The cloud computing center is a very large "market", and many companies offering cloud computing services have hundreds or thousands or even millions of servers. Companies that use private cloud computing often have hundreds or even thousands of servers. Cloud computing can bring a large number of computers together, giving users an unprecedented scale of storage space and computing power.

4. 1. 4. 3 Low Operation and Maintenance cost

When users obtain application services from the cloud through individual terminals, users do not need to know the specific location of operation and the number of participating servers. In this way, users can greatly save the human, material and financial resources spent on IT resources. Cloud computing avoids the complexity of processing users by abstractly simplifying the process. For the users, they only know that the service is running, but they do not know how the resource is being used. The resource pool takes some of the work that should be done by the user, such as maintenance, and hands it over to the provider.

4. 1. 4. 4 On-demand Services

Without any additional human intervention or total hardware investment, users can get the services they need at any time, anywhere. This is like eating a buffet without preparing, diners just take their own favorite things on the line.

4. 1. 4. 5　High reliability

On the one hand, cloud computing has huge resource advantages, which can easily solve the problem of resource redundancy; on the other hand, the establishment of cloud computing can achieve effective migration and recovery of resources in the case of hardware failure. At the same time, mature technologies such as deployment, monitoring and security in the cloud computing environment provide a strong guarantee for the stability of the network.

4. 1. 5　Development Status and Prospects of Cloud Computing ├──

Cloud computing is the foundation of data mining and artificial intelligence innovation. At present, the development of cloud computing shows the following characteristics of development.

Current state of cloud computing:

4. 1. 5. 1　Rapid Growth

The cloud computing market continues to grow. According to the *White Paper on Cloud Computing* (2023) released by the China Academy of Information and Communications Technology, the global cloud computing market in 2022 will be about 3. 5 trillion yuan, with a growth rate of 19%, and it is expected that under the stimulation of large models and computing power, the market will maintain stable growth, and the global cloud computing market will exceed about 10 trillion yuan by 2026. The size of China's cloud computing market will reach 455 billion yuan in 2022, an increase of 40. 91% from 2021, compared with the global growth rate of 19%, China's cloud computing market is still in a period of rapid development, and it is expected that the overall market size of China's cloud computing will exceed one trillion yuan in 2025.

4. 1. 5. 2　Diversification of Services

Cloud computing offers multiple service models. These include Software-as-a-Service (SaaS), Platform-as-a-Service (PaaS) and Infrastructure-as-a-Service (IaaS). Users can choose the appropriate service mode according to their needs.

4. 1. 5. 3　Large-scale Application

Cloud computing has been widely used in various industries and fields, including enterprise applications, mobile applications, big data analysis and so on. Many businesses and organizations have moved part or all of their IT infrastructure to the cloud.

4. 1. 5. 4　Continuous Innovation

New technologies and solutions continue to emerge in the field of cloud computing, such as container technology, server less computing, artificial intelligence, and so on. The development of these technologies has driven the further evolution of cloud computing.

4. 1. 6　Development Prospects of Cloud Computing ├──────────

4. 1. 6. 1　Huge Potential for Growth

With the advancement of digital transformation and the continuous growth of data volume, cloud computing will usher in a broader prospect in the future. More and more businesses and organizations will adopt cloud computing to increase efficiency, reduce costs and enable innovation.

4. 1. 6. 2 Intelligent Development

The combination of technologies such as artificial intelligence and machine learning with cloud computing will drive the development of intelligent applications. Cloud computing provides powerful computing and storage capabilities, providing infrastructure and support for intelligent applications.

4. 1. 6. 3 Edge Computing is on the Rise

With the rapid development of the Internet of Things, edge computing as an extension of cloud computing will be more widely used in the future. Edge computing can bring computing and storage resources closer to the end device, providing lower latency and more efficient services.

4. 1. 6. 4 Focus on Security and Privacy

With the popularity of cloud computing, security and privacy issues are also increasing concerns. In the future, cloud computing will strengthen data security and privacy protection measures to provide more reliable services.

4. 2   Convergence of Cloud Computing and Insurance

At present, the development of cloud computing is the first step for insurance institutions to achieve digital upgrading and technology-driven. The insurance business platform is built based on cloud computing capabilities, which has the advantages of flexible expansion of computing power, stable system operation and good customer experience.

4. 2. 1   Application Scenarios Combining Cloud Computing and Insurance

Figure 4. 3 shows the functional architecture of insurance consumer service platform based on cloud computing technology.

4. 2. 1. 1   Optimize the IT Resources of Insurance Companies and Reduce the Operation and Maintenance Costs of Insurance Companies

Traditional insurance companies need to build their own IT platform and resources, which will cost a lot of manpower, material and financial resources. Cloud computing technology can not only enable insurance companies to enjoy more reasonable IT resources, but also enhance the computing power and storage space of insurance institutions during the peak business period, ensure the high efficiency of underwriting claims, and reduce the operation and maintenance costs of IT resources for insurance companies.

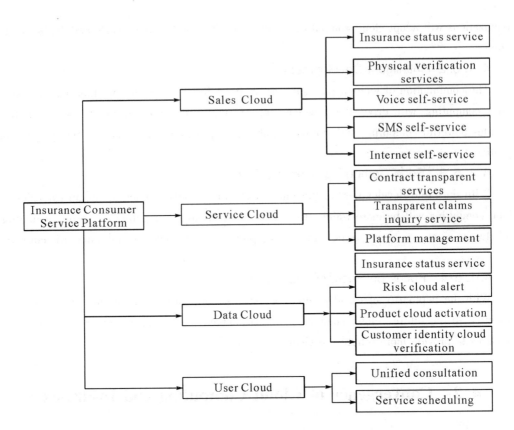

Figure 4. 3 **Functional architecture of insurance consumer**

service platform based on cloud computing technology

With the increasing demand for insurance and the rapid development of cloud computing, cloud computing and the insurance industry can be integrated in the following scenarios.

4. 2. 1. 2 Insurance Data Analysis and Risk Assessment

Cloud computing provides the insurance industry with powerful computing and storage capabilities to better handle massive policy information, such as customer information, claim records, market trends, and so on. On the cloud computing platform, through machine learning, data mining and other methods, deep mining of massive data, so as to achieve accurate assessment of its risks, and design a more reasonable security scheme.

4. 2. 1. 3 Online Insurance Sales and Services

Cloud computing provides the insurance industry with a highly available and flexible network architecture, and helps enterprises establish a stable and reliable online marketing and customer service system. Cloud computing technology is used to realize online insurance, online claims and other businesses, improve customer experience and improve business efficiency.

4. 2. 1. 4 Insurance Intelligence and Automation

Cloud computing technology provides a new technical means for the insurance industry and a new idea for the development of the insurance industry. For example, artificial intelligence, machine learning and other methods are used to establish an intelligent claims system to achieve automatic review and processing of claims. At the same time, cloud computing technology can also help enterprises complete the automation of business processes such as policy management and premium accounting, improve work efficiency and reduce human error.

4.2.1.5 Data Security and Privacy Protection

Cloud computing platforms often have advanced security and data encryption mechanisms, which can effectively protect the privacy of users. By storing data in the cloud, insurance companies can reduce the risk of data loss and leakage, and are better able to cope with network attack and threat to data security. Many companies are starting from scratch, buying IT equipment such as networks and servers, and then building their enterprise applications on top of it. However, when the business of the enterprise continues to expand, IT operators will face a variety of IT legacy problems, for example, the old system can not be completely replaced, and the migration of data is prone to problems. To start a new system, you have to spend a lot of money, you have to retrain, and you have to overcome the pressure of cost. The reason why more and more insurance companies want to replace their traditional IT systems with cloud computing is that cloud computing technology can avoid the problems of IT expansion in the enterprise, allowing users to focus on business development, so that users can adapt to the needs of the market more quickly.

4.2.2 Practical Examples of Cloud Computing in the Insurance Industry

4.2.2.1 ZA Insurance's Cloud Practice

ZA Online Property Insurance Co., LTD. (referred to as ZA Insurance) is the first company in China whose core business is cloud. As early as 2014, in order to meet the needs of rapid business development at that time, ZA Insurance decided to build the core insurance system— "Wujie Mountain 1.0" in the cloud; In 2019, ZA Insurance carried out a comprehensive upgrade of Wujie Mountain, and "Wujie Mountain 2.0" was officially launched. ZA Insurance has built a new core business system based on Alibaba Cloud platform and distributed architecture. This system not only supports external users to access the insurance front-end system through a variety of ways, but also provides interface gateways and industry solutions to external open platforms, and realizes mining new social needs through big data means and real-time docking with the insurance Regulatory Commission review.

In addition, ZA Insurance has built a "two-site, three-center" disaster recovery system based on cloud computing, which realizes second-level disaster recovery switchover of database, so that disaster applications in single-room are not affected, and disaster data loss in dual-room is less than 30 seconds. In order to ensure the smooth operation of ZA Insurance's business on the cloud, Alibaba Cloud has equipped a dedicated technical service manager (TAM) for ZA Insurance. On the one hand, TAM provides 7×24 hours quick response to daily problems through Dingding Group, and on the other hand, it regularly communicates with ZA Insurance team to follow up the daily needs and the advancement of major projects. Ali Cloud to ZA insurance protection escort.

4.2.2.2 TP Insurance's Cloud Practice

China TP Insurance Group Co., LTD. (hereinafter referred to as China TP) successfully deployed the Group's private cloud system-TP Cloud in 2017, focusing on the unified management of multi-regional and multi-data center resources, and providing unified, fast and on-demand infrastructure services for the whole group. The first phase of TP Cloud construction planning has been implemented, and the five sub-goals of TP Cloud platform have been realized (specifically to provide unified, fast and on-demand infrastructure distribution services for all units of the Group; application-oriented development can provide out-of-the-box development platform, application support, security protection and other PaaS services; unified management of multi-geographic, multi-data center resources; provide scheduling management and service charging functions in multi-tenant mode. To meet the resource needs of existing virtualization and support the flexible needs of the future), TP Group has a complete and advanced private cloud in the true sense of the architecture and function.

After the early accumulation in the cloud platform, storage and network and other IT infrastructure construction. China TP actively plans to build an innovative cloud computing platform to further improve the availability and reliability of IT infrastructure to meet the needs of business innovation and development. From promoting the transformation of IT infrastructure, including storage and network, to comprehensively upgrading to a cost-effective, more stable and more feature-rich cloud platform, China TP is building a more solid digital base, which can not only provide strong support for the group's digital transformation and accelerate digital transformation.

4.2.2.3 Cloud Practice of A Large Life Insurance Company

The large life insurance company grasped the cloud computing development opportunities, implemented the group's "science and technology" strategy, aimed at accelerating the construction of a more advanced, efficient, dynamic and flexible cloud data center, and made every effort to build a hybrid cloud with national longevity characteristics, built the first hybrid cloud platform in the domestic industry, and achieved an important breakthrough in the "cloud road" of China Life. Since 2012, it has made forward-looking plans based on the concept of cloud computing and landed the IT layout of "big back office + small front end" to build an industry-leading national life hybrid cloud. Since its release at the end of 2017, after continuous iterative upgrades, Hybrid Cloud has now provided cloud services to the whole Group, effectively guaranteeing the safe, stable and efficient operation of the IT systems of the Group and its member companies.

On the one hand, Hybrid Cloud gives full play to the advantages of rapid deployment, flexible expansion and low cost of public cloud resources; on the other hand, front-end applications are quickly deployed on the public cloud, and background data is securely stored in the private cloud, which effectively meets the requirements of regulators and enterprises for data security and independent control of core technologies. Through a unified management platform, resources can be managed, O&M, operated, and cloud services in a unified manner. Hybrid Cloud on demand, to achieve fast and efficient cloud services, such as cloud services to meet the challenges of large traffic live access, solve high concurrency online sales scenarios, quickly meet the needs of intelligent sales training. Relying on the powerful computing power provided by cloud computing, the intelligent world provides people with rich applications, but also generates massive data, greatly saves operating costs, and intelligently improves the quality of operations.

4.3 Foreign Cases of "Insurance + Cloud Computing"

4.3.1 The First Case

Case Tile:

API helps the insurance industry

Case Content:

L, the insurance company powered by artificial intelligence and behavioral economics, today launched its public API, allowing anyone to seamlessly offer L policies through their apps or websites.

Through its API platform, L will initially offer developers access to its renters, condo, and homeowners insurance, and expand the API as the company introduces new insurance products to market. Commerce sites, real estate apps, financial advisors, bots, smart home products will now be able to complement their offering with insurance, allowing their customers instant coverage and a hassle-free experience without ever leaving their app or website.

It takes years to pull together the licenses, capital and technology needed to offer insurance instantly through an app, which is why it's almost nonexistent. Today's API launch changes that. Anyone with a slight familiarity with coding can now include these capabilities in their app, in a matter of hours, we call on startups and entrepreneurs to use our platform to add insurance-related products and features to their apps and websites. We can't wait to see what entrepreneurs will create using our new API.

L's API is also ideal for established businesses such as real estate companies, mortgage originators, commerce sites and lifestyle brands to offer insurance to their customers, as a means to insure their residents or provide coverage for their valuable products.

Today's API launch comes on the heels of L's one year anniversary. Since its September 2016 launch in New York, the company has expanded to California, New Jersey, Illinois and Texas, and has been licensed-and will launch soon-in 15 more states, reaching more than 50% of the population. Most recently, L launched its Zero Everything product, offering new and existing L members a "zero deductible" upgrade, so they can make up to two claims each year with absolutely no deductible payments and no rate hikes.

Customers can buy homeowners and renters insurance in seconds at L. com, or through the L app, and choose a cause to "Giveback" to. In addition to digitizing the entire insurance process, L reduces costs and bureaucracy through giving. In a reversal of the traditional insurance model, L takes a flat 20% fee and treats premiums as belonging to the insured, not the insurer, returning unclaimed money during its annual "Giveback." Giveback is a unique feature of L, where each year leftover money (underwriting profit) is donated to a cause customers care about.

Case Comments:

As we all know, API is an important part of cloud computing and play a vital role in the development and application of cloud computing. L's API platform proved Cloud computing is producing a significant impact on the traditional insurance industry. By embracing cloud technology, L is not only streamlining insurance processes but also shorten the service time greatly in the insurance industry, ultimately reshaping how insurance services are delivered and experienced by customers.

Case Source:

BURKES J. Lemonade launches insurance API[EB/OL]. (2017 – 10 – 10) [2024 – 07 – 01]. https://www. prnewswire. com/news – releases/lemonade – launches – insurance – api – 650210233.html.

4.3.2 The Second Case

Case Tile:

G Life Insurance Company saved more than $ 3 million using container – based architecture on AWS

Case Content:

Mutual insurance provider G Life Insurance Company of America (G) wanted to deliver its growing list of products to customers even faster by going digital. In 2016, G began a company-wide digital transformation to improve innovation, speed to market, and the customer experience. The company chose to migrate its on-premises systems to the cloud using Amazon Web Services (AWS), closing its on-premises data center in 2018. Shortly after beginning its journey to the cloud, the company recognized the benefits of using a container-based solution to reduce costs and improve efficiency. A key part of G's container-based architecture is Amazon Elastic Kubernetes Service (Amazon EKS), which gives users the flexibility to start, run, and scale applications on AWS. Using Amazon EKS, G has achieved significant cost savings, an increase in employee productivity, and the agility to respond to customer demands in near real time. In 2021, 5 years into its digital transformation, G has further modernized its environment and runs 85 percent of its workloads on AWS and is focusing its future development on running new workloads as containers using Amazon EKS.

In G's efforts to adopt a cloud-first approach to building applications, the company began using container-based workloads to achieve elasticity, optimize cost savings, and decrease time to market. The company built an internal service called Launchpad, which its developers use to spin up infrastructure. The architecture for Launchpad includes Amazon Elastic Container Service (Amazon ECS), a fully managed container orchestration service that helps users deploy, manage, and scale containerized applications. As of July 2021, 123 of the company's micro services were built using Launchpad, saving the company $ 400,000 per year. As G started to increase its container capabilities, it expanded to Amazon EKS because of the integration flexibility. Today, G's core systems for its group benefits and individual markets applications run using Amazon EKS, and new workloads are run as containers on Amazon EKS. Instead of its teams spending time building and maintaining an on-premises infrastructure, they can now react quickly to customer feedback. Previously, when customers sent requests to fix technical issues, each request would be added to a queue and backlogged for weeks or months. "Using Amazon EKS, our teams can address technical requests in near real time", says CC. "They can start building fixes without engaging other teams." G has also reduced outages by 30 percent. "We pay penalties to our customers when we have an outage, so we have realized positive financial ramifications from that stability", says CC.

In addition, G has seen an increase in staff productivity and has enhanced its teams' cloud skill sets. Developers can go directly to Launchpad to provision infrastructure for development projects without involving the infrastructure team, significantly reducing time to market for new applications. "Using Amazon EKS, our developers' lead time to procure infrastructure decreased from 3-4 weeks to under 1 hour," says CC.

Through the scalability G has achieved using AWS services, the company has saved $ 3 million on computing costs over the past 18 months. "All unused workloads shut down at 6: 00 p. m. every day," says CC. "Once they're down, we're not paying for them. The cost savings has been a sizable benefit for us." Additionally, G has achieved a more secure environment through the use of AWS services such as Amazon Guard Duty, a threat detection service that continuously monitors for malicious activity and unauthorized behavior. "At G, security is embedded in everything we do", says CC. "Using AWS, we can build in controls at every stage of development and bring new technology to market quickly without compromising security."

To further modernize its large legacy environment, G will continue migrating its Amazon ECS workloads over to Amazon EKS. "There's a lot of appetite to run even more of our workloads on Amazon EKS", says CC. "We know there will be additional cost savings." Moreover, G plans to complete a full migration of its applications to AWS. Currently, 85 percent of its 450 applications run on AWS, and the company aims to migrate the remaining 15 percent by the end of 2024. G is also exploring the possibility of using AWS, a server less compute engine for containers, as a part of its ongoing digital transformation.

"When AWS says it's customer obsessed, that's not just lip service", says CC. "The AWS team members never say, 'We don't work on that' or 'We're not going to help you.' They bring the right resources to the table, even if the issue isn't in the AWS environment. They're always there for us."

Case Comments:

Overall, the case of G Life Insurance Company exemplifies how the strategic adoption of cloud computing technologies can improve the operational efficiency of the insurance industry and help reduce costs while increase customer experiences. It emphasizes the importance of embracing digital transformation to stay competitive and deliver value to customers in today's technology-driven world.

Case Source：

Amazonaws. cn. The guardian life insurance company of America saves over ＄3 million using container-based architecture on AWS［EB/OL］.（2021－06－06）［2024－07－01］. https：//aws.amazon.com/cn/solutions/case-studies/guardian-life-case-study/.

5 区块链与保险业

本章主要阐释区块链与保险业相互融合的基本思路与原理,并精选国内外相关典型案例与学生分享,启发学生探索区块链赋能保险科技应用场景和开发相关保险产品的思路。

5.1 区块链基本理论

5.1.1 区块链的基本概念

区块链(Blockchain)这一概念源自比特币。2008 年,中本聪(Satoshi Nakamoto)发表了一篇论文《比特币:一种点对点的电子现金系统》(*Bitcoin*:*A Peer-to-Peer Electronic Cash System*),该文将区块链描述为一种分布式账本技术(Distributed Ledger Technology)。区块链技术的发展历程如图 5.1 所示。

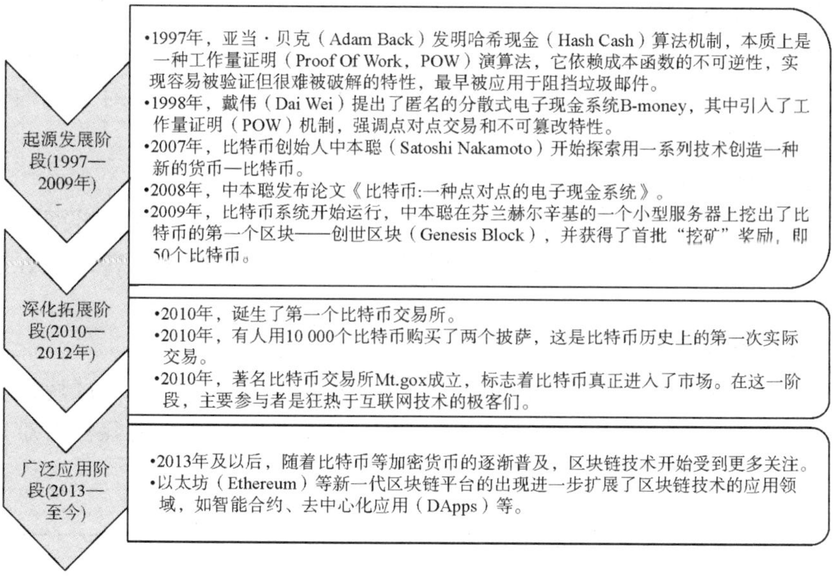

图 5.1 区块链技术的发展历程

资料来源:作者根据资料综合整理得到。

区块链是一种由多方共同维护，使用密码学保证传输和访问安全，能够实现数据一致存储、反篡改、防抵赖的核心技术体系。区块链的作用是存储信息，任何需要保存的信息都可以写入区块链，也可以从中读取。此外，区块链是一种分布式系统，意味着任何人都可以架设服务器，加入区块链网络，成为区块链上的一个节点。因此，区块链本质上是通过去中心化的方式集体维护一个可靠数据库的技术方案。

5.1.2　区块链的典型特征

随着比特币的出现，区块链也开始进入大众视野，逐渐引起政府、企业界和学界的关注。由于区块链的多重特征，学界对区块链的研究呈现加速发展态势。区块链被视为继大型计算机、互联网、个人电脑、移动社交网络之后的第五次计算机范式的革命。归纳而言，区块链有以下七种典型特征：

5.1.2.1　去中心化

区块链数据的验证、记账、存储、维护和传输等过程均是基于分布式系统结构，采用纯数学方法而非中心机构来建立分布式节点间的信任关系，从而形成去中心化可信任的分布式系统。

5.1.2.2　时序数据

区块链采用带有时间戳的链式区块结构存储数据，从而为数据增加了时间维度，具有极强的可验证性和可追溯性。

5.1.2.3　集体维护

区块链系统采用特定的经济激励机制来保证分布式系统中所有节点均可参与数据区块的验证过程，并通过共识算法来选择特定的节点将新区块添加到区块链。

5.1.2.4　可编程性

区块链技术可提供灵活的脚本代码系统，支持用户创建高级的智能合约、货币或其他去中心化应用。

5.1.2.5　自治共享

区块链采用基于协商一致的规范和协议，使得整个系统中的所有节点能够在去信任的环境下自由安全地交换数据，使得对个人或机构的信任改成了对系统的信任，任何人为的干预都将不起作用。

5.1.2.6　匿名安全

由于区块链各节点之间的数据交换遵循固定且预知的算法，区块链网络无须以信任为基础，可以基于地址而非个人身份进行数据交换。这种匿名的特征极好地保护了交易者的隐私。

5.1.2.7　难以篡改

区块链采用密码学的哈希算法机制，并由多方共同维护，每一个区块包含了前一个区块的加密散列、时间戳以及交易数据，这样的设计使得区块内容具有难以篡改的特性。

5.1.3　区块链的发展现状与前景

近年来，联合国、国际货币基金组织等机构以及多个发达国家先后发布了有关区块链的系列政策和研究报告。当前，区块链技术的应用领域已经超越金融领域，并逐步在供应链、征信管理、身份认证、公益慈善、物联网等领域展开实践创新。

5.1.3.1 美国区块链发展现状

美国是全球区块链技术研究和应用的重要推动者之一，众多科技公司、金融机构和研究机构都在积极投入区块链技术的研发和应用，区块链技术在美国呈现出蓬勃发展态势。一方面加强区块链技术的应用监管，另一方面与企业密切合作谋求新的研究议题。

在监管方面，2017 年 2 月，美国国会专门成立由两党成员组成的区块链核心小组，负责围绕区块链技术和数字货币完善相关的公共政策。以美国证券交易委员会（SEC）和美国商品期货交易委员会（CFTC）为代表，对包括区块链在内的数字经济监管越加严密。在加快布局区块链技术方面，美国除了加强对数字经济的开发监管外，也加大了区块链技术在医药开发应用和供应链管理中的监管力度。

此外，美国国土安全部支持用于国土安全分析的区块链应用研究；美国国防部高级研究计划局（DAPPA）则支持区块链用于保护高度敏感数据方面的探索，并积极探索区块链技术在军用卫星、核武器等多个场景中的应用。

5.1.3.2 英国区块链发展现状

英国对区块链发展持有积极态度，将发展分布式账本以及区块链技术提升到国家战略高度，并由财政部、数字经济部两部门共同主导推进。英国央行第一个提出数字法币模型，并主动进行开源，鼓励全世界共同研究。

与此同时，英国政府正在探索类似于区块链技术的分布式账本技术，并且探索区块链技术在传统金融行业的应用场景。2016 年 2 月，英国政府发布了一份关于区块链技术的首席科学顾问报告《分布式账本技术：超越区块链》（*Distributed Ledger Technology: Beyond Block Chain*）。该报告认为，分布式账本技术是一种强大的、具有颠覆性影响的创新，它将变革公共与私营服务供给方式，并可以有效提高生产力，强调要大力发展区块链在政府体系中的应用。

在区块链技术具体应用层面，2016 年 2 月，英国金融市场行为监管局（Financial Conduct Authority，FCA）明确表示将为区块链技术发展提供一定空间，因此不会对其进行严格管制。

5.1.3.3 中国区块链发展现状

我国非常重视区块链技术研究与应用探索，已经陆续制定一系列关于区块链监管方面的法律法规。在应用层面的区块链技术，正在向金融、互联网、供应链、物流以及医疗健康等多个行业延伸，具体呈现出以下趋势。

一是政策体系逐渐完善。目前中国政府出台了一系列关于区块链的相关政策，政策内容覆盖全面，涉及农业、商贸、交通、旅游、政务、教育、金融等各领域。各地方政府也持续强化区块链技术在数字经济与实体经济融合、公共服务治理、保障改善民生、金融科技服务等重点方向的布局和探索。

二是核心技术不断成熟。以中国高校为主的区块链研究团队实力不断增强，区块链人才培养持续输出。以企业为主的区块链技术研发不断深入，解决方案更新迭代。在政府政策的引导和支持下，高校、企业以及研究机构多方合作共促技术集成创新，技术研究实力不断增强，推动解决方案更新迭代，区块链产业规模稳步增长。

三是应用场景深入拓展。中国的区块链技术也呈现逐步渗透态势，开始注重区块链技术在推进平台经济、城市建设高质量发展等方面的重要作用。目前区块链技术已经涉及金融、供应链、医疗保健、物联网等多个领域，提供了更高效的支付和结算服务，减少了金融机构之间的中间环节，同时也为供应链管理、物联网设备身份验证和数据交换等提供了解决方案。

5.1.3.4 区块链技术发展前景

随着技术的不断成熟和市场需求的增加，区块链技术的应用场景将进一步拓展。未来区块链技术有望成为数字经济时代的重要基础设施，推动数字化转型，提高行业的透明度和效率。同时，区块链技术还将为物联网、人工智能等新兴领域带来新的机遇。此外，区块链技术与现实的中心化技术可以进行系统性互补，共同提高经济的交易率，进而促进经济高质量发展。总体而言，区块链技术发展现状良好，前景广阔。

然而，也需要注意到区块链技术面临的挑战与风险，如跨链难题、技术安全性、数据隐私保护以及信息纠错风险等问题。因此，在推动区块链技术发展的同时，也需要加强监管和采取风险防范措施，确保区块链技术健康、可持续发展。

5.2 区块链技术与保险业的融合发展

随着科学技术的不断发展，区块链技术已开始逐渐被运用到各个领域，其中包括保险行业。区块链技术的典型特征，如去中心化、可编程性、自治共享以及匿名安全等，为保险行业变革带来了前所未有的机遇。本节将从保险行业的痛点、难点出发，探讨区块链技术与保险业融合的应用场景，并分析其潜在的优势与挑战。

5.2.1 区块链技术在保险业的应用场景

区块链作为一种新型技术框架，区块链技术在保险领域的应用场景十分广泛，将驱动保险业实现数据价值提升、效率提升以及成本降低。以下是几个比较典型的应用场景，具体见图5.2。

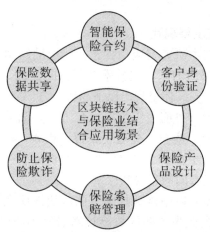

图5.2 区块链和保险业相结合的应用场景

资料来源：作者根据资料综合整理得到。

5.2.1.1 智能保险合约

区块链技术形成了基于去中心化系统建立的共识机制，可以自动执行协议，学界将此类协议称为智能合约。智能合约是区块链技术的重要组成部分，可以自动执行合同条款，确保合同的履行，具有高透明性、高安全性以及高效率性的典型特征。在保险领域，智能合约可以用于实现自动化的理赔流程，降低执行成本，提高理赔效率。例如，当保险事故发生时，智能合约可以自动触发理赔程序，将赔款直接支付给受益人，避免了烦琐的人工操作。

5.2.1.2 客户身份验证

区块链本身就是一个数据库，每个数据节点都可以参与验证信息的真实性和完整性过程。区块链技术基于更多维度的数据记录实现了保险数据价值的提升，可以实现去中心化的身份验证，使得客户无须提供大量的个人信息即可完成身份验证，极大地降低了保险系统的信任风险。这既保护了客户的隐私，又提高了身份验证的效率和准确性。

5.2.1.3 保险产品设计

区块链技术可以使得保险产品设计更加灵活多变，提供个性化定制保险服务。通过基于区块链技术的智能合约，保险公司可以根据客户的需求和风险偏好，设计出更加符合客户需求的保险产品。此外，区块链技术可以构建一个全球性的、去中心化的再保险市场，实现保险产品的交易和资金结算的自动化，推动保险产品创新。

5.2.1.4 保险索赔管理

保险公司可以事先约定基于不同场景承担的不同保险责任，如果一旦发生满足约定条件的风险，可以触发自动理赔程序。此外，区块链技术可以用于记录和验证索赔过程的所有信息，包括事故详情、损失评估、索赔状态等。这有助于保险公司更好地管理索赔流程，提高索赔处理的效率。

5.2.1.5 防止保险欺诈

区块链技术可以在被保险人身份识别中发挥重要作用，通过不可更改的身份证明信息降低保险欺诈风险。区块链技术的透明性和不可篡改性使得交易数据难以被篡改伪造，从而有助于防止保险欺诈行为，规避传统保险行业中的信息不对称问题。同时，区块链技术还可以用于追踪资金的流动，帮助保险公司更好地进行反洗钱工作。

5.2.1.6 保险数据共享

区块链技术可以实现保险公司之间的数据共享，打破数据孤岛。通过构建一个基于区块链的保险数据共享平台，保险公司可以共享客户信息、风险评估数据等，提高保险产品的设计水平和定价精度。同时，数据共享还可以帮助保险公司更好地了解市场需求，优化产品和服务，助力保险公司高质量发展。

总之，区块链技术在保险领域的应用场景非常广泛，从保险产品设计、销售、承保、理赔等各个环节，都可以实现效率提升、成本降低以及带来更好的用户体验。随着区块链技术的不断发展和成熟，其在保险领域的应用也将越来越广泛和深入。

5.2.2 区块链技术赋能保险业的优势与挑战

5.2.2.1 潜在优势

区块链技术与保险业融合发展可以带来诸多优势。首先，通过智能合约实现自动化的理赔流程，可以提高理赔效率，降低运营成本。其次，区块链技术的信任机制可以增强客户信任，提高保险公司的声誉和竞争力。最后，数据共享可以帮助保险公司更好地了解市场需求和风险评估，优化产品和服务。

5.2.2.2　现实挑战

尽管区块链技术与保险业融合发展具有巨大的潜力，但也面临一些挑战。首先，技术成熟度问题。区块链技术尚未完全成熟，可能存在安全风险和稳定性问题。其次，法律法规问题。如何在合法合规的前提下利用区块链技术开展保险业务，需要保险公司和相关监管机构共同摸索。最后，数据隐私保护问题。如何在保证数据共享的同时保护客户隐私，是保险公司需要高度关注的重要问题。

综上所述，区块链技术与保险业融合的应用场景为保险行业带来了前所未有的机遇。通过充分发挥区块链技术的优势，保险公司可以提高业务效率、增强客户信任、优化产品和服务。同时，也需要从技术成熟度、法律法规和数据隐私保护等方面关注到挑战，确保区块链技术在保险行业的健康发展。

5.3　"保险+区块链"国内案例

5.3.1　国内经典案例之一

案例题目：

上海保险交易所区块链保险服务平台

案例内容：

"保交链"是上海保险交易所（以下简称"上海保交所"）于2017年9月正式推出的区块链保险服务平台。该平台独立研发了Golang国密算法包，在电子保单存证场景中可以支持每秒五万笔的指纹数据验证上链，并能响应高并发的系统请求。该系统可以广泛应用于保险交易、金融清算结算、反诈骗和监管合规性等领域。

公开资料显示，保交链的主体服务架构包含了四个方面的内容：一是共识服务架构保证了链上数据的一致性；二是身份认证服务架构实现了身份数据的认证、审核、颁发和管理等功能；三是智能合约服务架构在保障智能合约安全性的前提下，实现了对智能合约的安装、应用和升级等服务功能，为区块链系统中的认证服务提供了强有力的支撑；四是平台服务架构满足了动态组网、同一底层平台下多链的配置和访问方式服务。与此同时，保交链实现了在数据安全和清洗、应用场景体系和数据交换服务在内的三大功能。

在系统应用方面，保交所在区块链技术上对安全性、可扩展性以及应用开发方面的能力进行了创新性的开发。首先，保交链开发并配备了支持国密Golang算法包，而且和上海交大密码与计算机安全实验室达成合作，验证了保交链系统的可行性和安全性。保交链在应用过程中会更加安全可控，同时满足国际标准的算法，拓展了国际业务的渠道。其次，保交链中的节点可以依据企业要求，提供本地部署和上海保交所的云托管两种类型的节点部署形式，满足众多企业的开发需求，节省了企业的开发成本，为不同类型机构的上链提供了便捷性服务。最后，保交链大大降低了应用开发的准入门槛，通过统一的 API 服务和功能分离的开发工具，满足了不同开发团队在应用层面、系统开发和运营的需求，提高了业务场景的开发速度和迭代更新。

保交链具有三大特点：一是监管审计，实现了监管合规性的审计要求；二是性能安全，通过调整配置参数和快捷的应用设计，可达到企业级应用标准；三是监控运维，完备的监控系统可以实时监控区块、数据、网络、CPU 内存及存储。

据了解，目前上海保交所在上线保交链之前已与数家保险机构在小范围内搭建了一条联盟链，由上海保交所和 9 家保险企业组成 10 个节点，测试区块链在保险业的可行性。上海保交所两大业务场景包括数字保单与保单质押登记两方面，未来还将有 9 个应用场景陆续落地。

案例评述：

上海保险交易所研发的"保交链"是国内保险业运用区块链的破冰之旅，这套系统在保险交易、金融清算结算、反诈骗和监管合规性等领域的应用或将成为行业标杆，引领该领域未来的发展方向。同时，上海保交所还牵头成立了区块链保险联盟，该联盟向成员开放区块链底层平台。这将由内而外地打通保险行业的区块链应用，打破供应链上下游禁锢，实现交易资源的数据分享，提升保险业的效率。

案例来源：

北京比特米拉. 区块链+保险行业案例介绍［EB/OL］.（2018－10－22）［2024－07－01］.https://zhuanlan.zhihu.com/p/47388337.

5.3.2 国内经典案例之二

案例题目：

ZA 保险将"区块链"引入保险设计

案例内容：

ZA 在线成立于 2013 年，由 MY 金服、TX、中国 PN 等知名企业联合发起，系国内首家互联网保险公司。相较于传统保险公司，ZA 在线不设任何分支机构，所有业务流程全程在线化，通过互联网进行承保和理赔服务，其中最著名也是最早的产品是基于 TB 场景的退货运费险。ZA 在线的保险业务主要集中在健康、消费金融、汽车、生活消费、航旅五大生态，并呈现个性化、定制化、智能化等趋势。ZA 在线拥有众多的在线合作伙伴，面向 ZFB、DD 等互联网平台提供场景化保险，同时为 XY、QD 及 LX 等互联网金融平台提供消费金融解决方案。截至 2018 年年底，ZA 在线已经服务约 4 亿用户，拥有 262 款保险产品。

2016 年 11 月，ZA 在线成立子公司 ZA 科技，将经过业务验证的科技产品和行业解决方案向国内国外输出，即"保险生态的信息化升级"，其中就涉及人工智能、区块链、云计算和大数据等技术。ZA 在线迫切需要找到新的且强有力的业绩增长点，进一步提升科技对业务增长的驱动力。区块链正是 ZA 在线目前最为重视的技术方向之一。

ZA 保险的安链云是基于人工智能、区块链和密码学的专业生态云服务平台。提供基于区块链技术的 BaaS 服务、基于人工智能技术的 AIaaS 服务、平台保障等云服务，针对金融、医疗健康、供应链、共享研发、文化产业、政务公益等不同领域的业务场景提供新型解决方案，通过开放资产协议（OAP）和新技术与更多的合作伙伴共创未来。

ZA 保险通过在保险场景应用区块链技术，可将保险索赔置于不可更改的总账下，有助于消除保险业中常见的欺诈源。该公司以智能合约形式载录的保单和共享账本可提高财产保险和意外伤害保险的承保效率，使得医疗记录可被加密保护并在健康服务提供者间共享，从而提高医疗保险生态系统的交互操作性；通过智能合约的形式保证再保险合同在区块链平台上的信息安全，简化保险人和被保险人之间的支付流程。

案例评述：

ZA 在线推出的"安链云"是区块链运用在保险领域的一次重要尝试，使得保险领域的自动理赔成为现实。随着区块链技术的不断发展和普及，未来将有更多的保险公司加入区块链技术的探索和应用中来。通过不断创新和突破，保险行业将提供更加高效、安全、便捷的服务，为人类社会的发展做出更大的贡献。

案例来源：

杨浩峰. 众安保险将"区块链"引入保险设计［EB/OL］.（2020-06-21）［2024-07-01］.https://zhuanlan.zhihu.com/p/149827518.

5.4 课程思政案例

案例题目：

"区块链+保险合同"守护助力诚信建设

案例内容：

2022 年 3 月，中共中央办公厅、国务院办公厅印发的《关于推进社会信用体系建设高质量发展促进形成新发展格局的意见》（以下简称《意见》）指出，完善的社会信用体系是供需有效衔接的重要保障，是资源优化配置的坚实基础，是良好营商环境的重要组成部分，对促进国民经济循环高效畅通、构建新发展格局具有重要意义。《意见》强调：培育和践行社会主义核心价值观，扎实推进信用理念、信用制度、信用手段与国民经济体系各方面各环节深度融合，进一步发挥信用对提高资源配置效率、降低制度性交易成本、防范化解风险的重要作用，为提升国民经济体系整体效能、促进形成新发展格局提供支撑保障。

保险业诚信建设是社会信用体系的重要组成部分，直接关系到行业兴衰和广大被保险人的切身利益，对保障人民生活、促进经济发展、构建和谐社会具有重大意义。保险业的诚信问题，存在于管理、经营的各个方面，突出表现为在设计保单时，用晦涩或所谓专业性的语言设置陷阱，待出险或理赔时逃避保险责任；对客户进行误导宣传，为获取业务不择手段；借助权力部门的力量，以联合发文、会议纪要、口头命令等方式发展业务；通过协议或借行业协会名义联合限价、划分市场进行垄断经营；展业理赔两张脸，通过拖延赔付、无理由拒赔等手段侵害被保险人利益；有的从业人员利用保险业人才缺乏和管理上的漏洞，非正常地频繁在公司间流动，并对原单位进行恶意诋毁或唆使老客户退保，扰乱市场秩序，损害被保险人利益。

区块链技术可以有效解决保险业面临的上述诚信问题，防范保险欺诈。区块链技术通过数字化合同将信用变成一个具有可管理的对象。区块链技术提供了公共的分类账，使得分散式数字存储库可以通过提供完整的历史记录独立验证客户和事务（如索赔）的真实性。因此，保险公司可以运用区块链技术轻而易举地发现赔付过程中是否存在重复交易或者是否存在可疑交易当事人的交易。区块链技术还可以跨行业实现与外部数据相通，验证真实性，如对货物所有权的验证、发生所有权变化的时间日期以及位置的变化、维修历史等。这样，可以确保我们所交易和消费的商品具有可靠来源，并且能够追踪到这些商品的整个生命周期。基于区块链技术协助保险公司验证信息能有效遏制欺诈性保险索赔数量的增加。

案例评述：

诚信是社会主义核心价值观的重要组成部分，也是保险行业可持续发展的重要原则。保险行业作为社会经济健康运行的重要保障，其诚信建设关乎投保双方的切身利益。

区块链技术的出现为保险行业的诚信建设提供了新的解决方案。通过区块链技术的去中心化、不可篡改等特性，可以有效解决保险业务中的信息不对称问题，提高保险合同的透明度和可信度。同时，区块链技术还可以实现跨行业的数据互通和验证，为保险公司提供更加全面、准确的客户信息，有效防范保险欺诈行为。

总之，在党和国家的高度重视下，区块链技术为保险行业的诚信建设提供了新的机遇。保险公司应该抓住这一机遇，积极推动区块链技术在诚信建设中的应用，提高行业的整体诚信水平，为社会和谐稳定和经济持续发展做出更大贡献。

案例来源：

新华社. 中共中央办公厅国务院办公厅印发《关于推进社会信用体系建设高质量发展促进形成新发展格局的意见》［EB/OL］.（2022-03-29）［2024-07-01］.https://www.gov.cn/zhengce/2022-03-29/content_5682283.htm.

5

Blockchain and insurance Industry

This chapter mainly explains the basic ideas and principles of the mutual integration of blockchain and the insurance industry, and selects relevant typical cases at home and abroad to share with students, inspiring them to explore the application scenarios of blockchain enabling insurance technology and the ideas of developing insurance-related products.

5.1 Basic Theory of Blockchain

5.1.1 The Basic Concept of Blockchain

The concept of blockchain comes from Bitcoin. In 2008, Satoshi Nakamoto published a paper titled *Bitcoin: A Point-to-Point Electronic Cash System*, which describes blockchain as a distributed ledger technology.

Blockchain is a core technology system that is jointly maintained by multiple parties, using cryptography to ensure the security of transmission and access, and can realize consistent data storage, anti-tampering and anti-denial. The role of a blockchain is to store information, and any information that needs to be saved can be written to the blockchain or read from it. In addition, blockchain is a distributed system, which means that anyone can set up a server, join the blockchain network, and become a node on the chain. Therefore, blockchain is essentially a technical solution to maintain a reliable database in a decentralized way. The development history of blockchain technology is shown in the Figure 5.1.

Origin and Development Stage (1997–2009)	•In 1997, Adam Back invented the Hash Cash algorithm mechanism, which is essentially a Proof of Work(POW) algorithm that relies on the irreversibility of the cost function to achieve easily verifiable but difficult to crack characteristics. It was first applied to block spam. •In 1998, Dai Wei proposed the anonymous decentralized electronic cash system B–moneey, which introduced Proof of Work (POW) mechanism, emphasizing peer-too-peer transactions and immutability. •In 2007, Bitcoin founder Satoshi Nakamoto began exploring the use of a series of technologies to create a new currency-Bitcoin. •In 2008, Satoshi Nakamoto published a paper titled *Bitcoin: A Peer to Peer Electronic Cash System*. •In 2009, the Bitcoin system began operating, and Satoshi Nakamoto dug up the first block of Bitcoin-the Genesis Block-on a small server in Helsinki, Finland, and received the first batch of "mining" rewards, which amounted to 50 Bitcoins.
Deepening and expanding stage (2010–2012)	•In 2010, the first Bitcoin exchange was born. •In 2010, someone purchased 2 pizzas with 10,000 Bitcoin, marking the first actual transaction in Bitcoin's history. •In 2010, the famous Bitcoin exchange Mt. gox was established, marking the true entry of Bitcoin into the market. At this stage, the main participants are geeks who are crazy about Internet technology.
Widely applied stage (2013 present)	•Since 2013, with the gradual popularization of cryptocurrencies such as Bitcoin, blockchain technology has begun to receive more attention. •The emergence of new generation blockchain platforms such as Ethereum has further expanded the application fields of blockchain technology, such as smart contracts and decentralized applications (DApps).

Figure 5. 1　**The development history of blockchain technology**

Source: The author has compiled the data comprehensively.

5. 1. 2　Typical Features of the Blockchain

With the emergence of Bitcoin, blockchain has come to attention of the public, gradually attracting the attention of the government, business and academic circles. Due to the multiple characteristics of blockchain, the academic research on blockchain has shown an accelerated development trend. Blockchain is seen as the fifth computer paradigm revolution after macro-computers, the Internet, personal computers, and mobile social networks. To sum up, blockchain has seven typical features:

5. 1. 2. 1　Decentralization

The processes of verification, bookkeeping, storage, maintenance and transmission of blockchain data are all based on the distributed system structure. Blockchain uses pure mathematical method rather than the central mechanism to establish the trust relationship between distributed nodes, so as to form a decentralized and trusted distributed system.

5. 1. 2. 2　Time Sequence Data

Blockchain uses a chain block structure with a time stamp to store data, thus adding a time dimension to the data, and has strong verifiability and traceability.

5. 1. 2. 3　Collective Maintenance

The blockchain system adopts a specific economic incentive mechanism to ensure that all nodes in the distributed system can participate in the verification process of data blocks, and uses the consensus algorithm to select specific nodes to add new blocks to the blockchain.

5.1.2.4 Programability

Blockchain technology provides a flexible scripting code system that enables users to create advanced smart contracts, currencies, or other decentralized applications.

5.1.2.5 Autonomy and Sharing

Blockchain adopts consensus-based norms and protocols, so that all nodes in the whole system can freely and safely exchange data in the environment of detrust, thus the trust of individuals or institutions is changed to the trust of the system, and any human intervention will not work.

5.1.2.6 Anonymous Security

Since the data exchange between the nodes of the blockchain follows a fixed and predictive algorithm, the blockchain network does not need to be based on trust, and can exchange data based on address rather than personal identity. This anonymous feature perfectly protects the privacy of the traders.

5.1.2.7 Hard to Tamper With

Blockchain uses the Hash algorithm mechanism of cryptography, and is jointly maintained by multiple parties. Each block contains the encryption hash, time stamp and transaction data of the previous block. This design makes the content of the block difficult to tamper with.

5.1.3 Development Status and Prospects of Blockchain

In recent years, the United Nations, the International Monetary Fund and other institutions as well as a number of developed countries have released a series of policies and research reports on blockchain. At present, the application field of blockchain technology has surpassed the financial field, and gradually carried out practical innovation in supply chain, credit management, identity authentication, public welfare and charity, Internet of Things and other fields.

5.1.3.1 Current Development Status of Blockchain in the United States

The United States is one of the important promoters of the global research and application of blockchain technology. Many technology companies, financial institutions and research institutions are actively investing in the research and development and application of blockchain technology. Blockchain technology shows a vigorous development trend in the United States. On the one hand, strengthen the application supervision of application of blockchain technology; on the other hand, work closely with enterprises to seek new research issues.

On the regulatory side, in February 2017, the US Congress set up a blockchain core group composed of two parties, responsible for improving public policies around blockchain technology and digital currency. Represented by the Securities and Exchange Commission (SEC) and the Commodity Futures Trading Commission (CFTC), the regulation of the digital economy, including blockchain, is tightening. In terms of accelerating the layout of blockchain technology, the United States has not only strengthened the supervision of the development of the digital economy, but also strengthened the supervision of blockchain technology in the pharmaceutical development and application and supply chain management.

In addition, the Department of Homeland Security supports blockchain application research for homeland security analysis, and the Defense Advanced Research Projects Agency (DAPPA) supports the exploration of blockchain for protecting highly sensitive data, and actively explores the application of blockchain technology in military satellites and nuclear weapons.

5. 1. 3. 2　The Development Status of Blockchain in the UK

The UK has a positive attitude towards the development of blockchain, and promotes the development of distributed ledger and blockchain technology to a national strategic height, which is jointly led by the Ministry of Finance and the Ministry of Digital Economy. The Bank of England was the first to propose a digital fiat model and actively open source to encourage the world to research.

At the same time, the UK government is exploring a distributed ledger technology similar to the blockchain technology, and is exploring the application scenarios of the blockchain technology in the traditional financial industry. In February 2016, the British government issued a chief scientific adviser on block chain technology report the distributed book technology: beyond block chain, the report that distributed book technology is a powerful and disruptive innovation, it will change the public and private service supply, and can effectively improve productivity, facilitate the application of the block chain in the government system.

In terms of the specific application of blockchain technology, in February 2016, the UK Financial Conduct Authority made it clear that it would provide some space for the development of blockchain technology, so it will not be strictly regulated.

5. 1. 3. 3　The Development Status of Blockchain in China

China attaches great importance to the research and application of blockchain technology, and has successively formulated a series of laws and regulations on blockchain supervision. At the application level, blockchain technology is being extended to finance, Internet, supply chain, logistics, medical and health care and other industries, specifically showing the following trends.

First, the policy system has been gradually improved. At present, the Chinese government has issued a series of policies related to blockchain, covering a comprehensive range of agriculture, trade, transportation, tourism, government affairs, education, finance and other fields. Local governments have also continued to strengthen the layout and exploration of blockchain technology in the integration of the digital economy and the real economy, public service governance, safeguard and improvement of people's livelihood, and fintech services.

Second, the core technologies continue to mature. The strength of the blockchain research team dominated by Chinese universities is constantly enhanced, and the blockchain talent training continues to boom. The enterprise-based research and development of blockchain technology continues to deepen, and the solutions are updated and iterated. Under the guidance and support of government policies, universities, enterprises and research institutions cooperate to promote technology integration and innovation, the technological research strength is contin-

5

Blockchain and insurance Industry

uously enhanced, and the update and iteration of solutions are promoted, and the scale of the blockchain industry is steadily growing.

Third, the application scenarios are further expanded. China's blockchain technology also shows a gradual trend of penetration, and begins to pay attention to the important role of blockchain technology in promoting platform economy, high-quality and high-level development of urban construction. At present, blockchain technology has involved finance, supply chain, healthcare, Internet of Things and other fields, providing more efficient payment and settlement services, reducing the intermediate links between financial institutions, and also providing solutions for supply chain management, Internet of Things device authentication and data exchange.

5.1.3.4 Development Prospects of Blockchain Technology

With the continuous maturity of technology and the increase of market demand, the application scenarios of blockchain technology will be further expanded. In the future, blockchain technology is expected to become an important infrastructure in the digital economy era, promoting digital transformation and improving the transparency and efficiency of the industry. At the same time, blockchain technology will also bring new opportunities for emerging fields such as the Internet of Things and artificial intelligence. In addition, blockchain technology and realistic centralized technology can be systematically complementary, jointly improving the transaction rate of the economy, thus promoting high-quality economic development. Overall, blockchain technology is in good development and has broad prospects.

However, it is also necessary to pay attention to the challenges and risks faced by blockchain technology, such as cross-chain problems, technical security, data privacy protection, and information error correction risks. Therefore, while promoting the development of blockchain technology, it is also necessary to strengthen supervision and risk prevention measures to ensure the healthy and sustainable development of blockchain technology.

5.2　Integrated Development of Blockchain Technology and Insurance Industry

With the continuous development of science and technology, blockchain technology has begun to be gradually applied to various fields, including the insurance industry. Typical features of blockchain technology, such as decentralization, programmability, autonomous sharing, and anonymous security, bring unprecedented opportunities for change in the insurance industry. This section will start from the pain points and difficulties of the insurance industry, discuss the application scenarios of the integration of blockchain technology and the insurance industry, and analyze its potential advantages and challenges.

5.2.1 Application Scenarios of Blockchain Technology in the Insurance Industry

Blockchain, as a new technology framework, blockchain technology has a wide range of application scenarios in the insurance field, which will drive the insurance industry to achieve data value improvement, efficiency improvement and cost reduction. Here are several typical application scenarios, as shown in Figure 5.2.

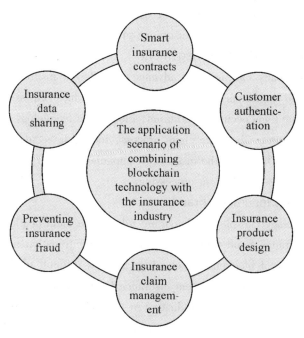

Figure 5.2 **Application scenarios of combining blockchain technology and insurance industry**

Source: The author has compiled the data comprehensively.

5.2.1.1 Smart Insurance Contract

Blockchain technology has formed a consensus mechanism based on decentralized systems that can automatically execute protocols, which are called smart contracts. Smart contracts are an important part of blockchain technology, which can automatically execute contract terms and ensure the performance of contracts, which is typical of high transparency, high security and high efficiency. In the insurance sector, smart contracts can be used to automate the claims process, reduce execution costs and improve claims efficiency. For example, when an insurance accident occurs, the smart contract can automatically trigger the claim procedure, paying the claim directly to the beneficiary, avoiding cumbersome manual operations.

5.2.1.2 Customer Authentication

Blockchain itself is a database, and each data node can participate in verifying the authenticity and integrity of the information. Based on more dimensions of data records, blockchain technology can improve the value of insurance data, and can realize decentralized authentication, so that customers can complete the authentication without providing a large amount of personal information, and greatly reduce the trust risk of the insurance system. This not only protects customer privacy, but also improves the efficiency and accuracy of authentication.

5.2.1.3 Insurance Product Design

Blockchain technology can make insurance product design more flexible and provide personalized and customized insurance. Through smart contracts, insurance companies can design insurance products that can further meet customers' needs according to their demands and risk preferences. In addition, blockchain technology can build a global and decentralized reinsurance market, realize the automation of transactions and fund settlement of insurance products, and promote the innovation of insurance products.

5.2.1.4 Insurance Claim Management

The insurance company can agree in advance on different insurance liabilities based on different scenarios, and the automatic claim settlement procedure can be triggered if the risk of meeting the agreed conditions occurs. In addition, blockchain technology can be used to record and verify all the information about the claim process, including accident details, loss assessment, claim status, etc. This helps the insurance companies to better manage the claim process and improve the efficiency of the claim processing.

5.2.1.5 Prevent Insurance Fraud

Blockchain technology can play an important role in the identification of the insured, reducing the risk of insurance fraud through unchangeable identification information. The transparency and immutability of blockchain technology make it difficult for transaction data to be falsified and forged, thus helping to prevent insurance fraud and avoid the information asymmetry problem in the traditional insurance industry. At the same time, blockchain technology can also be used to track the flow of funds and help insurance companies to better conduct anti-money laundering work.

5.2.1.6 Insurance Data Sharing

Blockchain technology can realize the data sharing between insurance companies and break the data islands. By building a blockchain-based insurance data sharing platform, insurance companies can share customer information, risk assessment data, etc., to improve the design and pricing accuracy of insurance products. At the same time, data sharing can also help insurance companies better understand the market demand, optimize their products and services, and help insurance companies achieve high-quality development.

In short, blockchain technology has a wide range of application scenarios in the field of insurance, from insurance product design, sales, underwriting, claims, reinsurance and other links, which can achieve efficiency improvement, cost reduction and better user experience. With the continuous development and maturity of blockchain technology, its application in the insurance field will be more and more extensive and deep.

5. 2. 2　Advantages and Challenges of Blockchain
Technology to Empower the Insurance Industry

5. 2. 2. 1　Potential Advantages

The integrated development of blockchain technology and the insurance industry can bring many advantages. First, an automated claims settlement process through smart contracts can improve the efficiency of claims settlement and reduce operating costs. Secondly, the trust mechanism of blockchain technology can enhance customer trust and improve the reputation and competitiveness of insurance companies. Finally, data sharing can help insurance companies better understand market needs and risk assessment, and optimize products and services.

5. 2. 2. 2　Practical Challenges

Despite the great potential of the integrated development of blockchain technology and the insurance industry, it also faces some challenges. First of all, the technology maturity problem. The blockchain technology is not fully mature, there may be security risks and stability problems. Secondly, laws and regulations. How to use blockchain technology to carry out insurance business under the premise of legal compliance needs to be explored by insurance companies and relevant regulatory agencies. Finally, the issue of data privacy protection. How to protect customer privacy while ensuring data sharing is an important issue that insurance companies need to pay special attention to. To sum up, the application scenarios of the integration of blockchain technology and the insurance industry bring unprecedented opportunities for the insurance industry. By leveraging the advantages of blockchain technology, insurance companies can improve business efficiency, enhance customer trust, and optimize products and services. At the same time, it also needs to pay attention to the challenges in terms of technology maturity, laws and regulations, and data privacy protection to ensure the healthy development of blockchain technology in the insurance industry.

To sum up, the application scenarios of the integration of blockchain technology and the insurance industry have brought unprecedented opportunities and challenges to the insurance industry. By leveraging the strengths of blockchain technology, insurance companies can improve business efficiency, enhance customer trust, and optimize products and services. However, we also need to focus on challenges such as technology maturity, laws and regulations, and data privacy protection to ensure the healthy development of blockchain technology in the insurance industry.

5.3 Foreign Cases of "Insurance + Blockchain"

5.3.1 The First Case

Case Tile:

Ethereum Blockchain on insurance

Case Content:

French insurance giant A is using the Ethereum public blockchain to offer automated compensation for delayed flights to air travelers. With this new blockchain insurance product, called Fizzy, A now claims to be "the first major insurance group to offer an insurance product using blockchain technology". If the flight is delayed by more than two hours, the "smart contract" insurance product will reimburse the passenger directly and automatically. A describes Fizzy as a "100% automated, 100% secure platform that provides parametric insurance against flight delays".

They use the public Ethereum blockchain to record insurance product purchases and trigger automatic payments by using smart contracts on the blockchain. Ethereum smart contracts are also linked to a global air traffic database to constantly monitor flight data. When a flight is delayed by more than 2 hours, the compensation mechanism will be automatically implemented and sent directly to the policyholder's "credit card" account, independent of A's decision.

However, A probably did not know that as early as last year, S Insurance launched a blockchain insurance card for airline extension insurance. With this new blockchain insurance product, called Fizzy, A now claims to be "the first major insurance group to offer an insurance product using blockchain technology". If the flight is delayed by more than two hours, the "smart contract" insurance product will reimburse the passenger directly and automatically. A describes Fizzy as a "100% automated, 100% secure platform that provides parametric insurance against flight delays".

Case Comments:

The integration of blockchain technology in the insurance sector, as demonstrated by A's Fizzy product, represents a significant advancement in enhancing customer experience and operational efficiency. By leveraging the Ethereum public blockchain, A has introduced a novel approach to automating compensation for delayed flights through smart contracts, thereby streamlining the claims process and ensuring transparency. The author believes with the development of blockchain technology, blockchain technology will be used more and more frequently in the insurance industry and companies like A must continue to innovate and differentiate their offerings to stay ahead in the market. Overall, the combination of blockchain technology and insurance holds great promise for improving operational efficiency, enhancing customer trust, and driving innovation in the industry.

Case Source:

KEATING C. French insurance giant a boss proposes new climate alliance for insurance sector[EB/OL].(2020-12-15)[2024-07-01].https://www.greenbiz.com/article/french-insurance-giant-axa-boss-proposes-new-climate-alliance-insurance-sector.

5.3.2 The Second Case

Case Tile:

A Insurance company "Le" to Use Blockchain to Deliver "Affordable and Instantaneous" Climate Insurance

Case Content:

Le to use blockchain to deliver "affordable and instantaneous" climate insurance.

InsurTech firm Le has announced the launch of the Le Crypto Climate Coalition, which will offer climate insurance to the worlds most vulnerable farmers.

The climate insurance will be architected as a stable coin-denominated, decentralised application (dApp) on Avalanche-an eco-friendly proof-of-stake blockchain. This will allow farmers to make and receive payments with ease from their mobile phones by using global stable coins and local currencies.

This new service is being launched through Le non-profit foundation-The Le Foundation which promotes the use of AI, data and software to build socially impactful products and programs.

The coalition is being constituted as a Decentralised Autonomous Organisation (DAO), dedicated to building and distributing at-cost, instantaneous, parametric weather insurance to subsistence farmers and livestock keepers in emerging markets.

The Le Foundation will provide the initial capital to backstop the DAOs smart contracts, and in time all crypto investors will be able to fund the DAOs liquidity pool. The DAO will also issue a governance token to reward participation by the broader community.

Alongside the Le Foundation, founding coalition members include Hannover Re, Avalanche, DAOstack, Chainlink, Etherisc, Pula, and Tomorrow. io.

Director of the Le Foundation, Daniel Schreiber said: The Le Foundation was established to build exponentially-impactful technologies. "By using a DAO instead of a traditional insurance company, smart contracts instead of insurance policies, and oracles instead of claims professionals, we expect to harness the communal and decentralized aspects of web3 and real-time weather data to deliver affordable and instantaneous climate insurance to the people who need it most."

An initial rollout of the coalition in Africa is expected within the year.

"Africa has an estimated 300 million smallholder farmers. The majority face real climate risks to their livelihoods, as traditional, indemnity-based insurance is often unaffordable or unavailable to them", said Rose Goslinga, co-founder of Pula, a Kenya-based insurTech that specializes in digital and agricultural insurance to de-risk millions of smallholder farmers across Africa.

She continues: "This is where the power of the Le Crypto Climate Coalition comes in: An on-chain solution that can be immediately impactful at scale will allow farmers to finally get financially protected against the increasingly frequent risks such as drought."

Addressing the coalition, S. N, co-founder of Chainlink, the market-leading blockchain oracle said: Weve been helping developers and institutions usher in a new age of economic fairness and transparency with web3. The Le Crypto Climate Coalition is a prime example of how innovative solutions built on the blockchain can drive global financial inclusion previously unavailable.

"We plan to make the Chainlink team and platform available to L3C in an effort to protect the millions of farmers who depend on what they grow from the devastation of climate change."

The Le Crypto Climate Coalition will be presented at the Avalanche Summit on March 23, 2022.

Case Comments:

The initiative by Le to utilize blockchain technology for delivering affordable and instantaneous climate insurance through the Le Crypto Climate Coalition is an important process towards using insurance technology to solve traditional problems and dilemmas. The author considers, by combining blockchain's transparency, efficiency, and decentralization with the mission of providing climate insurance to those most in need, Le is paving the way for a more inclusive and sustainable insurance ecosystem.

Case Source:

WILLARD J. Lemonade to use blockchain to deliver "affordable and instantaneous" climate insurance[EB/OL]. (2022-0322)[2024-07-01]. https://www.reinsurancene.ws/lemonade-to-use-blockchain-to-deliver-affordable-and-instantaneous-climate-insurance/.

6

机器人与保险业

本章主要阐释机器人与保险业融合发展的基本思路与原理，并精选国内外相关典型案例与学生分享，启发学生探索机器人技术赋能保险科技的应用场景和开发相关保险产品的思路。

6.1　机器人基本理论

6.1.1　机器人的基本概念

1920 年，捷克著名作家卡雷尔·卡佩克（Karl Capek）在剧本《罗萨姆的万能机器人》（*Rossum's Universal Robots*）中首次提到"机器人"一词。1959 年，乔治·德沃尔（George Devol）与约瑟夫·英格伯格（Joseph Engelberger）合作制造了第一台工业机器人"尤尼梅特"（Unimate）；随后约 450 台"尤尼梅特"在通用汽车公司（General Motors Corporation）投入使用，标志着第一代机器人诞生。机器人发展历程详见图 6.1。

国际机器人联合会（International Federation of Robotics，IFR）将机器人（Robot）定义为一种自动控制、可编程和多用途的机器。维基百科将机器人定义为一种机器，尤其是能够自动执行一系列复杂的动作的、可由计算机编程的机器。

一般来说，机器人是一种自动执行命令的自动化机械，具有与人相似的感知能力、决策能力和执行能力，可以帮助或者替代人类完成重复、烦琐且危险的任务，从而提升人类的工作效率和品质，服务于人们的生产和生活，扩大人类的行动和能力范围。

机器人包括工业机器人和服务机器人。工业机器人是完全自主的机器，不需要人工操作，可以通过编程执行多项手动任务，如焊接、喷漆、组装、搬运材料或包装。需要说明的是，纺织机、电梯、起重机、运输带或咖啡机不是工业机器人，因为它们有独特的用途，不能重新编程以执行其他任务或需要人工操作才能执行其他任务。服务机器人主要从事维护保养、修理、运输、清洗、保安、救援、医疗、监护、陪伴等一系列服务工作。

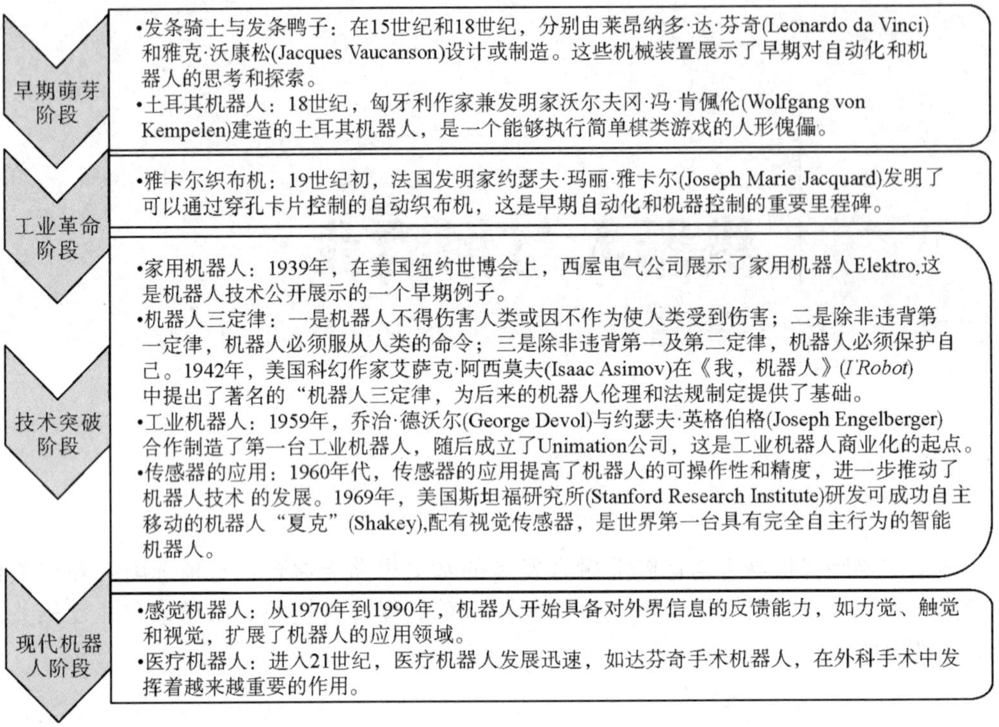

早期萌芽阶段	•发条骑士与发条鸭子：在15世纪和18世纪，分别由莱昂纳多·达·芬奇(Leonardo da Vinci)和雅克·沃康松(Jacques Vaucanson)设计或制造。这些机械装置展示了早期对自动化和机器人的思考和探索。 •土耳其机器人：18世纪，匈牙利作家兼发明家沃尔夫冈·冯·肯佩伦(Wolfgang von Kempelen)建造的土耳其机器人，是一个能够执行简单棋类游戏的人形傀儡。
工业革命阶段	•雅卡尔织布机：19世纪初，法国发明家约瑟夫·玛丽·雅卡尔(Joseph Marie Jacquard)发明了可以通过穿孔卡片控制的自动织布机，这是早期自动化和机器控制的重要里程碑。
技术突破阶段	•家用机器人：1939年，在美国纽约世博会上，西屋电气公司展示了家用机器人Elektro,这是机器人技术公开展示的一个早期例子。 •机器人三定律：一是机器人不得伤害人类或因不作为使人类受到伤害；二是除非违背第一定律，机器人必须服从人类的命令；三是除非违背第一及第二定律，机器人必须保护自己。1942年，美国科幻作家艾萨克·阿西莫夫(Isaac Asimov)在《我，机器人》(I'Robot)中提出了著名的"机器人三定律，为后来的机器人伦理和法规制定提供了基础。 •工业机器人：1959年，乔治·德沃尔(George Devol)与约瑟夫·英格伯格(Joseph Engelberger)合作制造了第一台工业机器人，随后成立了Unimation公司，这是工业机器人商业化的起点。 •传感器的应用：1960年代，传感器的应用提高了机器人的可操作性和精度，进一步推动了机器人技术 的发展。1969年，美国斯坦福研究所(Stanford Research Institute)研发可成功自主移动的机器人"夏克"(Shakey),配有视觉传感器，是世界第一台具有完全自主行为的智能机器人。
现代机器人阶段	•感觉机器人：从1970年到1990年，机器人开始具备对外界信息的反馈能力，如力觉、触觉和视觉，扩展了机器人的应用领域。 •医疗机器人：进入21世纪，医疗机器人发展迅速，如达芬奇手术机器人，在外科手术中发挥着越来越重要的作用。

图 6.1 机器人发展历程

资料来源：作者根据资料综合整理得到。

6.1.2 机器人的典型特征

随着人工智能、大数据以及云计算等数字技术的迅速发展，机器人开始进入大众视野，逐渐引起政府、企业界和学界的关注。由于机器人的多重特征，近年来，学界对机器人的研究呈现加速发展态势。机器人作为一种具有高度灵活性的自动化机器，具有以下四重特征：

6.1.2.1 自主性

机器人具有自主学习、感知和执行的能力。一些先进的机器人可通过机器学习和深度学习等技术，从经验中学习并优化其性能，以适应不断变化的环境和任务，并可以自主地调整或者改变工作方式。例如，机器人可以在流水线上完成重复、危险或高精度的工作，不需要人为干预，由此可以提高生产效率和产品质量，同时减少劳动力成本。此外，基于感知信息，机器人能够进行自主决策和规划，选择合适的行为和动作来完成任务，从而在不同情境下做出正确的决策。

6.1.2.2 灵活性

机器人的结构和功能是可定制的，可以按照不同的需求进行个性化设计。机器人可以根据不同产品的制造要求进行不同的装备和程序调整，实现多种生产流程的自动化。家庭机器人可以根据不同的家庭需求，安装不同的功能模块，例如，智能语音控制、自动清洁等，从而提高家庭生活的便利程度。

6.1.2.3 高效性

机器人通过执行器（如电机、服务器等）控制身体的运动和行为，实现自主的行动。这使得机器人能够执行各种任务，如搬运物体、操作工具、移动位置等。机器人可以持续地执行高负载、高强度的工作任务，并且不会出现因为疲劳或者人为因素导致的操作失误。

6.1.2.4 精度性

机器人通常配备多种传感器，如视觉、听觉、触觉等，用于获取环境信息，实现自主感知。这些传感器使得机器人能够感知并理解其周围的环境，包括物体、声音、光线、温度等。机器人在执行任务时可以达到高精度的效果，通常比人工操作更稳定和准确。例如，无人机可以通过各种遥感技术将目标物的具体情况记录下来，通过分析目标物的特征，实现精确观测。医疗机器人可以在手术中准确地定位、切割和缝合，从而最大限度地减小手术风险，提高治疗效果。

这些特征使得机器人在许多领域具有广泛的应用价值，如工业自动化、医疗服务、家庭服务、救援行动等。它们能够辅助甚至替代人类完成危险、繁重、复杂的工作，提高工作效率与质量，扩大或延伸人的活动及能力范围。

6.1.3 机器人的发展现状

机器人技术起源于 20 世纪 50 年代，最初被应用于工业生产领域，也即工业机器人。据国际机器人联合会数据，截至 2022 年年底，全球工厂共安装了 553 052 台工业机器人，同比增长 5%。按地区划分，73% 的工业机器人安装在亚洲，15% 的工业机器人安装在欧洲，10% 的工业机器人安装在美洲。

据统计，中国是迄今为止全球最大的工业机器人市场。2022 年，中国年度安装量达到 290 258 台，同比增长 5%。为了服务这个充满活力的市场，国内外机器人供应商纷纷在中国建立生产工厂，并不断提高产能。日本的工业机器人市场规模仅次于中国，位居全球第二。日本是全球主要的机器人制造国，占全球机器人产量市场份额的 46%。2022 年，日本的机器人安装量达到 50 413 台，超过了 2019 年的 49 908 台的水平。美国是最大的区域市场，2022 年占美洲安装量的 71%，机器人安装量增长 10%，达到 39 576 台，仅略低于 2018 年 40 373 台的峰值水平。

从以上数据可以看出，机器人产业已经成为当今世界的重要产业之一。随着技术的不断进步，机器人的应用范围越来越广泛，种类也越来越多。目前，机器人已经应用于工业生产、医疗保健、农业、服务业等各个领域。

一般来说，机器人产业链包括核心技术支撑、生产销售和终端应用等多个层面。机器人生产环节涵盖了一系列用于实际生产的各类产品型号及其配套服务体系。机器人终端市场层面，即各种商业化场景中的具体运用实例，例如，工厂自动化作业流程以及管理方案设计实施等。目前，中国成功构建了全面且成熟的机器人产业生态链，可有力支持工业生产、医疗保健、农业、服务业等领域的机器人发展。特别是在机器人生产和终端市场层面，中国机器人产业链较为完整。

2022 年全球前 15 个国家或地区工业机器人安装量见图 6.2。

6.1.4 机器人的发展前景

机器人技术的发展前景十分广阔，随着科技的不断进步和需求的日益增长，机器人将在各个领域发挥越来越重要的作用。

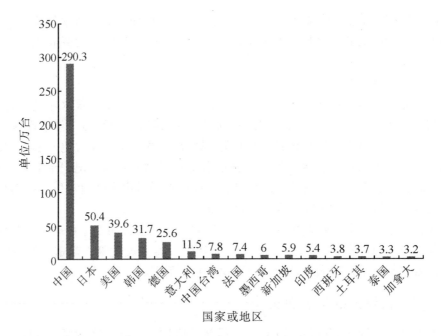

图 6.2　2022 年全球前 15 个国家或地区工业机器人安装量

数据来源：https://www.istis.sh.cn/cms/news/article/75/26664。

6.1.4.1　核心技术不断创新

机器人行业的发展受到技术进步的推动。随着大数据、人工智能、机器学习、物联网等技术的持续进步，机器人的智能化水平将不断提高，其应用领域也将更加广泛。例如，生成式人工智能的发展为机器人发展提供了新方案，使机器人能够通过训练进行新知识创造。这种技术的发展将使机器人更加智能化，能够更好地适应各种复杂环境并完成任务。同时，企业界正在开发生成式人工智能驱动界面，将使用户能够更直观地通过自然语言对机器人进行编程，降低使用门槛，使得更多人能够利用机器人技术。因此，技术的持续创新将推动机器人行业的持续发展。

6.1.4.2　应用领域深入拓展

机器人在制造业中有着广泛的应用。未来随着机器人在医疗、农业、物流等领域的应用不断拓展，将进一步推动机器人行业的快速发展。特别是在医疗领域，机器人的运用有助于提高医生的诊疗水平，更好地治疗疾病。此外，人机协作也是机器人发展的一个重要趋势。随着传感器、视觉技术和智能抓取器的快速发展，机器人能够实时响应环境变化，从而与人类协同联动。在制造业、医疗领域和服务行业，机器人和人类的协作将变得更加普遍，这种协同联动有望提高生产和服务效率、降低成本，并创造更安全的工作环境。

6.1.4.3　市场规模不断增长

随着机器人应用的普及、技术的不断进步以及教育、医疗、安防等领域需求的增长，机器人行业的市场规模将持续扩大。据相关统计数据，未来几年全球机器人市场的年复合增长率将维持在 10% 以上，市场规模的扩大也将为机器人行业提供更多的发展机遇和空间。

虽然机器人的发展前景广阔，但也应意识到，机器人的发展仍面临着一些挑战。

例如，机器人的感知与决策能力仍需进一步提高，以适应更加复杂和多变的环境。同时，随着机器人技术的普及，如何确保机器人的安全性、隐私保护以及道德伦理等问题也需要得到重视和解决。

总之，尽管目前仍存在技术难题和人才短缺等挑战，但随着技术不断创新以及人才培养和引进的加强，这些问题将得到有效解决，机器人行业将迎来更加美好的发展前景。

6.2　机器人与保险结合的应用场景

机器人的迅速发展正在推动保险行业生态系统的重塑。机器人在助力保险信息整合、业务流程优化、降低运营成本以及保险勘察方面发挥了重要作用（如图6.3所示），为保险业的持续进步和创新提供了有力支撑。未来如何利用机器人提升保险业务处理效率、优化客户体验、降低运营成本以及增强风险管理能力，是数字经济时代保险行业面临的重要机遇和挑战。

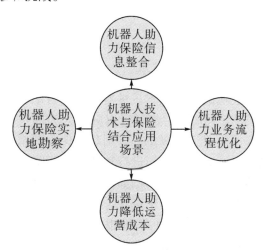

图6.3　机器人技术与保险结合应用场景

资料来源：作者根据资料综合整理得到。

6.2.1　机器人助力保险信息整合

机器人的应用可以替代人类执行大量机械重复的任务，如标准化的手动操作和大规模生产，这有助于减少对人力的过度依赖并推进智能运营模式的发展。目前，保险公司处理理赔工作的员工需要频繁地跳转系统界面来获取客户资料、核实赔偿情况等基础业务。由于人工操作难以确保信息的精确性，这种烦琐的过程使得案件堆积严重、效率低下，容易出现错误。借助机器人技术，可以在事前设定好与理赔相关的标签，包括客户的投保数据、事故详情及支付记录等。机器人利用自然语言处理技术和机器学习算法，从索赔申请中提取关键信息，并与数据库进行对比。一旦满足特定条件，机器人就会自动提取这些关键信息并将它们整理在一个页面上，自动决定是否批准理赔。如此就无须再去寻找规则、匹配信息或验证结果，从而大大提高了响应速度和服务质量。此外，机器人技术还可以进一步筛选和过滤复杂的信息，以提高其针对性和专业性，实现保险业内部信息资源的优化配置，进而改善客户的服务感受，优化客户体验。

6.2.2 机器人助力业务流程优化

机器人可以自动处理大量的保险业务，包括理赔处理、保单更新、保单照片上传、保单取消等。通过利用自然语言处理技术和机器学习技术，机器人能够理解并分析客户的多样化需求，快速准确地完成相关操作，大大提高了业务处理效率。例如，对于一例严重的车体损伤案例来说，传统做法是让工作人员进入系统的后端去核实汽车的具体信息，包括车型信息的比较分析、备品的价格检讨、比价的结果确认等一系列复杂的程序。然而，借助机器人技术，只需单击一下按钮就可以启动所有相关设备的信息搜索功能，而该智能化机器人会依据事故车的损失状况自行完成所有的数据收集和对照检查的工作，并将最终的数据呈现至用户界面。这样处理理赔的速度和效率将大幅提升，而且理赔总体质量的提升也更加显著。此外，在处理保单更新、保单照片上传、保单取消等任务时，机器人可以自动从文本文件中提取保单数据，跨系统处理数据，并自动更新到应用程序的不同页面之中，或者代替人工自动上传照片影像信息，大大节省了时间，优化了保险业务流程。

6.2.3 机器人助力降低运营成本

机器人有助于降低保险业的运营成本。机器人通过自动化处理保险业务，可以减少人工操作，降低人力成本。同时，它们还可以减少人为的错误和疏漏，提高业务处理的准确性，进一步降低保险业运营成本。特别是对保险营销员的培训，都有一定的程序且具有重复性，机器人可对部分工作进行替代，进而降低保险公司人力资源管理成本，逐步提升保险营销员的服务能力。例如，机器人可以帮助保险营销员在销售过程中做好前期的简单解答工作。保险营销员在与客户的交流过程中，可以使用机器人智能助理，线上24小时不间断回答客户关于保险产品的问题，并提供咨询和个性化建议，使用户对其产生信任感。这种即时性和个性化的服务方式，使得客户在购买保险产品时能够获得更好的体验，从而增强了对保险公司的信任度和满意度，助力保险业高质量发展。

6.2.4 机器人助力保险实地查勘

机器人运用于保险实地查勘方面，可以减少人工成本和时间成本，提高查勘效率，同时减少人身风险和查勘误差。在农业查勘方面，可以利用机器人来查勘受灾面积。例如，利用无人机遥感技术实现空中拍摄和地面工作的实时联动，使得保险查勘定损更加快速、精确和高效，大大提高了农业保险查勘定损效率。在房屋查勘方面，机器人可以替代查勘人员进行保险勘察，大大提高了检查效率，也可以确保查勘人员的安全。同时，机器人可以利用复杂技术如热成像传感或者激光测量设备等观测房屋建筑的具体情况，多角度观测建筑物，从而更全面地测量建筑物的受损程度，实现高效精确的查勘。此外，通过机器人采集的信息可以建立一个高效的保险信息数据库，简化风险建模与损失评估流程。

总之，机器人的应用为保险业的高质量发展提供了有力支撑。未来，随着技术的不断进步和应用场景的不断拓展，机器人将在保险业发挥更加重要的作用，推动行业的持续创新和发展。

6.3 "保险+机器人"国内案例

6.3.1 国内经典案例之一

案例题目：

RPA 助力 ZGRS 实现业务自动化

案例内容：

2022 年 1 月，中国银保监会办公厅发布了《关于银行业保险业数字化转型的指导意见》，为银行、保险机构的数字化转型提供了顶层设计，推动金融行业高质量发展。

随着业务范围的拓展和业务量的持续增加，ZGRS 迫切需要采用自动化工具来减轻运营成本压力，同时更好地满足客户的需求。在这一背景下，机器人流程自动化（RPA）的概念开始进入中国大众的视野。作为中国保险行业的领军企业，ZGRS 决定率先尝试采用 RPA 技术来解决公司内部的自动化难题。

以 ZGRS 江苏省分公司为例，该公司的流程自动化工程由 RPA 技术和自动业务数据平台两部分组成，通过利用机器劳动力代替人工重复工作，实现了降低成本、提高效率的目标。

ZGRS 江苏省分公司以"众智、敏捷、迭代"为科技创新行动准则，推动流程自动化技术在保险业务应用过程中不断探索和迭代。从财务领域开始探索，逐步向一线生产部门推广，促进科技与公司经营发展深度融合。

财务领域是 ZGRS 江苏省分公司最早尝试 RPA 技术的领域。公司财务经历省级集中管理后，已经将分散在市县的财务业务集中起来，并按照统一的业务流程进行处理。业务量庞大、规则标准统一且工作内容重复率高等特点为 RPA 技术的应用提供了场景和规模优势。

2020 年 ZGRS 的 IT 部门陆续协助保险理赔部门、财务部门、人事行政部门和 IT 部门完成了 RPA 部署，涉及自动化改造的业务流程包括理赔快速打印、人事考勤管理、财务核销、系统性能监控等。ZGRS 在原有基础上加大创新，进一步对十几项业务流程进行了 RPA 部署，包括保单自动录入、快速理赔、发票打印、智能员工报销、自动对账、人事招聘等。随着 RPA 实践的不断深入，RPA 工具已逐渐成为 ZGRS 每个员工的"机器人助手"。

"自动化优先思维"正在重塑业务流程。RPA 可以解放人力，将人们从重复劳动中解放出来，从而将他们投入更具价值的工作中。由于机器人操作精准、错误率低，许多原本耗费大量精力的重复性工作都可以交给 RPA 来完成。机器人可以 24 小时不间断运行，不受工作时间限制。这不仅可以降低成本，还可以为更加灵活地安排工作时间带来益处。

RPA 不仅是一种简单的自动化工具，更是一种思维方式。企业可以充分利用 RPA

的特性和技术思路来革新业务流程。我们相信，每家公司在真正了解 RPA 之后，都会对其产生很大的需求。

回顾 ZGRS 的 RPA 之旅，RPA 不仅能提高服务效率，还能为客户提供更完善的产品和服务支持。与客户和合作伙伴一起推广"自动化优先思维"，有助于人们重塑未来的工作和生活。

案例评述：

保险 RPA 机器人在保险行业中发挥着重要作用，它可以自动执行烦琐、重复的任务，如理赔处理、保单管理等，可以大大提高工作效率，减少人力资源的浪费，并且能够提高数据处理的准确性和一致性。这样，可以更快速地响应客户需求，提供更高效的服务，从而提升客户满意度。

总之，保险 RPA 机器人的应用可以带来诸多好处，包括提高效率、降低成本、减小错误概率和提升客户体验，有助于推动保险行业的数字化转型和提升竞争力。

案例来源：

中国人寿江苏省分公司. 以数字化转型赋能金融高质量发展［EB/OL］（2022-08-05）［2024-07-01］.https://baijiahao.baidu.com/s? id = 1740313201749788863.

6.3.2 国内经典案例之二

案例题目：

无人机+卫星遥感，塑造智能理赔新生态

案例内容：

"无人机航拍就是不一样，大棚的受损情况一目了然。" 2023 年夏天，依托某财险南通中心支公司工作人员航拍画面，家住通州湾示范区的农户范先生利用保险查勘"无人机"视角看到了风雨后受损的大棚。

2023 年 6 月 10 日，通州湾示范区出现强对流天气，短时风力高达 12 级，并伴有雷暴、冰雹，给广大农户带来巨大财产损失。为了快速、精准地摸排受损情况，ZJ 财险启用无人机以及农险地理位置系统协助定损。

农险部负责人介绍，与普通的拍照无人机不同，保险查勘无人机对图片、图像质量的要求极高，且需要在重点查勘区域设计严密的飞行路线并精准定位，飞行结束后需要快速回收数据。"收回的照片经过专业化软件的算法处理以后，就能够清晰地识别每个田块的灾害发生情况和灾害发生范围。"

RB 财险是省内最早运用无人机的公司，配置有固定翼无人机 1 架，多旋翼无人机 8 架。公司相关负责人表示，使用 Pix4D 专业测绘软件，可快速对地块信息进行整合处理，实现"按图承保、按图理赔"，极大地提高验标、查勘的效率。

记者走访多家保险公司发现，与无人机一样用于理赔查勘的还有卫星遥感技术，该技术适用于大面积监测，精准选取不同长势地点进行精准查勘，减少查勘点数工作量，提高查勘定损速度。

无人机与遥感技术齐上阵，用"城市上空的眼睛"解决了传统作业方式下面积厘定、大面积下的精准查勘难、定损理赔难等难题，也塑造了南通保险业智能理赔新生态。

案例评述：

无人机查勘在很多领域都表现出了巨大的优势，包括但不限于农业、房地产、自然灾害评估等。无人机能够实现高效的勘查和监测，进入一些危险或难以进入的场所。配备各种先进的传感器和摄像设备，无人机可以获取高分辨率的影像和数据，实现实时监测和数据传输。相对于传统的查勘方式，无人机查勘通常具有更低的成本，无人机与保险的结合将更加紧密。

综上所述，无人机查勘具有高效、安全、精准、成本效益高等优点，在多个领域都发挥着重要作用，成为现代科技手段在保险勘查领域的重要应用之一。

案例来源：

南通日报. 科技农险奔向数智化"升维"之路［EB/OL］.（2023－09－19）［2024－07－01］. https：//www. nantong. gov. cn/ntsrmzf/ntxw/content/69ff25e0－be74－4acc－bc76－a98f8c47795a.html.

6.4　课程思政案例

案例题目：

无人机赋能农业保险，助力乡村振兴

案例内容：

2019 年《关于加快农业保险高质量发展的指导意见》的出台，标志着我国农业保险将朝着提质目标迈进。近年来，保险科技在农业保险发展中扮演了"新引擎"的角色，为农业保险行业解决问题和实现突破提供了可能性。随着科技在农业保险领域应用的推广和深入，从哪些层面评估检验保险科技对农业保险发展的驱动效应，如何梳理其有效的驱动路径，对提升科技应用效果和推动农业保险发展具有重要意义。

一人多高的玉米地如何看长势？ 2017 年之前，农业定损专家们搬梯子、爬树的招数都要用上，现在兜里揣个"小助手"就能搞定。今年，扶沟的某承包了 700 多亩（1 亩＝666.67 平方米）地，这是他第一次承包这么多地，但当他真正种植的时候发现，700 多亩连片的玉米地，管理和自然灾害防护都是问题。玉米地土质不一，一场大雨过去，有的地块上的作物安然无恙，有的田地被雨水冲成了沟壑。虫害、干旱、水灾冲毁、刮风倒伏，这 700 多亩玉米地面临的种植难题各有不同。想要查验受灾情况，查验者要在比人还高的玉米地中穿梭。

无人机技术，可以完美解决这一查勘痛点问题。2022 年 9 月，ZY 农险扶沟县支公司派出无人机为某地玉米定损，操作员只需在田间地头就能精准定位受损地块，并完成了查勘、取景工作。某在无人机操作台屏幕端，就可以"俯瞰"自家 700 多亩玉米地全貌，以及不同地块中的玉米生长情况。在查勘完成后，他只需要安心等 10 月份的保险赔付到账就可以了。

那些适用于无人机勘查的场景，往往人工作业耗时费力。扶沟团队也因为无人机技术的应用，工作效率提升超过一倍，原本一个月才能干完的查勘工作现在 15 天内就可以完成，大大缩短了查勘时间，提升了理赔效率。对于农户们来说，就可以更快地拿到这笔理赔费用，安心等到下个季节播种了。科技的创新和应用为农业保险发展注入了新活力，有力地提升了我国政策性农业保险的服务效率。

综上所述，ZY 农业保险公司围绕国家战略和乡村振兴，拓宽服务领域、拓展服务功能，将服务质效提升贯穿农业生产全链条，为农业增收、农民致富提供更加全面的风险保障，为农村的发展提供更加多元的服务功能，助力农业高质量发展和幸福乡村建设。

案例评述：

随着全面建成小康社会和脱贫攻坚目标的如期实现，国家"三农"工作的重点由脱贫攻坚转移到全面实施乡村振兴战略上来。习近平总书记也曾说：要"坚持把解决好'三农'问题作为全党工作的重中之重，举全党全社会之力推动乡村振兴"。保险公司积极响应党的号召，为实现乡村振兴贡献自己的力量。

无人机在农业保险领域的应用具有重要的价值和积极的作用。通过集成高清数码相机、光谱分析仪、热红外传感器等设备，无人机能够准确测算投保地块的种植面积，为保险公司评估农作物风险和保险费率厘定提供依据。同时，无人机还能对农作物进行实时监测，特别是在灾害发生后，能够快速准确地判断农作物的生长情况和损失程度，为保险公司提供第一手资料，加快理赔速度。

总之，无人机助力农业保险能够提升保险服务的效率和质量，为农民和保险公司带来更多益处，为乡村振兴保驾护航。

案例来源：

河南商报. 给田野安上"眼睛"，揭秘金融豫军无人机战队如何为农业保险赋能 [EB/OL].（2022-10-11）［2024-07-01］.https://mq.mbd.baidu.com/r/1gDrZMF57YQ? f=cp&u=f4d380756d1b028a.

Robotics and the Insurance

This Chapter mainly explains the basic ideas and principles of the integration and development of robots and the insurance industry, and selects typical domestic and international cases to share with students, inspire students to explore the application scenarios of robot technology empowering insurance technology and develop ideas for related insurance products.

6.1　Basic theory of robots

6.1.1　Basic Concepts of Robots

In 1920, the famous Czech writer K first mentioned the term "robot" in his play "Rossum's Universal Robots". In the end of the play, the robots took over the earth and destroyed their creators. In 1959, GD and JE collaborated to create the first industrial robot, "Unimate". Subsequently, about 450 "Unimates" were put into use at GM Corporation, marking the birth of the first generation of robots.

The International Federation of Robotics (IFR) defines robots as automatic, programmable, and versatile machines. Wikipedia defines robots as machines, especially those programmable by a computer, capable of performing a series of complex actions.

Generally speaking, robots are automated machines that execute commands automatically. They have similar perception, decision-making, and execution capabilities as humans. They can assist or replace humans in completing repetitive, tedious, and dangerous tasks, thereby improving work efficiency and quality, Serving people's production and life, expanding the scope of human action and capabilities. Robots include industrial robots and service robots. Industrial robots are fully autonomous machines that do not require manual operation. They can be programmed to perform a variety of manual tasks, such as welding, painting, assembly, material handling, or packaging. It is worth mentioning that textile machines, elevators, cranes, conveyors, or coffee machines are not industrial robots because they have unique purposes and cannot be reprogrammed to perform other tasks or require manual operation. Service robots are mainly engaged in a series of service work such as maintenance, repair, transportation, cleaning, security, rescue, medical care, supervision, and companionship.

6.1.2 Typical Features of Robots

With the rapid development of artificial intelligence, big data, and cloud computing, robots have begun to enter the public's field of vision and have gradually attracted the attention of governments, enterprises, and academia. Due to the multiple characteristics of robots, research on robots has shown an accelerating development trend in recent years. As a highly flexible automated machine, robots have the following four characteristics:

6.1.2.1 Autonomy

Robots have the ability to learn, perceive, and execute autonomously. Some advanced robots can learn from experience and optimize their performance through machine learning and deep learning technologies to adapt to changing environments and tasks, and autonomously adjust or change their work methods. For example, robots can perform repetitive, dangerous, or high-precision work on assembly lines without human intervention, thereby improving production efficiency and product quality, while reducing labor costs. In addition, based on perceptual information, robots can make autonomous decisions and plans, choose appropriate behaviors and actions to complete tasks, and make correct decisions in different situations.

6.1.2.2 Flexibility

The structure and functions of robots are customizable and can be designed according to different needs. Robots can be equipped and programmed differently according to the manufacturing requirements of different products, achieving automation in various production processes. Household robots can be installed with different functional modules according to different household needs, such as intelligent voice control, automatic cleaning, thereby improving the convenience of home life.

6.1.2.3 Efficiency

Robots control the movement and behavior of their bodies through actuators (such as motors, servos, etc.) to achieve autonomous action. This enables robots to perform various tasks such as object handling, tool operation, and movement. Robots can continuously perform high-load and high-intensity tasks without operational errors caused by fatigue or human factors.

6.1.2.4 Precision

Robots are usually equipped with various sensors, such as vision, hearing, touch, etc., to obtain environmental information and achieve autonomous perception. These sensors enable robots to perceive and understand their surroundings, including objects, sounds, lights, temperatures, etc. Robots can achieve high precision in task execution, usually more stable and accurate than manual operation. For example, unmanned aerial vehicles can record the specific conditions of target objects through various remote sensing technologies, and achieve precise observation by analyzing and deciphering the characteristics of target objects. Medical robots can accurately locate, cut, and suture in surgery, minimizing surgical risks and improving treatment effects.

These features make robots have wide application value in many fields, such as industrial automation, medical services, home services, rescue operations, etc. They can assist or even replace humans in completing dangerous, heavy, and complex work, improve work efficiency and quality, and expand or extend human activities and abilities.

6.1.3 Current Development Status of Robots

Robot technology originated in the 1950s and was initially applied in the field of industrial production, namely industrial robots. According to the data from the International Federation of Robotics, as of 2022, a total of 553 052 industrial robots have been installed in factories worldwide, with a year-on-year growth of 5%. In terms of regions, 73% of industrial robots are installed in Asia, 15% in Europe, and 10% in the Americas.

According to statistics, China is the largest industrial robot market in the world so far. In 2022, China's annual installation reached 290, 258 units, a year-on-year increase of 5%. In order to serve this vibrant market, domestic and foreign robot suppliers have established production factories in China and continuously improved their production capacity. Japan's industrial robot market size is second only to China, ranking second in the world. Japan is a major robot manufacturing country, accounting for 46% of the global market share of robot production. In 2022, Japan's robot installation reached 50, 413 units, surpassing the level of 49, 908 units in 2019. The United States is the largest regional market, accounting for 71% of the installation volume in the Americas in 2022. The installation volume of robots in the United States increased by 10% to reach 39, 576 units, slightly lower than the peak level of 40, 373 units in 2018.

From the above data, it can be seen that the robotics industry has become one of the important industries in the world today. With the continuous advancement of technology, the application scope and types of robots are becoming more and more extensive. Currently, robots have been applied in various fields such as industrial production, healthcare, agriculture, and services.

Generally speaking, the robotics industry chain includes core technology support, production and sales, and terminal applications at multiple levels. The production process of robots includes a series of product models and supporting service systems used for actual production. The terminal market level of robots refers to the specific application examples in various commercial scenarios, such as factory automation processes and management scheme design and implementation. Currently, China has successfully built a comprehensive and mature robotics industry ecosystem, which can effectively support the development of robots in industrial production, healthcare, agriculture, and services. Especially in the production and terminal market levels, China's robotics industry chain is relatively complete. Figure 6.1 shows the industrial robot installations in the top 15 countries or regions in 2022.

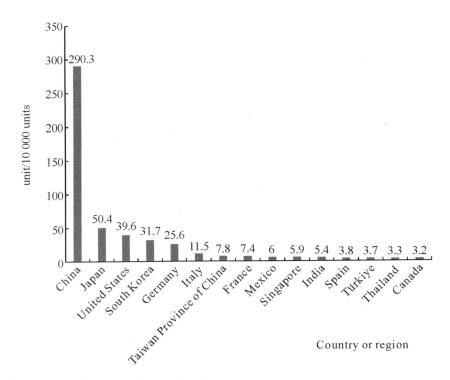

Figure 6. 1　**Industrial robot installations in the top** 15 **countries or regions in** 2022

Source：https://www.istis.sh.cn/cms/news/article/75/26664.

6. 1. 4　Prospects of Robot Development

The prospects of robot technology development are very broad, and with the continuous advancement of science and technology and the increasing demand, robots will play an increasingly important role in various fields.

6. 1. 4. 1　Continuous Innovation of Core Technology

The development of the robotics industry is driven by technological progress. With the continuous advancement of technologies such as big data, artificial intelligence, machine learning, and the Internet of Things, the intelligence level of robots will continue to improve, and their application areas will also become more extensive. For example, the development of generative artificial intelligence provides new solutions for the development of robots, allowing robots to create new knowledge through training. This development will make robots more intelligent and better adapted to various complex environments and tasks. At the same time, the industry is developing generative artificial intelligence-driven interfaces that allow users to program robots more intuitively through natural language, reducing the barriers to use and enabling more people to utilize robot technology. Therefore, continuous technological innovation will drive the continuous development of the robotics industry.

6. 1. 4. 2　Deepening Application Areas

Robots have wide applications in the manufacturing industry, and in the future, with the continuous expansion of robots' applications in fields such as healthcare, agriculture, and logistics, the rapid growth of the robotics industry will be further promoted. Especially in the healthcare field, the use of robots helps improve the diagnostic and treatment capabilities of doctors in treating diseases. In addition, human-robot collaboration is also an important trend in robot development. With the rapid development of sensors, visual technology, and intelligent grippers, robots can respond to environmental changes in real time and collaborate with humans. In the manufacturing, healthcare, and service industries, human-robot collaboration will become more common, and this collaboration is expected to improve production and service efficiency, reduce costs, and create a safer working environment.

6. 1. 4. 3 Continuous Market Growth

With the popularization of robot applications, continuous technological advancements, and the growth of education, healthcare, and security demands, the market size of the robotics industry will continue to expand. According to relevant statistics, the annual compound growth rate of the global robot market in the coming years will remain above 10%, and the expansion of the market size will provide more development opportunities and space for the robotics industry.

Although the prospects of robot development are broad, it should also be noted that the development of robots still faces some challenges. For example, the perception and decision-making capabilities of robots still need to be further improved to adapt to more complex and changing environments. At the same time, with the popularization of robot technology, issues such as ensuring the safety, privacy protection, and ethical considerations of robots also need to be taken seriously and addressed. Overall, although there are still technical challenges and talent shortages at present, these problems will be effectively resolved with continuous technological innovation and the strengthening of talent cultivation and introduction. The future robotics industry will have a brighter development prospect.

6. 2 Application Scenarios of Robot-Insurance Integration

The rapid development of robots is reshaping the ecosystem of the insurance industry. Robots play an important role in assisting insurance information integration, optimizing business processes (See Figure 6. 2), reducing operating costs, and insurance surveying, providing strong support for the continuous progress and innovation of the insurance industry. How to utilize robots to improve the efficiency of insurance business processing, optimize customer experience, reduce operating costs, and enhance risk management capabilities is an important opportunity and challenge facing the insurance industry in the digital economy era.

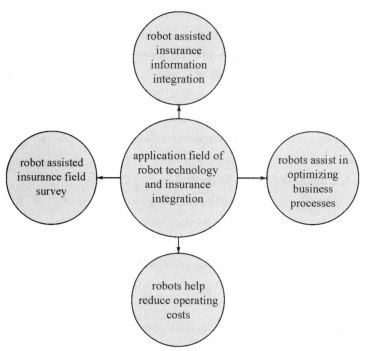

Figure 6. 2 **Application scenarios of robot technology combined with insurance**

Source: Compiled by the author based on comprehensive information.

6. 2. 1　Robot Assisted Insurance Information Integration

The application of robots can replace humans in performing a large number of mechanical repetitive tasks, such as standardized manual operations and mass production. This helps reduce excessive reliance on manpower and promotes the development of intelligent operation models. Currently, employees in insurance companies who handle claims work need to frequently switch system interfaces to obtain customer information and verify compensation situations, among other basic tasks. This cumbersome process leads to severe case backlog, low efficiency, and is prone to errors because it is difficult to ensure the accuracy of information through manual operations. With the help of robot technology, it is possible to preset labels related to claims, including customer insurance data, accident details, and payment records. Using natural language processing technology and machine learning algorithms, key information can be extracted from claim applications and compared with databases. Once specific conditions are met, the robot will automatically extract these key information and organize them on a page, automatically deciding whether to approve the claim. This eliminates the need to search for rules, match information, or verify results, greatly improving response speed and service quality. In addition, robot technology can further filter and refine complex information to improve its pertinence and professionalism, optimize the allocation of internal information resources in the insurance industry, and improve customer service experience.

6. 2. 2 Robots Assist Business Process Optimization ├──────────

Robots can automate a large amount of insurance business, including claim processing, policy updates, policy photo uploads, policy cancellations, and more. By leveraging natural language processing and machine learning technologies, robots can understand and analyze diverse customer needs, quickly and accurately complete relevant operations, greatly improving business processing efficiency. For example, in a severe case of vehicle body damage, the traditional approach involves staff entering the backend system to verify specific vehicle information, including complex procedures such as comparing and analyzing vehicle model information, reviewing spare part prices, confirming price comparisons, and more. However, with the help of robotics technology, the information search function of all relevant devices can be activated with just a click of a button, and the intelligent robot will independently complete all data search and comparison checks based on the loss situation of the accident vehicle, and present the final data to the user interface and display it. This will significantly improve the speed and efficiency of claims processing, and the overall quality level of claims will be more significantly improved. Additionally, when handling tasks like policy updates, policy photo uploads, policy cancellations, robots can automatically extract policy data from text files, process data across systems, automatically update different pages in the application, or replace manual photo image uploads, saving time and optimizing insurance business processes.

6. 2. 3 Robots Help Reduce Operating Costs ├──────────

Robots contribute to reducing operating costs in the insurance industry. By automating insurance business processes, robots can reduce manual operations and lower labor costs. They can also reduce human errors and omission, improve business processing accuracy, further lowering insurance industry operating costs. Particularly in terms of increasing and training insurance sales agents, which involve certain procedural and repetitive tasks, robots can substitute for some work, thereby reducing insurance companies' human resource management costs and gradually enhancing the service capabilities of insurance sales agents. For example, robots can assist insurance sales agents in providing preliminary simple answers during the sales process. During the communication process with customers, insurance marketers can use robot intelligent assistants online to answer customers' questions about insurance products 24 hours a day, provide consultation and personalized suggestions, and build a sense of trust among users. This real-time and personalized service approach allows customers to have a better experience when purchasing insurance products, enhancing trust and satisfaction with the insurance company, supporting high-quality development in the insurance industry.

6. 2. 4 Robots Facilitate Insurance Field Surveys ├──────────

Utilizing robots for insurance field surveys can reduce labor and time costs, improve survey efficiency, and decrease personal risks and survey errors. In agricultural surveys, robots can be used to survey disaster-affected areas. For instance, using drone remote sensing technology for real-time coordination between aerial photography and ground work streamlines insurance survey and loss assessment, significantly enhancing agricultural insurance survey efficiency. In house surveys, robots can replace surveyors to conduct insurance inspections, greatly improving inspection efficiency and ensuring surveyors' safety. Additionally, robots can utilize complex technologies such as thermal imaging sensors or laser measurement devices to observe specific conditions of house structures, observe buildings from multiple angles, thereby more comprehensively measuring the extent of building damage, achieving efficient and accurate survey efficiency. Furthermore, information collected by robots can build an efficient insurance information database, simplifying risk modeling and loss assessment processes.

In short, the application of robots provides strong support for the high-quality development of the insurance industry. In the future, with continuous technological advancements and expanding application scenarios, robots will play a more significant role in the insurance industry, driving continuous innovation and development in the industry.

6.3   Foreign Cases of "Insurance + Robot"

6.3.1   The First Case

Case Tile:

Insurance Industry Use of Drone, Aerial Imagery Soared After 2018 Southeast Disasters

Case Content:

The importance of drones and aerial imagery rose to a new level in the wake of 2018 natural catastrophes as insurers made them an integral part of their disaster recovery procedures, particularly following the hurricanes in the Southeast.

From the images of Hurricane Florence's floods across North and South Carolina to Hurricane Michael's devastation in the Florida Panhandle, insurers were able to see the impact immediately and get straight to work handling claims for their customers, and gather data from the events from aerial images.

"Usually what we find is we have carriers that are very anxious to get airplane imagery right after a catastrophe. They want that data as fast as possible", said S. "This was the first year that we started getting requests from insurance carriers to have drone inspections executed shortly thereafter [the events] as well. Usually they're more hesitant and they're of the opinion, "Okay, we can wait this out, we'll send drones if we need them."

The company, formed five years ago as a spin-off of claims estimating software company X, currently works with four of the top 10 insurers in the country while nine of the top 10 work with its sister company X, according to S. He said in the five years since G started, the use of aerial imagery and drone technology by insurers has been growing fast, particularly for claims.

G focuses on geospatial operations, specifically airplanes, satellites, drones and gathering data. It currently has 12 operational hubs with airplanes and other remote sensing devices used to gather data. Shelton said the company has its own fleet of airplanes, as well as drones and drone technology and tools that are used to support insurance carriers that also deploy their own drones.

S said after insurers had an opportunity to vet drone services and use drones in their workflows for storms like Harvey and Maria in 2017, they were anxious to deploy them after this year's catastrophes to view overall damage to their books as well as start claims inspections for policyholders. S said some carriers were even impatient about getting drone teams out to inspect damage right away.

S said because of the scale of the Hurricane Florence, which was primarily a flood event, G relied more on aircrafts to gather data and received many more requests from insurers for that data than for drones.

"It's because of the scale of the disaster and that's where airplanes shine", he said. "You just don't have the ability to gather as much data with drones as you do in airplanes."

Still, the use of drones after Hurricane Florence was "incredibly prevalent", according to ID, vice president and general manager of drone technology provider PH's pilot network of 15,000 commercially licensed drone pilots called Droners. io.

PH announced a partnership with EV, which provides high-resolution aerial imagery, property data analytics and structural measurements to the insurance industry, shortly before Hurricane Florence made landfall on Sept. 14. Through the partnership, EV collects insurance claims imagery using drones piloted by PH's network and the drone operators can use EV's claims technology for remote claims inspections.

Case Comments:

The insurance industry is witnessing a great transition with the integration of drone technology. Drones are revolutionizing how insurers inform underwriting decisions, streamline claims adjustments, and gain valuable insights to evaluate risk. Insurance professionals can enhance their efficiency, accuracy, and customer satisfaction by harnessing the power of drones for pre-loss inspections, property measurements, roof damage inspections, wide area damage assessments, fraud monitoring, risk assessments, insurance inspections, and boiler inspections. With drones as their aerial allies, insurers can confidently navigate the evolving landscape of risk assessment, claims management, and fraud detection, ultimately propelling the industry to new heights of success.

Case Source:

AMY O'CONNOR. Insurance Industry use of drone, aerial imagery soared after 2018 southeast disasters[EB/OL].(2024-01-24) [2024-07-01].https://www.insurancejournal.com/news/southeast/2019/01/24/515622.htm.

6.3.2 The Second Case

Case Tile:

Global Insurance Leader H Achieves Sustainable Growth With Communications Automatio.

Case Content:

As a major specialist insurance provider, H aims to deliver the best protection available through high-quality products, excellent service, and claims support. H also strives to grow its international insurance business, taking on more clients and offering more new product, however, with growth comes greater complexity, higher demand and, above all, more communications to process.

To achieve the company's strategic goals and fulfill its service promise to customers, the European change and IT teams at H turned to robot automation.

Competitive service depends on swift communication. Half of customers are less likely to do business with a company that takes longer than expected to respond. Yet service teams at H were feeling the pressure as the company's growth drove more demand and more client emails to their mailboxes.

So, an automated solution that could rapidly reduce this repetitive workload by 28%, while reducing average response time, held the promise of improving both customer and employee satisfaction—critical for H's long-term success.

The change team was eager to find a way to streamline, or even automate, the email triage process at H. However, in a business where swift response and exceptional service are critical, they needed greater accuracy and sophistication than what keyword matching could provide. Fortunately, H Europe found a solution in U Communications Mining, and Guilherme played a key role in its design and implementation.

The European change team was particularly impressed with how easy it was to use Communications Mining. "The tool got very positive feedback. It's very easy to use. It almost makes model training fun. It's very user friendly and easy to use, with a lot of features that are quite convenient. I felt like, whenever we had a problem or question on how to train something, we quickly found an easy way to handle it within the tool."

Following a successful pilot of U Communications Mining, Guilherme and the IT team hit the ground running with their deployment. After an initial use case with the insurance administration team, they soon applied Communications Mining for intelligent triage in the company's high-stakes claims function. As soon as an email landed in an agent's mailbox, Communications Mining got to work extracting the relevant information, helping H rapidly identify what the message was about and allocate it to the right person or team.

"We started seeing value very quickly", Guilherme said. "In claims, we went from talking about the idea to achieving a 28% automation rate in just three to four months."

The claims team was able to automate over a quarter of its entire message volume, with the emails accurately triaged to the correct team for processing without any human intervention. In the past two months, H managed to save nearly 480 working hours using Communications Mining.

One of the key benefits of triage automation for H was the ability for their service team to focus more on valuable tasks. This included devoting more time to responding to customer inquiries.

Case Comments:

The increasingly widespread and in-depth application of robots is creating more value for insurance companies, which can help them more efficiently complete claim information classification. Undoubtedly, in the coming years, robots will continue to deepen its integration with the industry, bringing new changes to the industry. While seeing opportunities, insurance companies also need to be aware of the challenges that still exist in terms of personnel, data, regulation, and actively seek solutions.

Case Source:

By the website of Uipath.

7

生物科技与保险业

本章主要阐释生物科技与保险业相互结合的基本思路与原理，并精选国内外相关案例与学生分享，启发学生借助生物科技开发保险科技应用场景和相关保险产品的思路。

7.1 生物科技基本理论

7.1.1 生物科技基本概念

随着全球科技革命和产业变革，生物技术领域迅猛发展。生物科技是应用生物学、化学和工程学的基本原理，利用生物体（包括微生物，动物细胞和植物细胞）或其组成部分（细胞器和酶）来生产有用物质、为人类提供服务的科学，是一门新兴的、综合性学科。

生物科技领域涵盖基因工程、细胞工程、酶工程（也称作蛋白质工程）和发酵工程等。生物科技有力推动了人类社会发展。基因测序带动了各种相关技术发展并推进了临床应用；精准医学改变了传统的疾病诊疗模式、推动了医药产业变革；干细胞技术与基因治疗技术为治疗疾病开启了新思路；基因编辑技术、合成生物技术、基因驱动技术以及功能获得性研究等推动了生命科学的发展。如图7.1所示。

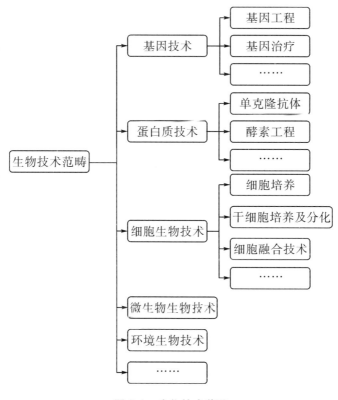

图 7.1　生物技术范畴

7.1.2　生物技术的发展历程

现代生物技术的发展历程如图 7.2 所示。生物技术的发展大致经历了以下几个阶段：

7.1.2.1　传统生物技术

古代人类利用发酵技术生产酒、酱油等食品，也使用传统的草药治疗疾病，这可以看作是古代生物技术的起源。

7.1.2.2　现代生物技术的萌芽

随着技术的逐渐发展，人们开始研究细菌、酵母等微生物，发现了遗传学基础知识，为现代生物技术的发展奠定了基础。

7.1.2.3　基因工程技术的兴起

基因工程技术的发展推动了生物技术的快速发展，人们可以通过改变生物体的基因来实现特定的目的，如生产药物、改良作物等。

7.1.2.4　生物信息学的发展

随着计算机技术和生物学的结合，生物信息学逐渐兴起，为生物技术的研究提供了强大的工具和方法。

7.1.2.5　合成生物学的崛起

随着合成生物学成为生物科技的新兴领域，设计和构建新型生物系统，为生物制造、医疗等领域带来了新的可能性。

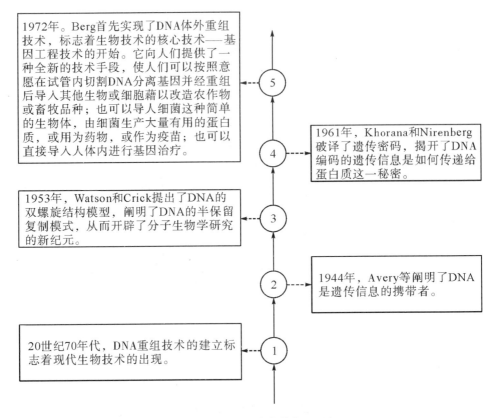

图 7.2　现代生物技术的发展历程

7.1.3　生物科技的特点

从研究逐步走向应用，现代生物技术的发展逐步呈现出以下四个特点：

7.1.3.1　多学科的交叉性

生物技术涉及生物工程、化学、物理学、工程学等多个学科，不仅需要掌握微生物学、动物学，还要掌握有生化、分子生物学等方面的知识，综合运用各种知识和技术。

7.1.3.2　应用的广泛性

生物技术更加注重实际应用，其决定了研究的方向。生物技术在医药、康养、农林业、养殖业、食品、物种保护、环境保护、金融、保险、案件侦破等领域有着广泛的应用，对人类社会的生产和生活以及地球的生态保护有着重要影响。

7.1.3.3　科技的先进性

传统生物技术往往以酶工程和发酵工程为代表；现在的生物技术则更加重视基因工程和细胞工程，需要非常先进的科技手段作为支撑。

7.1.3.4　伦理道德要求高

现代生物科技涉及基因干预和克隆技术等，有可能触及人类伦理道德等敏感问题，对从业者的伦理道德水平要求极高。

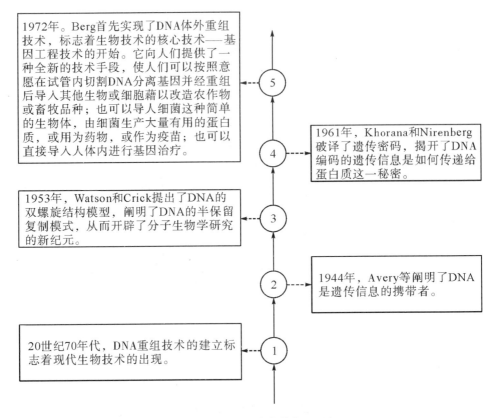

1972年。Berg首先实现了DNA体外重组技术，标志着生物技术的核心技术——基因工程技术的开始。它向人们提供了一种全新的技术手段，使人们可以按照意愿在试管内切割DNA分离基因并经重组后导入其他生物或细胞藉以改造农作物或畜牧品种；也可以导人细菌这种简单的生物体，由细菌生产大量有用的蛋白质，或用为药物，或作为疫苗；也可以直接导入人体内进行基因治疗。

5

1961年，Khorana和Nirenberg破译了遗传密码，揭开了DNA编码的遗传信息是如何传递给蛋白质这一秘密。

4

1953年，Watson和Crick提出了DNA的双螺旋结构模型，阐明了DNA的半保留复制模式，从而开辟了分子生物学研究的新纪元。

3

2

1944年，Avery等阐明了DNA是遗传信息的携带者。

20世纪70年代，DNA重组技术的建立标志着现代生物技术的出现。

1

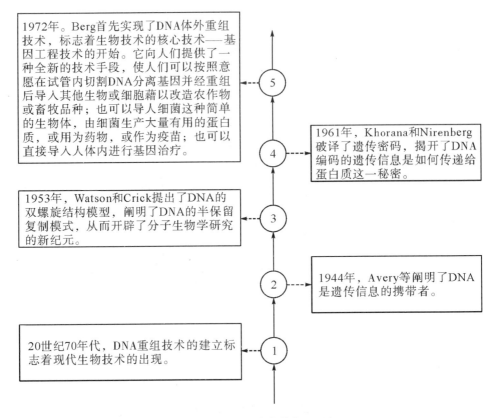

7.1.4 生物科技的现状与前景

生物科技的发展为很多与人们生产生活切实相关的问题找到了解决的方法。目前生物科技的专业研究综合了基因工程、分子生物学、生物化学、遗传学、细胞生物学、胚胎学、免疫学、有机化学、无机化学、物理化学、物理学、信息学及计算机科学等多学科技术，在医疗领域、农林养殖、军事科技、工业应用、环境保护等领域应用广泛。

7.1.4.1 医疗领域

生物科技以加速新药开发、助力精准医疗的优势在医疗领域的研究受到了极大关注。干细胞技术可应用于再生医学领域，不仅可以治疗白血病、免疫系统疾病等过去难以医治的疾病，还可以延展出类器官技术，有望实现再生医学的飞跃。基因治疗作为新疾病治疗的新手段，给一些难治疾病的根治带来了光明。利用微阵列核酸芯片或蛋白质芯片，可寻找致病基因。利用抗体技术，可将毒素送入具有特殊标记的癌细胞，用于精准治疗癌症。利用基因克隆技术，可对某些疑难病症进行基因治疗等。基因治疗还能利用分子生物学方法将目的基因导入患者体内，使之表达目的基因产物，从而使疾病得到治疗。

7.1.4.2 农林养殖

人口数量快速膨胀，粮食问题正是生物科技应用的切入点。对基因克隆农作物进行开发，利用克隆技术，不仅研究出了抗虫害基因和抗冻基因等有用基因，还培育出了含有维生素 A 的稻米等农作物，大大提高了农作物的品质；利用组织培养技术，提高了观赏性花卉的质量；利用遗传工程技术，使乳牛产出凝血因子可用于医疗方面。制作的生物肥料主要是利用微生物技术，不仅给作物提供养料、改善品质、增强抗寒抗虫害能力，还改善了土壤通透性、保水性、酸碱度等理性化特性，可为农作物根系创造良好生长环境，保证作物的增产。研制生物农药，利用微生物、抗生素和基因工程等产生有杀灭虫病效果的毒素物质，生产出广谱毒力强的微生物菌株制作而成的农药，虽不像化学农药般见效快，但效果持久，与化学农药相比，对环境、人体和作物的危害性更小。

7.1.4.3 工业应用

在工业上利用工业菌种的特殊代谢路径来替代一些化学反应，除专一性提高外，在常温常压下还更节约能源。由于专一性高，产生的废弃物量低，因此被称为绿色工业。

7.1.4.4 环境保护

当环境受到破坏，可以利用生物科技的处理方式，让环境免于第二次受害。生物具有高度专一性，能针对特殊的污染源进行处理。例如，运输原油的邮轮，因事故，将重油污染海域，可以利用分解重油的特殊微生物菌株，对于重油进行分解，代谢成环境可以接受的短链脂肪酸等，排解污染。此外，土壤遭受重金属污染，亦可利用特定植物吸收污染源。

7.2　生物科技与保险结合的应用场景

目前，生物科技主要可以与人身保险、种植保险、养殖保险相结合。

7.2.1　生物科技与人身保险相结合

生物科技中的基金检测技术和基因治疗技术正逐步应用于保险行业。

基因检测是指通过分析个体的基因组信息，来评估其患病风险或者预测其健康状况的科学技术。基因检测技术的运作机理是从个体的生物样本（唾液、血液或口腔黏膜细胞）中提取遗传物质，对样本主体的 DNA 进行测序和分析，甄别突变或异常基因，对个体患疾病的可能性做出预测性判断。目前，科学家们已经发现 6 500 余种疾病与基因之间存在的密切联系，多种疾病已能够利用基因检测技术进行预测。保险公司可以利用基因检测技术来为客户提供更加个性化的保险产品和定价策略。例如，保险公司可以根据客户的基因检测结果来评估其患某种疾病的风险，从而为其提供相应的保险保障和个性化的保险定价。这可以更好地满足客户的需求，也可以降低保险公司的承保风险。

基因治疗是指利用生物科技手段来修复或改变个体的基因，以治疗或预防疾病。保险公司可以与基因治疗机构合作，一方面为客户提供基因治疗相关的保险产品。例如，为鼓励更多人参与基因治疗，保险公司可以为客户提供给付基因治疗费用的保险产品，以确保客户在接受基因治疗时能够在经济上得到额外的支持。另一方面，可深入研究和探索基因治疗中存在的潜在风险，开发出应对基因检测风险、基因边际风险的保险产品，推动保险产品的创新。

人身保险是以人的身体和生命作为保险标的、以人的生（生育）、老（衰老）、病（疾病）、亡（死亡）等为保险事故的一种保险。若按照保险范围划分，人身保险可分为人寿保险、意外伤害保险和健康保险。

基因信息对于不同类型的人身保险，其应用价值存在不同：

（1）对于人寿保险，被保险人向保险人转嫁的是被保险人的生存或死亡风险，被保险人的寿命长短直接关系保险人的保费收入与保险金给付。因此，能否充分掌握信息，以识别可能使被保险人寿命显著缩短的潜在风险因子，将成为保险人能否实现经济利益的关键。基因检测技术的产生和发展成为保险人评估被保险人生存寿命的有力工具，对提升人寿保险中风险定级与保险费率厘定的准确性具有重要意义。

（2）对于意外伤害保险，满足出险条件的意外伤害应是外来的、突发的、非本意的、非疾病的使身体受到伤害的客观事件。基因信息仅具有疾病预测功能，而对外在事故发生概率的预测上无能为力。因此，就目前的研究成果，基因信息在意外伤害保险领域暂无可利用空间。

（3）对健康保险产品进行细化的分类考察，可以发现：在团体健康保险和个人短期健康保险中，基因技术的应用价值较为有限；在个人长期健康保险中，应用价值较高。

在团体健康保险中，团体中的每个成员共同分担整个群体的风险，保险人以团体为风险计量单位，对团体规模、新成员流入量、所属行业、团体稳定性等整体因素进行考量评价，而不要求对成员个体信息进行逐一审查。所以，基因信息作为一种个人信息，对团体健康保险的应用价值有限。

在个人健康保险中，除少数承保特定危险的健康保险（重大疾病保险、长期护理保险等）以外，大多数健康保险（尤其是医疗保险）的保险期限一般较短，被保险人短期健康变化是保险人的关注点。此时，基因信息对于短期疾病并不具备特别优势。因此，在个人短期健康险当中，保险人对基因信息使用的经济动因较弱。相反地，对于个人长期健康保险，保险人更倾向于收集、利用被保险人的基因信息，以提高其预测风险的精准性，有效降低保险人风险评级的难度。

综上所述，由于人身保险险种之间的差异，以及其相对应的风险评估对象与风险关注侧重点的不同，基因信息的应用对于不同人身保险具有不同的应用价值，如图 7.3 所示。

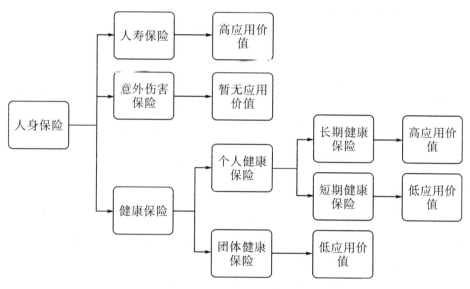

图 7.3 基因检测对人身保险的应用价值

7.2.2 生物科技与种植保险相结合

随着生物科技的发展，生物技术已经开始在种植保险中得到应用，促进了农业保险高质量发展。生物科技在种植保险中的应用主要体现在以下八个方面：

7.2.2.1 生物育种技术

通过生物育种技术，可以培育出具有抗病虫害、抗旱、抗盐碱等特性的优良品种，提高作物的产量和质量，减少因自然灾害和病虫害造成的损失，从而降低农业保险的赔付风险。

7.2.2.2 生物识别技术

利用生物识别技术，可以对作物进行精准识别，确保保险标的的真实性和准确性。例如，通过识别作物的生物特征信息，可以防止虚假承保和理赔，提高保险业务的透明度和效率。

7.2.2.3　生物信息学

生物信息学可以帮助分析作物基因组数据，预测作物的生长状况和产量，为农业保险提供更精确的风险评估和定价依据。

7.2.2.4　生物监测技术

通过生物监测技术，可以实时监控作物的生长环境和健康状况，及时发现并预警可能的风险，为保险理赔提供及时、准确的信息。

7.2.2.5　生物肥料和生物农药

利用生物肥料和生物农药，可以减少化学肥料和农药的使用，提高作物的抗病虫能力，减少环境污染，同时也有助于降低农业保险的赔付成本。

7.2.2.6　基因编辑技术

基因编辑技术可以精确修改作物基因，培育出具有特定优良性状的新品种，提高作物的适应性和稳定性，减少保险赔付。

7.2.2.7　微生物应用

利用微生物技术，如接种有益微生物以改善土壤结构和提高营养，增强作物的抗病能力，从而降低因病害导致的保险赔付。

7.2.2.8　生物传感器

生物传感器可以用于监测作物生长环境中的各种生物活性物质，如植物激素、病原体等，为农业保险提供风险预警。

通过这些生物科技的应用，种植保险可以更有效地进行风险管理和控制，提高保险服务的质量和效率，同时也有助于推动农业的可持续发展。

7.2.3　生物科技与养殖保险相结合

随着生物科技的发展，生物技术已经开始在种植、养殖中得到应用，促进农业保险的高质量发展。生物科技在养殖保险中的应用主要体现在以下七个方面：

7.2.3.1　生物识别技术

利用生物识别技术，如面部识别、耳标、DNA 鉴定等，可以对牲畜进行精准识别，确保承保和理赔的准确性。这些技术可以创建牲畜的唯一身份标识，防止重复投保和理赔。

7.2.3.2　生物传感器

生物传感器可以用于监测养殖场环境中的微生物、毒素、污染物等，为养殖保险的风险评估和管理提供科学依据。

7.2.3.3　基因技术

基因技术可以帮助改良牲畜品种，提高其抗病性和生产效率，降低养殖风险，从而减少养殖保险的赔付概率。

7.2.3.4　生物信息学

通过分析牲畜的基因组数据，可以预测疾病发生的概率，为养殖保险的产品设计和定价提供依据。

7.2.3.5　微生物应用

利用有益微生物改善饲料质量和养殖环境，提高牲畜的免疫力和健康水平，减少疾病发生，降低养殖保险的赔付风险。

7.2.3.6 生物标记物

通过检测牲畜体内的生物标记物，可以评估其健康状况和生产性能，为养殖保险的承保和理赔提供参考。

7.2.3.7 生物统计模型

利用生物统计模型分析牲畜的生长发育、疾病发生等数据，可以更准确地评估养殖风险，为养殖保险的定价和风险管理提供科学依据。

通过这些生物技术的应用，养殖保险可以更有效地进行风险识别、评估和管理，提高保险服务的质量和效率，同时也有助于推动养殖业的可持续发展。

7.3 "保险+生物科技"国内案例

7.3.1 国内经典案例之一

案例题目：

从"买保险送基因"到"基因+保险"

案例内容：

近年来，随着基因测序技术的迅速发展和成本的不断降低，其临床能力和商业价值正在被不断挖掘；与此同时，商业健康险正在寻求突破口，试图改变"先天不足"的现状，通过提供健康管理服务增强后天竞争力。但何不将二者结合起来，实现合作共赢？

北京 LPK 生物科技有限公司（以下简称"LPK"）是一家专注于基因检测和生物信息分析的公司。他们提供易感基因检测、安全用药指导、靶向药物检测等服务，致力于通过基因大数据服务帮助消费者进行疾病预防、安全用药和个性化健康管理。LPK 在"基因+保险"领域进行了一些创新性的探索和合作。

LPK 推出的"LPK ⓒ G+"系列产品，是一个结合基因检测和保险服务的健康管理服务闭环。用户不仅可以享受全基因扫描检测服务，还能根据检测结果提供遗传咨询、健康管理服务，以及在确诊重大疾病时提供专家预约和保险偿付服务。LPK 的健康管理系统依托各大医院的专家资源，为用户提供基因风险筛查、遗传咨询、靶向药物检测、大病诊疗指导等一站式服务。目前，LPK 已经与多家保险机构建立合作关系，如 TP 人寿、YD 人寿、AB 保险、ZGRM 保险等，通过提供基因检测服务来增强保险服务能力，提高客户满意度。

LPK 这种从"买保险送基因"的模式向"基因+保险"的战略转型，不仅深挖基因检测技术和保险公司合作潜力，还兼顾了保险机构和用户双方的利益。因为对于大病重病而言，早预防、早发现、早诊断、早治疗，既是增加患者生存率和幸福感的重要路径，也是医疗成本控制的有效方法。无论对于保险用户，还是对于保险公司，都十分重要。

不仅如此，在政策支持与行业自律方面，LPK 的商业思路符合政策大势，受益于国家对基因检测等新型医疗技术的大力支持。同时，LPK 也在积极探索行业自律，以应对基因检测与商业保险结合中存在的伦理和数据安全问题。

案例评述：

LPK 的这些实践展示了如何将基因检测技术与保险服务相结合，为用户提供更全面的健康风险管理方案，同时也为保险业带来了新的服务模式和增长点。LPK 发现并抓住了市场机会，通过与保险机构的合作，不仅为客户提供了更全面的健康管理服务，也为保险机构提供了增值服务，增强了客户黏性。

案例来源：

王方怡. 从"买保险送基因"到"基因+保险"利普康如何深挖基因服务［EB/OL］.（2017－12－11）［2024－07－01］. https://www.cn-healthcare.com/article/20171211/content-498132.html.

7.3.2 国内经典案例之二

案例题目：

生物识别技术助力养殖保险

案例内容：

在养殖保险中，牛险保单均保费、保额高，养殖周期长，存在虚假理赔或重复理赔等痛点。传统检验标的做法是通过"打耳标+标的拍照"方式，对投保标的进行唯一性判断。但是，打耳标成本较高、操作不便。人员在作业过程中操作危险性较高，同时耳标易掉落、被替换。

于是，PA 产险新疆分公司推出了牛脸识别项目。牛脸识别是一种基于牛的脸部特征信息进行身份识别的生物识别技术，类似于人脸识别。这项技术通采集到的牛的脸部特征，如牛漩、眼纹、毛发纹理的分布和位置等信息录入系统，使养殖户的每头牛都有专属"身份证"，确保保险标的真实、精准、唯一。这个项目自上线以来，已经在全国进行推广应用，牛脸抓拍准确率96%，牛脸识别准确率97%。2023 年12 月，在由《ZGYH 保险报》主办的第三届保险业数字化转型大会暨第十六届保险信息技术大会上，PA 产险"牛脸识别项目"成功入选"2023 中国保险业自主科技创新优秀案例"。

其实，早在2018 年，PA 产险就联合 PA 科技在内蒙古对其承保的奶牛、母猪进行了现场影像身份信息收集，实现了牲畜识别等 AI 创新科技试点应用。将多模态生物识别系统、牲畜识别、声纹识别、图像识别技术等融入农牧业保险应用，可实现农户投保人自动识别、农场信息化管理、牲畜养殖管理等，用科技服务农牧业发展。其中，多模态生物识别将 3D 人脸识别、声纹识别和唇语识别三大高精度识别引擎融为一体，通过采集三种不同的生物特征，通过分析、判断三种识别方式的特征值，结合数据融合技术，使得认证和识别过程更加精准、安全；牲畜识别主要基于卷积神经网络，通过学习获取牲畜唯一性标签来实现，PA 科技在国际猪脸识别、狗脸识别大赛上，均位居第一，对猪、牛、狗种类识别精准度高达98%以上。利用牲畜识别技术可以快速确定牲畜身份，将牲畜的信息从系统中调出，实现一键报案，智能核损。

目前，多家财险公司也正在积极推动生物识别技术在畜牧业保险领域的落地，探索更多保险服务"三农"的新举措、新模式，为我国畜牧业高质量发展保驾护航。

案例评述：

牛脸识别技术作为生物技术中的生物识别技术，不仅可以提高畜牧业的管理效率和了解牲畜的健康状况，还可以有效防范保险领域的欺诈行为。在承保牛只时，可以通过这种技术确保所承保的牛只的真实性、准确性和唯一性；在理赔环节，可以利用这种技术快速准确地识别死亡牛只的身份，对比死亡牛只脸部影像与特征数据库影像，精准识别，有效防范重复理赔、虚假理赔等情况的发生。这不仅可以大大提高理赔的准确度，还可以减少保险公司的风险和损失。

案例来源：

冉虎. 平安产险新疆分公司"牛脸识别"为牛精准上保险［EB/OL］.（2022-08-05）［2024-07-01］.http://xj.news.cn/zt/2024-01/22/c_1130064923.htm.

7.4　课程思政案例

案例题目：

"保险+基因"，为巩固脱贫攻坚成果提供有力保障

案例内容：

乳腺癌在全球的发病率约 11.7%，死亡率约 6.9%。在我国女性中，乳腺癌发病率位居第一。研究表明，乳腺癌发病率的升高与人们生活水平的提高，饮食、营养结构改变，生活压力增大以及环境恶化等关系密不可分。目前，乳腺癌治疗已进入靶向精准时代，基因检测已成为乳腺癌靶向治疗的必要手段。基因检测应用主要指导乳腺癌患者靶向、免疫用药以及遗传筛查两个方面，多基因检测被认为具有辅助临床决策的重要作用。

2015 年 6 月，ZA 保险联合 HD 基因推出国内首款互联网基因检测保险计划"知因保"，客户通过基因检测得知患乳腺癌的概率，保险公司根据检测结果提供相应的乳腺癌专项体检服务和保障计划。

"知因保"是以基因检测为支撑、以健康体检为手段、以保险为保障的个人健康管理计划，首款产品"知因保·乳腺癌"基因检测保险计划于 2015 年 6 月末正式在 TB 保险频道公开发售。此产品面向 18～50 周岁的客户群体，提供包括乳腺癌基因检测、乳腺癌专项健康体检（针对中、高风险人群）、一年期 10 万元乳腺癌癌症保险和 1 万元乳腺原位癌保险等在内，集前端疾病预防、中端管理防控、后端风险处置功能于一体的全流程、专项健康管理计划。在合作中，ZA 保险提供了 1 年期 10 万元乳腺癌重疾保险和 1 万元乳腺原位癌保险；HD 基因提供乳腺癌基因检测，包含 BRACI、BRAC2 等与乳腺癌高度相关的 8 种基因、21 个位点。如果客户检测出中等风险，ZA 保险免费提供未来 2 年，每年 1 次的乳腺癌专项体检；如果客户检测出高等风险，ZA 保险免费提供未来 2 年，每年 2 次的乳腺癌专项体检。这个产品创新地使用了口腔刷取样，无须采血，用快递寄送样本，跳过传统医院、诊所等中间环节，售价超过 400 元。消费者在成功购买上述保障计划后需要提交个人基因。在 25 个工作日内，消费者便可在 ZA 保险或 HD 基因官网查询到检测结果、饮食建议等。"知因保"还将根据检测结果提供相应的乳腺癌专项体检服务。

"知因保"是国内保险业与基因检测的首次结合，旨在利用基因检测技术，为保险客户提供从前端风险预防、中端风险管理到后端风险处置的闭环式、全流程健康管理方案，实现互联网"保险+基因"的"1+1>2"的效果。该计划的推出表明，基因检测

和保险的结合，有助于保险以基因检测作为健康管理的切入点。根据客户的检测结果管理客户的健康、提升风险管理能力，提供针对性的后续健康管理服务，这是一整套积极、温暖的保障服务。

HD基因，是全球最大的基因测序中心、人类基因组计划中国部分的承担者。此次合作的"知因保·乳腺癌"基因检测保险计划，以国内外报道的乳腺癌权威文献为基础，结合数万中国国家基因库特有的中国人群基础数据，筛选了与乳腺癌高度相关的8个基因共21个位点进行检测，并通过严谨科学的数学模型计算和信息分析解读进行风险界定。通过基因检测，客户可以更好地了解自身的基因信息，并通过报告中的健康建议来调整生活方式。如果检测结果提示为高、中风险人群，从遗传背景来看，终生乳腺癌发生概率就会明显增高，特别需要对诱发疾病的环境因素进行改变，例如，遵从"知因保"计划提供的体检和健康管理指导等。

保险公司通过基因检测的手段，一方面，可以获取客户的健康数据，依据客户患病的风险概率进行更精准的定价；另一方面，又可为客户提供有针对性的后续健康管理服务，降低发病率从而减少赔款，增加保险公司的盈利。

案例评述：

我国脱贫攻坚于2021年2月取得全面胜利，但因病返贫的风险仍然存在。重大疾病不但威胁健康，还侵蚀财产。虽然目前我国的社保覆盖面广，但是一旦遭遇重大疾病，很容易因病返贫。这个时候，重疾险就起到了应有的经济救助及保障功能。"保险+基因"模式使保险不再只是事后的弥补，它可以让保险企业更加清楚地了解人们的身体状况，让重疾险从一项事后补偿的保障变为一项健康风险管理手段，有效防止因病返贫的发生。保险与基因检测相结合，为以妇女为代表的弱势群体构建了一道应对因病返贫的坚固防线，为巩固来之不易的脱贫攻坚成果提供了有力保障。

案例来源：

中金在线综合. 保险+基因如何1+1>2？众安保险知因保计划亮剑[EB/OL].（2015-7-1）[2024-07-01]. http://www.china-insurance.com/news-center/newslist.asp? id=257951.

7

Biotechnology and Insurance

This chapter mainly explains the basic ideas and principles of the mutual integration of biotechnology and insurance industry, and selects relevant domestic and international cases to share with students and inspire them to develop insurance technology application scenarios and related insurance products with the help of biotechnology.

7.1 Basic Biotechnology Theory

7.1.1 Basic Concepts of Biotechnology

With the global scientific and technological revolution and industrial changes, the field of biotechnology is developing rapidly. Biotechnology is an emerging and comprehensive discipline that applies the basic principles of biology, chemistry and engineering to utilize living organisms (including microorganisms, animal cells and plant cells) or their components (organelles and enzymes) to produce useful substances and provide services to human beings.

The field of biotechnology covers genetic engineering, cell engineering, enzyme engineering (also known as protein engineering) and fermentation engineering. Biotechnology has vigorously promoted the development of human society. Gene sequencing has led to the development of various related technologies and promoted clinical applications; precision medicine has changed the traditional mode of disease diagnosis and treatment and promoted the transformation of the pharmaceutical industry; stem cell technology and gene therapy technology have opened up new ideas for the treatment of diseases; gene editing technology, synthetic biotechnology, gene drive technology, and acquired function research have promoted the development of life sciences (See Figure 7.1).

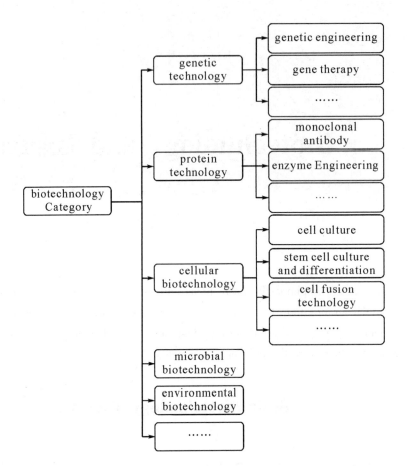

Figure 7.1 **Scope of biotechnology**

7.1.2 Development History of Biotechnology

The development of biotechnology has roughly gone through the following stages:

7.1.2.1 Traditional Biotechnology

Ancient human beings utilized fermentation technology to produce foodstuffs such as wine and soy sauce, and also used traditional herbs to treat diseases, which can be regarded as the origin of ancient biotechnology.

7.1.2.2 Germination of Modern Biotechnology

With the gradual development of technology, people began to study microorganisms such as bacteria and yeast, and discovered the basics of genetics, which laid the foundation for the development of modern biotechnology.

7.1.2.3 The Rise of Genetic Engineering Technology

The development of genetic engineering technology has promoted the rapid development of biotechnology, and people can change the genes of organisms to achieve specific purposes, such as the production of drugs and crop improvement.

7.1.2.4 Development of Bioinformatics

With the combination of computer technology and biology, bioinformatics has gradually emerged, providing powerful tools and methods for biotechnology research.

7. 1. 2. 5　Rise of Synthetic Biology

As synthetic biology has become an emerging field of biotechnology, the design and construction of new biological systems has brought new possibilities in biomanufacturing, medical care, and other fields. Figure 7. 2 shows the evolution of modern biotechnology.

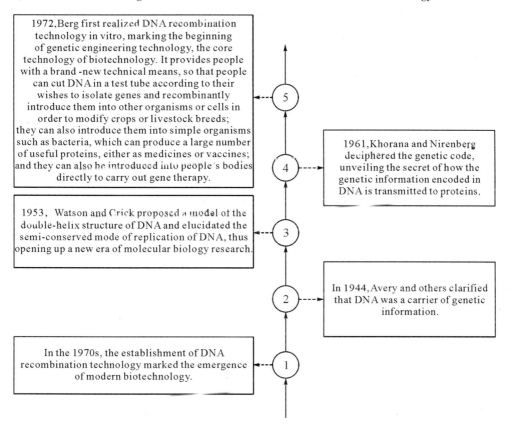

1972, Berg first realized DNA recombination technology in vitro, marking the beginning of genetic engineering technology, the core technology of biotechnology. It provides people with a brand -new technical means, so that people can cut DNA in a test tube according to their wishes to isolate genes and recombinantly introduce them into other organisms or cells in order to modify crops or livestock breeds; they can also introduce them into simple organisms such as bacteria, which can produce a large number of useful proteins, either as medicines or vaccines; and they can also be introduced into people's bodies directly to carry out gene therapy.

1961, Khorana and Nirenberg deciphered the genetic code, unveiling the secret of how the genetic information encoded in DNA is transmitted to proteins.

1953, Watson and Crick proposed a model of the double-helix structure of DNA and elucidated the semi-conserved mode of replication of DNA, thus opening up a new era of molecular biology research.

In 1944, Avery and others clarified that DNA was a carrier of genetic information.

In the 1970s, the establishment of DNA recombination technology marked the emergence of modern biotechnology.

Figure 7. 2　The evolution of modern biotechnology

7. 1. 3　Characteristics of Biotechnology

Gradually moving from research to application, the development of modern biotechnology has been progressively characterized by the following features:

7. 1. 3. 1　Interdisciplinarity

Biotechnology involves the intersection of many disciplines, such as bioengineering, chemistry, physics, engineering, etc., and requires not only the mastery of microbiology, zoology, but also biochemistry, molecular biology and other aspects of knowledge, and the need to synthesize the use of a variety of knowledge and technology.

7. 1. 3. 2　Wideness of Application

Biotechnology pays more attention to practical application, which determines the direction of research. Biotechnology has a wide range of applications in the fields of medicine, recreation, agriculture and forestry, aquaculture, food, species protection, environmental protection, finance, insurance, case detection, etc., and has an important impact on the production and life of human society and the ecological protection of the earth.

7.1.3.3 Advanced Nature of Science and Technology

Traditional biotechnology is often represented by enzyme engineering and fermentation engineering; today's biotechnology places more emphasis on genetic and cellular engineering, which requires very advanced scientific and technological means for support.

7.1.3.4 High Ethical and Moral Requirements

Modern biotechnology involves genetic intervention and cloning technology, etc., which may touch upon sensitive issues of human ethics and morality, and requires a very high level of ethics and morality from practitioners.

7.1.4 Status and Prospects of Biotechnology

The development of biotechnology has found solutions to many problems that are practically related to people's production and life. At present, the specialized research on biotechnology integrates multidisciplinary technologies such as genetic engineering, molecular biology, biochemistry, genetics, cell biology, embryology, immunology, organic chemistry, inorganic chemistry, physical chemistry, physical informatics and computer science, etc., and is widely used in the fields of medical care, agriculture, forestry, farming, military science and technology, industrial applications, environmental protection, and so on.

7.1.4.1 Medical Field

Biotechnology has attracted great attention in the medical field with the advantages of accelerating the development of new drugs and facilitating precision medicine. Stem cell technology can be applied in the field of regenerative medicine, which can not only treat leukemia, immune system diseases and other diseases that were difficult to treat in the past, but also extend organ-like technology, which is expected to promote regenerative medicine to achieve a leap, and gene therapy, as a new means of treatment for new diseases, has brought a bright future for the eradication of some difficult-to-treat diseases. Using microarray nucleic acid chips or protein chips, we can search for disease-causing genes. Using antibody technology, toxins can be delivered to cancer cells with special markers for precise treatment of cancer. Using gene cloning technology, gene therapy can be used for certain difficult diseases, etc. Gene therapy can also be used to treat diseases by using molecular biology methods to introduce the target gene into the patient's body so that it expresses the target gene product.

7.1.4.2 Agroforestry Farming

The population is expanding rapidly, and the food problem is exactly the entry point for the application of biotechnology. The development of genetically cloned crops, using cloning technology, not only researched the useful genes of anti-pest genes and anti-freezing genes, but also bred rice and other crops containing vitamin A, which greatly improved the quality of crops, the use of tissue culture technology to improve the quality of ornamental flowers, and the use of genetic engineering technology so that the output of coagulation factors from dairy cows can be used for medical purposes. The production of bio-fertilizers, mainly using microbial technology, not only provides crops with nutrients, improves quality, enhances resistance to cold and pests, but also improves the permeability of the soil, water retention, acidity and alkalinity and other physiological properties, which creates a good growing environment for the root system of crops and ensures the increase of crop yields. The development of biopesticides, the use of microorganisms, antibiotics and genetic engineering to produce toxins that have the effect of killing pests and diseases, and the production of microbial strains of pesticides with strong broad-spectrum virulence, which, although not as fast as chemical pesticides, have a long-lasting effect and, compared with chemical pesticides, are less harmful to the environment, human beings and crops.

7. 1. 4. 3　Industrial Applications

In industry, the special metabolic pathways of industrial strains are utilized to replace some chemical reactions, which, in addition to increased specificity, are more energy-efficient at ambient temperature and pressure. Due to the high specificity and the low amount of waste produced, it is called green industry.

7. 1. 4. 4　Environmental Protection

When the environment is damaged, biotechnology can be utilized to deal with it and save it from a second victimization. Biological organisms have a high degree of specificity and can eliminate special sources of pollution. For example, if a cruise ship transporting crude oil pollutes the sea with heavy oil due to an accident, special microbial strains that decompose heavy oil can be used to decompose the heavy oil and metabolize it into environmentally acceptable short-chain fatty acids, thus eliminating the pollution. In addition, when soil is contaminated with heavy metals, specific plants can be used to absorb the source of contamination.

7. 2　Application Scenarios of Combining Biotechnology and Insurance

Currently, biotechnology can be combined mainly with life insurance, planting insurance and farming insurance.

7. 2. 1　Integration of Genetic Testing and Life Insurance ├───────

Fund detection technology and gene therapy technology in biotechnology are gradually being applied to the insurance industry.

Genetic testing is the scientific technique of analyzing an individual's genomic information to assess his or her risk of disease or predict his or her health status. The operation mechanism of genetic testing technology is to extract genetic material from individual biological samples (saliva, blood or oral mucous membrane cells), sequence and analyze the DNA of the sample body, screen for mutations or abnormal genes, in order to make predictive judgments on the likelihood of individuals suffering from diseases. At present, scientists have found that there are close links between more than 6,500 diseases and genes, and a variety of diseases can be predicted using genetic testing technology. Insurance companies can use genetic testing technology to provide customers with more personalized insurance products and pricing strategies. For example, an insurance company can assess a customer's risk of developing a certain disease based on his/her genetic test results, and then provide him/her with appropriate insurance coverage and personalized insurance pricing, which can better meet the needs of the customer and reduce the risk of the insurance company.

Gene therapy refers to the use of biotechnological means to repair or alter an individual's genes in order to treat or prevent diseases. Insurance companies can cooperate with gene therapy organizations to provide customers with gene therapy-related insurance products on the one hand. For example, in order to encourage more people to participate in gene therapy, insurance companies can provide customers with insurance products for gene therapy expenses, so as to ensure that customers can receive unexpected financial support when undergoing gene therapy. On the other hand, they can conduct in-depth research and explore the potential risks in gene therapy, develop insurance products to deal with gene testing risks and gene editing risks, and promote the innovation of insurance products.

Life insurance is a kind of insurance that takes human body and life as the subject matter of insurance, and takes birth, senility, sickness and death as the insured accidents. According to the insurance scope, life insurance can be divided into life insurance, accident insurance and health insurance.

The application value of genetic information for different types of life insurance varies:

(1) For life insurance, the insured passes on to the insurer the risk of survival or death of the insured, and the length of the insured's life is directly related to the insurer's premium income and benefit payment. Therefore, the ability to grasp sufficient information to identify potential risk factors that may significantly shorten the life expectancy of the insured becomes the key to whether the insurer can realize economic benefits. The emergence and development of genetic testing technology gives insurers a powerful tool to assess the life expectancy of the insured, which is of great significance in improving the accuracy of risk rating and premium rate setting in life insurance.

(2) For accidental injury insurance, the accidental injury that satisfies the conditions of insurance should be an external, sudden, non-disease objective event that causes bodily injury. Genetic information only has the function of disease prediction, but can do nothing to predict the probability of occurrence of external accidents. Therefore, as far as the current research results are concerned, there is no room for the utilization of genetic information in the field of accidental injury insurance.

(3) A fine-grained categorical examination of health insurance products reveals that the application of gene technology is of more limited value in group health insurance and individual short-term health insurance, and of higher value in individual long-term health insurance.

In group health insurance, each member of a group shares the risk of the entire group, and the insurer uses the group as the unit of risk measurement and considers and evaluates overall factors, such as the size of the group, the inflow of new members, the industry to which it belongs, and the stability of the group, rather than requiring a case-by-case review of individual member information. Therefore, genetic information, as a kind of personal information, has limited application value for group health insurance.

In individual health insurance, with the exception of a few health insurance policies that cover specific perils (critical illness insurance, long-term care insurance, etc.), most health insurance policies (especially medical insurance) are generally of short duration, and short-term changes in the health of the insured are the focus of the insurer. At this time, genetic information does not have a particular advantage for short-term illnesses. Therefore, the economic incentives for insurers to use genetic information in individual short-term health insurance are weak. On the contrary, insurers of individual long-term health insurance are more inclined to collect and utilize the insured's genetic information to improve the accuracy of their risk prediction and effectively reduce the difficulty of the insurer's risk rating.

In summary, due to the differences between life insurance types and the corresponding risk assessment objects and risk focus, the application of genetic information has different application values for different life insurance, as shown in Figure 7.3.

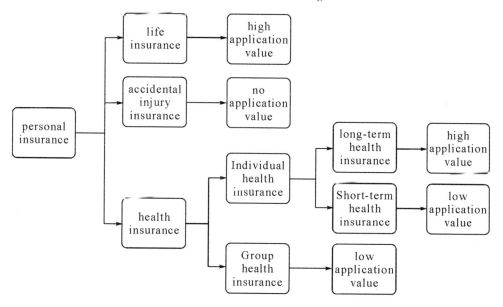

Figure 7.3 **The value of genetic testing for life insurance applications**

7.2.2 Integration Biotechnology and Plantation Insurance

With the development of biotechnology, biotechnology has begun to be applied in plantation insurance to promote the high-quality development of agricultural insurance. The application of biotechnology in planting insurance is mainly reflected in the following aspects:

7.2.2.1 Bio-breeding Technology

Through bio-breeding technology, it is possible to cultivate excellent varieties that are resistant to pests and diseases, drought, salinity and so on, so as to improve the yield and quality of crops and reduce the losses caused by natural disasters and pests and diseases, thus reducing the risk of paying out in agricultural insurance.

7.2.2.2 Biometrics

By utilizing biometrics, crops can be accurately identified to ensure the authenticity and accuracy of the insurance subject matter. For example, by recognizing the biometric information of crops, false underwriting and claims can be prevented, and the transparency and efficiency of insurance business can be improved.

7.2.2.3 Bioinformatics

Bioinformatics can help analyze crop genomic data, predict crop growth and yield, and provide a more accurate risk assessment and pricing basis for agricultural insurance.

7.2.2.4 Bio-monitoring Technology

Through bio-monitoring technology, the growing environment and health status of crops can be monitored in real time, so that possible risks can be detected and warned in a timely manner, and timely and accurate information can be provided for insurance claims.

7.2.2.5 Bio-fertilizers and Bio-pesticides

The use of bio-fertilizers and bio-pesticides can reduce the use of chemical fertilizers and pesticides, improve the resistance of crops to diseases and pests, and reduce environmental pollution, while also helping to reduce the cost of agricultural insurance claims.

7.2.2.6 Gene Editing Technology

Gene editing technology can accurately modify crop genes to breed new varieties with specific excellent traits, improve crop adaptability and stability, and reduce insurance payouts.

7.2.2.7 Microbial Application

Utilizing microbial technology, such as inoculation of beneficial microorganisms to improve soil structure and nutrition, to enhance the disease resistance of crops, thereby reducing insurance claims due to diseases.

7.2.2.8 Biosensors

Biosensors can be used to monitor various biologically active substances in the growing environment of crops, such as plant hormones, pathogens, etc., to provide risk warning for agricultural insurance.

Through the application of these biotechnologies, plantation insurance can carry out risk management and control more effectively, improve the quality and efficiency of insurance services, and at the same time help promote the sustainable development of agriculture.

7.2.3 Combining Biotechnology and Farming Insurance

With the development of biotechnology, biotechnology has begun to be applied in farming to promote the high-quality development of agricultural insurance. The application of biotechnology in farming insurance is mainly reflected in the following aspects:

7.2.3.1 Biometrics

The use of biometrics, such as facial recognition, ear tagging, and DNA identification, allows for the precise identification of livestock to ensure the accuracy of underwriting and claims. These technologies can create unique identifiers for livestock, preventing duplicate insurances and claims.

7.2.3.2 Biosensors

Biosensors can be used to monitor microorganisms, toxins, pollutants, etc. in the farm environment, providing a scientific basis for risk assessment and management of farming insurance.

7.2.3.3 Gene Technology

Gene technology can help improve livestock breeds, increase their disease resistance and productivity, and reduce farming risks, thus reducing the probability of payouts from farming insurance.

7.2.3.4 Bioinformatics

By analyzing the genomic data of livestock, the risk of disease occurrence can be predicted, providing a basis for product design and pricing of farming insurance.

7.2.3.5 Microbial Application

Use of beneficial microorganisms to improve feed quality and the breeding environment, enhance the immunity and health of livestock, reduce the occurrence of diseases and lower the risk of paying out on farming insurance.

7.2.3.6 Biomarkers

By detecting biomarkers in livestock, it is possible to assess their health status and production performance, which provides reference for underwriting and claim settlement of farming insurance.

7.2.3.7 Biostatistical Models

Using biostatistical models to analyze the growth and development of livestock, the occurrence of diseases and other data, we can more accurately assess the risk of farming and provide a scientific basis for the pricing and risk management of farming insurance.

Through the application of these biotechnologies, farming insurance can more effectively identify, assess and manage risks, improve the quality and efficiency of insurance services, and at the same time help promote the sustainable development of the farming industry.

7.3 Foreign Cases of "Insurance + Biotechnology"

7.3.1 The First Case

Case Tile:

ABO/Rh Testing, Antibody Screening, and Biometric Technology as Tools to Combat Insurance Fraud

Case Content:

After claiming to have exhausted every alternative form of pain management, a patient with diabetes requested a total knee replacement. A week before the elective surgery, the patient's physician ordered pretransfusion tests. The laboratory performed a blood-type test and an antibody screen. This patient was determined to be O positive with a negative antibody screen. On the day this patient was scheduled for her operation, the physician ordered preoperative blood work which was ordered and collected per hospital policy. This hospital's policy on surgical procedures required a final check of ABO/Rh and antibody screening to be performed on all patients if those tests had been performed more than 72 hours earlier. This patient did not provide a photographic identification (ID) card to the registration clerk; she claimed to have left it at home. After she explained that she had received care at that hospital in the past, she was then instructed to type in her social security number on a keypad; the clerk then took her picture. The clerk then placed a wristband on the woman and directed her to the waiting area for surgery.

After hospital staff performed another ABO/Rh check and antibody screening on the day of the scheduled operation, the patient's blood type was verified to be O positive, as before; however, the results of her antibody screen were positive. This finding was very strange because the results for this patient from one week earlier were negative for unexpected antibodies. According to her medical records, this patient had not received a transfusion or organ transplant in the past 3 months. She had 2 adult children and no history of a recent pregnancy. The laboratory notified the surgical unit's nursing staff of the possible discrepancy and that further testing would be required. The nurse who was notified informed the surgeon, who decided that the operation should be rescheduled.

A different blood bank technologist repeated all tests to ensure that no testing errors had been made. The results of the antibody screen were again positive. The technologist performed an antibody identification procedure, which identified anti-K, an antibody that reacts at the anti-human globulin phase, in the patient's plasma. The blood bank supervisor asked the nurse whether the patient had received care at another hospital after the anti-K was identified. The nurse stated that the patient had told her that she had not obtained any medical care since her most recent preoperative visit to the hospital, which had taken place 1 week earlier. Because the blood bank stores all specimens for 10 days per laboratory policy, another blood-bank technologist obtained the patient's specimen that had been collected from the previous week and performed blood typing and antibody screening on it, to compare those results with the previous results on file.

This technologist performed the test-tube (manual) method and gel technology to verify the patient's antibody results. The antibody screen result was negative; this was in agreement with the result from one week earlier. Two different specimens from the same patient, collected one week apart, with no health or medication changes on the part of the patient, had yielded different antibody screen results. This finding is an anomaly because anti-K is one of the antibodies that require a Kantigen negative individual to be exposed to the antigen through transfusion, transplantation, or pregnancy. Because none of these possibilities was true of this patient, the laboratory findings presented a clinical dilemma.

A nurse unit coordinator informed the patient that to reschedule her surgery, another blood sample had to be collected because of a discrepancy with her laboratory results. The phlebotomist followed the venipuncture protocol; she remarked that the patient seemed oblivious to what was happening and did not seem to be concerned about the discrepancy. The phlebotomist stated that this patient was very cooperative during the second venipuncture. The nurse unit coordinator requested more information about this patient because of the discrepancy. At some point in the conversation, the patient confessed to the unit coordinator that she was in need of a total knee replacement and explained that she had no health insurance. She explained that she assumed that because her friend had the same blood type, O positive, she could safely undergo the operation in her friend's name and have the procedure covered by her friend's insurance policy. The patient also admitted that the only medically related visit her friend had made was for the original laboratory tests (which had yielded negative antibody-screening results) and payment of her deductible. It was later discovered that the first visit was the only time that a form of photo ID had been presented during the entire process. This incident led to the hospital requiring patients to present a photo ID during registration and to implement a procedure of scanning a barcode on patient wristbands before patients could receive any care or treatment, to prevent such a situation from happening again.

Case Comments:

Medical insurance fraud affects everyone and fraud triggered higher premiums. But if a hospital or insurance company can use the biometric technology described in this case, the patient attempting to impersonate her friend would not have been authenticated to undergo the scheduled operation because the patient's biometric template would not have been linked to the friend's electronic health record, in this way, a hospital or an insurance company can not only streamline patient identification processes but also reduce financial losses due to fraud, and uphold the integrity of the healthcare system as a whole.

Case Source:

JATOR E K, HUGHLEY M K. ABO/Rh testing, antibody screening, and biometric technology as tools to combat insurance fraud: An example and discussion [J]. Laboratory Medicine, 2014, 45 (1): E3-E7.

7.3.2 The Second Case

Case Tile:

Explore the current issues regarding life insurance and genetics-related information in Australia.

Case Content:

James (pseudonym) was in his early 20s when he started receiving letters from a familial bowel cancer registry, run by a genetics service, recommending that he consider genetic testing for Lynch syndrome. Lynch syndrome (previously known as hereditary non-polyposis colorectal cancer) is an inherited cancer syndrome caused by a mutation in a mismatch repair gene. Compared with the general population, carriers have an increased risk of colorectal and other types of cancer, with an earlier age of onset. Colonoscopic screening significantly improves survival among carriers of Lynch syndrome. James's mother had been diagnosed with uterine cancer at

50 years of age. However, James was not particularly interested in undertaking a genetic test at this stage.

Several years later, he discussed genetic testing for Lynch syndrome with a doctor, who advised him to ensure that he had a life insurance policy first. James had an existing life insurance policy, which he had applied for when he started working. For this policy, he had declared his mother's uterine cancer. After a substantial increase in his salary, he applied for an increase in cover and was approved with no conditions. On the application form, there was a question asking whether he was planning to seek any medical advice, treatment or tests, to which he replied "no", notwithstanding the fact that he had made an appointment to see a genetic counsellor.

He then went to the genetics service to discuss testing. They gave him "a lot of information" and followed up with a letter, which "was very descriptive about… what I discussed with the counsellor… that got me a bit worked up because I thought this kind of thing was a conversation with a counsellor and wouldn't end up in official correspondence".

James was concerned that the written record of his discussion with the genetics service (including reference to a discussion about genetic testing) would render his insurance invalid. He disclosed all correspondence between himself and the genetics service to the insurance company. Based on this information, he was denied cover for cancer in his upgraded policy.

He decided to "just stick with the cover that I had when I initially applied as a graduate, as that includes everything", and he "left it at that for another couple of years".

After researching Lynch syndrome further, James recognised the need to test and potentially begin surveillance before 30 years of age. He underwent testing at 27 years of age and was found to carry a mutation in the MSH6 gene, a mutation associated with Lynch syndrome.

He applied to a second company for life insurance, disclosing his genetic test result. Once again, he was offered cover excluding cancer.

I left it for a little bit and then I thought to myself, "All right. I'm going to try someone else"… I thought I'm going to get everything in writing and I'm not going to let them push me around … I got all fired up and I did some research.

James read published epidemiological research articles and communicated with their authors. He worked out that his risk of colorectal cancer, if he underwent yearly colonoscopy, was the same as the population risk. He presented this in a lengthy document with his application to a third insurance company. He included a table of risks to illustrate that he should not be considered at higher risk of colorectal cancer if he adhered to yearly colonoscopy (Box).

He was once again denied cover for cancer.

I said to them, "show me the actuarial evidence of why you can do this"… they just ignored that request… They wrote me some terrible letter saying that even though I'm getting this surveillance, it doesn't eliminate my risk of cancer, which is irrelevant. The relevant part is my level of risk of getting cancer compared with the general population.

James carried out further research and decided on a course of action. He made a complaint to the Australian Human Rights Commission, submitting all documentation between himself and the third life insurance company. Soon after informing the insurance company that he had made the complaint, he was offered full cover, with the minor exclusion of any claim caused as a result of a colonoscopy.

At the time of James's application to the first life insurance company, he had discussed the possibility of genetic testing for Lynch syndrome with a doctor but had not undergone genetic testing. There was some family history information available, which he had disclosed. His application for increased cover was initially approved. It was only after he voluntarily disclosed his dealings with the genetic service after receiving correspondence from them that the insurer withdrew approval for the increased cover, alleging that he had failed to make full disclosure at the time of application. However, in terms of actuarial evidence, there was no new information on which this insurer could base its decision to exclude cancer from his insurance cover. Significantly, James did not have more information about his risk status than the insurer, and the advice from his doctor, quite appropriately, had been to get his life insurance in order before undertaking genetic testing. Viewed objectively, this decision was not justified by any actuarial or statistical data and amounted to unlawful discrimination outside the scope of the insurance exemption. At most, this may have justified postponing the processing of the application to ascertain whether James would proceed with genetic testing. It certainly did not justify the insurer's decision to exclude for cancer cover and, in the absence of any relevant evidence, the decision was clearly inappropriate.

By the time of James's second and third insurance applications, his circumstances had changed, as he had undergone a genetic test and was found to carry a mutation in the MSH6 gene, which had implications for his risk status. In these further applications for life insurance cover, James fully disclosed his genetic test result. In both instances, the insurance companies offered restricted cover that excluded cancer.

Case Comments:

The case of James primarily focuses on issues related to genetic testing, disclosure of genetic information, and the implications of genetic test results on insurance coverage.

And we can learn from this case that biotechnology, particularly in the form of genetic testing, plays a significant role in this case as James underwent testing for Lynch syndrome, which influenced the insurance companies' decisions whether to offer him restricted cover that excluded cancer.

Case Source:

KEOGH L, OTLOWSKI M. Life insurance and genetic test results: a mutation carrier's fight to achieve full cover [J]. Medical Journal of Australia2013, 199 (5): 363-366.

8 | 物联网与保险业

本章主要阐释物联网与保险业相互结合的基本思路与原理，并精选国内外相关案例与学生分享，启发学生借助物联网开发保险科技应用场景和相关保险产品的思路。

8.1 物联网的基本理论

8.1.1 物联网是什么

物联网概念最早出现于 1995 年比尔·盖茨的《未来之路》一书。1998 年，美国麻省理工学院创造性地提出了当时被称作 EPC 系统的"物联网"的构想。在中国，物联网最早被称为传感网。中国科学院早在 1999 年就启动了物联网的研究，并取得了一些科研成果。同年，在美国召开的移动计算和网络国际会议提出了"传感网是下一个世纪人类面临的又一个发展机遇"。

物联网（Internet of Things，IoT）是指基于通信感知技术等传播媒介，将不同的物体与互联网相互连接，使其能够进行信息交换与通信，通过万物互联，以实现智能化的识别、管理等功能。

8.1.2 物联网的特点

"物联网"问世打破了之前的传统思维。在物联网时代，钢筋混凝土、电缆等各种设备将与互联网整合为统一的基础设施。物联网的本质就是物理世界和数字世界的融合，是为了打破空间限制，实现物物之间按需进行的信息获取、传递、存储、融合、使用等服务的网络。归纳而言，物联网至少具有三个特征。

8.1.2.1 整体感知

整体感知是物联网的基本特征之一。物联网利用各种感知设备来获取物体的信息，这些感知设备包括射频识别标签、二维码标签、温度传感器、湿度传感器等。通过这些设备，物联网能够实时感知物体及其所处环境的状态，并将这些信息转换为人们可处理的数据。

8.1.2.2　同步传递

通过对互联网、无线网络的融合，将物体的信息实时、准确地传递给需要的人们，以便信息交流、分享。这种传输过程需要保证信息的准确性和安全性，防止信息在传输过程中被篡改或窃取。为了实现可靠传输，物联网采用了多种通信协议和技术。

8.1.2.3　智能处理

物联网利用云计算、模糊识别等各种智能计算技术，对海量数据和信息进行分析和处理，对物体进行实时智能化控制，实现通过各种设备更加智能地监测、控制、获取处理信息。这种处理过程通常涉及数据挖掘、机器学习等技术，能够对大量的数据进行处理和分析，提取出有价值的信息。

综上所述，物联网的基本特征包括整体感知、同步传递和智能处理。这些特征相互协作，共同实现了对物体的智能化管理。例如，在智能家居中，通过整体感知技术，物联网能够实时感知家居环境的状态和变化；通过可靠传输技术，物联网能够将感知到的数据传输到云端进行处理；通过智能处理技术，物联网能够对收集到的数据进行分析和处理，从而实现智能化的家居管理。

随着物联网技术的不断发展，这些特征将更加突出，为人们的生活和工作带来更多的便利和价值。

8.1.3　物联网的发展现状与前景

虽然物联网起源于国外，但我国早在 1999 年就开始了对物联网的研究。2009 年，国内掀起了集中研究物联网技术的浪潮，物联网科技突飞猛进。2010 年，物联网技术首次被写入政府工作报告。2021 年，工业和信息化部等八部门联合印发了《物联网新型基础设施建设三年行动计划（2021—2023 年）》。政策层面的支持带动了产业的创新突破发展。目前，我国物联网技术已经初步形成完整的产业体系。2022 年，我国物联网市场整体产业规模达到 2 105.09 亿美元，市场前景巨大。据 Statista 统计数据，2022 年全球物联网市场规模达到 9 702.2 亿美元（如图 8.1 所示）。中国物联网行业发展历程如图 8.2 所示。

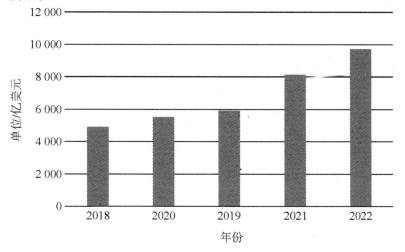

图 8.1　2018—2022 年全球物联网市场规模走势

资料来源：Statista 前瞻产业研究院。

2003年及之前：萌芽期	2004—2008年：初步发展期	2009年至今：快速成长期
• 1993年，"金卡工程"启动，开启了我国信息化建设新纪元 • 2000年金卡工程率先启动物联网RFID应用试点，开启智能化新时代	• 2003年,召开"物流信息新技术——物联网及产品电子代码(EPC)研讨会暨第一次物流信息新技术联席会议" • 2004年，启动"物联网+12个重点行业"应用试点与工程示范。 • 2005年，成立了RFID标准工作组和中国RFID产业联盟	• 2009年开始,工业和信息化部开始统筹部署宽带普及、三网融合、物联网及下一代互联网发展 • 2011年,《物联网"十二五"发展规划》正式印发，物联网步入产业化发展 • 2017年,《物联网发展规划(2016—2020年)》发布，物联网技术研发水平和创新能力显著提高 • 2021年,《物联网新型基础设施建设三年行动计划(2021—2023年)》

图8.2 中国物联网行业发展历程

资料来源：Statista 前瞻产业研究院。

8.1.3.1 物联网基础设施建设成效显著

以智能手机、传感器、工业设备、车辆等为代表的蜂窝物联网用户快速增长，截至 2023 年年末，根据工业和信息化部最新统计数据，1—11 月我国蜂窝物联网用户较快增长，三家基础电信企业发展蜂窝物联网终端用户 23.12 亿户，比上年末净增 46 772 万户，占移动网终端连接数的 57.3%。与此同时，物联网业务收入同比增长 22.7%，成为拉动通信行业增长的生力军。

8.1.3.2 物联网的应用促进万物互联

在农业发达地区，广阔的田野竖立着一个个传感设施，农户们无须看天气预报就能准确预知田地里的温度、湿度等指标，也能精确预知哪块区域发生了病虫害，稻田中的水位高度，并随时调节。

工业和信息化部数据显示，截至 2023 年 8 月末，应用于公共服务、车联网、智慧零售、智慧家居的物联网终端规模已分别达 7 亿户、4.4 亿户、3.2 亿户、2.4 亿户。另据市场研究机构 IoT Analytics 统计数据，中国物联网行业应用中制造业/工业，占比 22%，排在首位；其次是交通/车联网，占比 15%；智慧能源、智慧零售、智慧城市、智慧医疗和智能物流占比分别为 14%、12%、12%、9% 和 7%。随着社会经济的发展，科技创新的进步，物联网逐渐覆盖到生活生产中的各个领域。目前，物联网已广泛应用于工业制造、农业生产、交通车联、健康医疗、电力能源、环境保护等领域。

8.1.3.3 物联网的应用创新不断

2023 年中国物联网大会在无锡召开，"移动设备生物特征识别标准创新和实施应用、Wi-Fi 网联无源 RFID 分布式读写系统及应用、家居物联网边端智能解决方案、小蜘蛛低轨卫星互联网星座及宽带物联网应用、广义确定性智融标识网络系统及核心设备、异构自适应的边缘协同智能计算技术与应用、近零功耗软件定义物联网关键技术与核心芯片……"。物联网领域内的重要科技被广泛讨论，很多前沿科技正逐步落地应用。随着新一代信息技术将物联网推入新发展时期，整个社会对物联网的未来有了更多期待，高速发展下还有更多的应用空间有待开发。

随着人工智能、大数据、云计算等新科技相互融合。物联网技术将会应用到更多的领域，发挥更大的作用。例如，智慧家居，将一家一户的智能设备统筹结合，提升生活质量，让家居生活更加高效、便捷、舒适；智能交通通过大数据，优化出行路线，促进交通安全。此外，智能医疗、智能电网、智能物流、智能农业、智能电力、智能安防、智慧城市等更多领域在未来都将出现物联网技术的身影。

8.2 物联网技术在保险行业的应用

物联网拥有将物理设备与网络结合在一起，能在信息传递的基础上实现万物互联。物联网强大的信息交互能力，对于传统保险行业的发展，在技术上有着颠覆性的作用。欧洲金融管理协会（EFMA）在其报告《物联网：颠覆保险模式》中描绘了物联网保险的发展趋势。首先，物联网设备的数量将呈指数级增加。预计到 2035 年，物联网设备将增长至 1 万亿台，物联网相关应用程序的数量也将达到 1 亿个。其次，该报告指出与物联网相关的保险业务是近年来财险业务中增长势头最为迅猛的领域。世界各地的保险公司在过去一年中推出了大量以物联网为基础的保险产品和服务。最后，调查还显示，45%的保险公司认为物联网将会是未来三年推动保险客户增长的主要驱动力。

基于物联网技术的新型保险产品服务模式如图 8.3 所示。

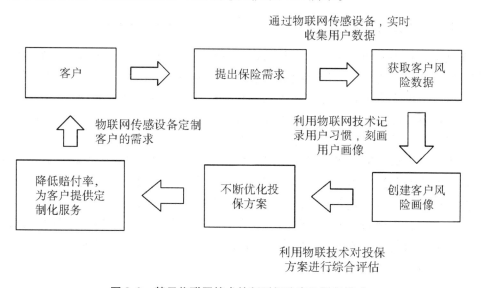

图 8.3 基于物联网技术的新型保险产品服务模式

8.2.1 物联网赋能寿险和健康险

在保险核保层面，物联网技术可以使保险行业在传统的人工核保基础上，实现动态核保。在寿险、健康险中，传统核保主要依靠客户所提供的过往数据，体检报告等，并依据生命周期表来核定费率。由于信息的不对称，传统核保可能会出现难以预料的道德风险。而物联网技术的应用，可以通过健康感知设备，追踪投保人的近期身体指标，为客户匹配最合适的投保方案以及最准确的保险费率，并为客户定制一系列的健康守护方案。

8.2.2　物联网赋能养老保险和医疗保险

目前，中国多数老年人最满意的养老方式是居家养老。然而，并不是所有家庭子女都能有时间和意愿去照护老人，但同时国内专业的护理人员又比较短缺。随着老龄化社会的加剧，国家、社会层面对老年人的医养问题越来越关注，各家保险企业都积极推出相应的养老保险产品以满足老年客户群体的需求。基于物联网的智慧养老的新模式可以通过部署智能产品，接入物联网的智能设备，让子女随时随地监护老人在家中的状态，实时提醒用药、监测居家安全、监控生命体征，必要时还可以直接通话、一键报警急救等，为投保人提供高质量远程康养监护服务。

8.2.3　物联网赋能企业财产保险、农业保险和环责保险

在未来，保险所起到的作用不该只是出险后的赔付，而应该在投保后的每个环节为客户提供增值服务。在企业财产保险领域，保险企业可以通过引入物联网技术，为企业安装传感智能设备，实时掌握安全生产、工厂动态，及时预警危险情况。在农业保险领域，物联网技术的引入可以让农户在家里就可以监测到农田里的湿度、气温、病虫害等情况或者饲养的鸡、鸭、鱼、牛、羊、猪等情况，从而帮助农户精准防控各种风险。在环责保险方面，物联网技术可以使保险与环保监测部门深化合作，高效获得各种环境监测信息，提高对风险的实时监控水平和快速反应能力。

8.2.4　物联网赋能车险

车联网是物联网的一个分支，是通过传感技术，将车与车、车与人、车与路之间协同互联，通过对获取的大量数据进行智能化的分析、处理与决策，从而实现智能化的行车管理。保险公司通过对车辆及其驾驶人员的信息进行分析处理，得出其驾驶习惯，从而能够准确为投保人匹配相适应的费率，降低骗保率，提高承保收益。对保险事故的发生由被动承受变为主动管理，缩减理赔成本。

UBI 车险是基于车主驾驶行为和使用车辆相关数据的可量化的保险，通过 OBD 车载智能终端实时监控里程、油耗等数据，评估车主风险等级，提供定制化的保单和差异化的保险定价。UBI 车险搜集的数据并不局限于驾驶里程，通过车内的传感器与行车记录仪的数据，车辆的实际驾驶时间、地点、具体驾驶方式、车辆状态等都是被考虑在内的因素。目前，全球车联网保险市场正处于高速发展期，UBI 车险势必将成为我国车险发展的重要方向。

8.3　"保险+物联网"国内案例

8.3.1　国内经典案例之一

案例题目：
深度解析：UBI 车险在 LB 车险业务中的应用与影响

案例内容:

自 1998 年 Progressive Insurance 推出第一款 UBI 车险产品以来,美国、日本、英国等国家的 UBI 车险已经发展 20 多年,逐渐成熟。然而,相较之下,中国的 UBI 车险业务仍处于市场探索阶段。2013 年,某保险企业与第三方企业合作,首次进行 UBI 项目测试。2014 年,中国保险信息技术管理有限公司成立,为 UBI 车险市场提供了技术支持。

1. 2C 到 2B

LB 车险(下文简称"LB")成立于 2014 年 12 月,隶属于深圳某科技有限公司,是一家专业的 UBI 车险与车联网平台。

LB 通过智能车载硬件采集数据,辅之数据分析处理工具,致力于推广基于车主驾驶行为的 UBI 保险,为保险公司提供 UBI 保险全系统解决方案。

LB 曾直接为 C 端用户提供 UBI 服务,后来发现这条路径相对缓慢,改为与 B 端企业合作。2016 年 7 月,LB 与某地图公司共同推出"某度招财车险",以某地图车险平台为依托,面向全国车主售卖 UBI 车险,充分发挥双方在 UBI 精算技术及行车大数据上的优势。LB 以此为出发点,已与多家保险公司、车厂、车联网平台、互联网平台等达成 UBI 方向的合作。

公开数据表明,LB 可触达国内主机厂近 80% 的车联网数据和新能源车数据;在联网车辆中,LB 实现了私家车品牌全部覆盖,部分品牌车辆的接入数据量达到 90%。

2. 借助大数据平台助力为用户进行风险定价

UBI 车险属于大数据驱动型产品,需要基于用户的驾驶行为、出行习惯、用车信息和生活环境等综合因素进行风险定价和风控管理,实现车险的合理定价。按照实际风险进行车险的差异化定价,能够让车主享受到合理的车险保费,进而享受价格低、理赔快、出险少的实惠。因此,众多保险公司都设立了 UBI 车险事业部,监控驾驶员行车过程中的使用数据。目前,主流的数据采集多通过 OBD(车载自动诊断系统)完成。

LB 采用业内专业的 CDH 大数据平台,支持资源可视化管理、监控、告警;提供快速不宕机的可视化操作配置、完成水平扩容;选择基于 docker 的容器编排、完成资源动态调整。具体来看,LB 的数据抓取分为抓取驾驶信息和用户画像两部分。

对于驾驶信息,LB 通过速度、里程、驾驶事件、天气、路况等多维数据,利用驾驶评测精算模型对驾驶情况进行综合评估,反映驾驶风险水平,为保险风险定价、客户风险识别等提供抓手。

对于用户画像,LB 基于用户的驾驶行为、用车习惯、出行规律等驾驶数据,利用用户人口属性、社会属性、生活习惯等信息,构建用户忠诚度、用户价值等多种模型,为精准营销、用户统计、效果评估等提供决策依据。

3. 建设路车联网数据连接器"LB 云"

为实现保险公司 UBI 车险的成功落地,LB 前端携手多家主机厂,后端对接各保险公司,积极构建车联网大数据布局服务体系,建设了 LB 车联网数据商业化的连接器——数据、用户信息运营平台"LB 云"。

"LB 云"通过汽车硬件传感器采集数据,由前端应用、运营管理、数据交互三大系统组成。

对于用户资料、用户需求等敏感性私人信息,LB 基于 PKI 技术、密码学技术、分布式平台部署的云端技术及国家相关标准规范要求，构建了一套数据安全防护系统和运行管理机制，将客户资料、客户需求高度保密，确保数据安全。

对于公开数据和共享数据，LB 则采取开放共赢的态度与保险公司合作，向保险公司输出可供保险行业使用的数据。LB 通过数据平台打通数据壁垒，建立起跨行业的数据通道，满足合作方各类产品的风险数据查询需求，衔接保险公司各业务流程和环节，让合作方能快速落地 UBI 创新产品。

具体来看，LB 同互联网平台、主机厂合作时，主要通过标准接口的方式接入，对接完成后平台方只需按照要求传送数据；同保险公司对接时，则会根据保险公司的技术能力数据直接对接或者封装处理之后传送。

4. 区分风险，降低赔付率

车险市场整体赔付压力较大，行业赔付率达 50%~60%。除人民保险公司、平安保险公司、太平保险公司前三大巨头外，国内大部分中小车险公司都处于亏损状态。

车险赔付率关键的三个因素分别为出险率、案均赔款、已赚件均保费。LBUBI 模型结果显示，驾驶收益越高，出险率越低。LB 通过行业数据整合分析以及上万车主试用和校准，对驾驶模型不断迭代更新，从出险率层面削减赔付成本。

根据不同的数据结构以及行业标准，截至 2020 年 8 月，LB 已对超过 1 000 万车辆进行数据分析、校验、修正，精算建模预测结果区分度达 7 倍，远超非驾驶模型。

UBI 模型效果的衡量标准是对车主风险的区分度，LB 模型区分的好用户、坏用户风险可相差十几倍，相较于行业内的 45% 出险率，LB-UBI 优质客户的出险率最低降至 16%。在此基础上，LB 能够将车险赔付率压降 10~20 个百分点，赔付率在 40% 左右。

5. 对接车险上下游全产业

LB 的业务模式是与平台方、保险公司合作，其中平台方承担获客、与用户交互的角色，LB 负责系统搭建与对接、UBI 产品设计与定价，并在后端对接保险公司，由保险公司承保。具体而言，LB 目前的业务模式分为三种：

一是后端赋能保险公司，提供创新车险产品；前端赋能主机厂商、车联网平台，售卖创新车险，收取保险公司保费佣金和赔付分成。

二是整合主机厂数据，面向保险公司和各行业提供车主基于驾驶行为的精算定价及相应数据化产品，收取数据查询费以及项目费。

三是面向主机厂、保险公司和 B 端渠道客户提供适合车辆销售、保险承保和第三方监测平台的硬件技术和服务，收取硬件设备销售收入和服务费。

LB 的服务对象主要包括保险公司、车联网平台、主机厂。对于传统保险公司，LB 已为国内主流保险公司及中小型保险公司提供全流程产品落地服务；对于车联网平台，LB 通过车联网数据应用，服务 UBI 产品等场景；对于主机厂，LB 与其携手打造贯通车主用车场景的产品服务体系。

案例评述：

随着物联网技术的迅速发展，车载传感器、智能手机应用程序和车辆连接平台等先进技术已经成熟并广泛被应用于车辆领域。这些技术的普及使得收集驾驶行为数据变得更加容易和实时化，为 UBI 车险提供了更为可靠和精确的数据支持。

中国保险公司通过与物联网技术企业合作，积极探索 UBI 车险市场，借助先进的物联网技术实现对驾驶行为的实时监测和评估。通过安装车载传感器或者利用智能手机应用程序，车主可以方便地与保险公司共享行车数据，从而获得个性化的保险费率。

物联网技术的高速发展不仅为 UBI 车险提供了更为准确和实时的数据支持，还为保险公司提供了更多的商业模式和创新空间。未来，中国的 UBI 车险市场潜力巨大。

案例来源：

卜彬彬. UBI 车险案例：路比车险业务分析［EB/OL］.（2021-06-04）［2024-07-01］. https://www.sohu.com/a/470308072_120022804.

8.3.2 国内经典案例之二

案例题目：

守护文物遗产，平安相随——平安产险古建筑保障计划全国首发

案例内容：

2019 年 4 月，法国巴黎圣母院发生了一场大火，全球为之震惊。保险公司尽管支付了巨额赔款，但人们更加关注的是这种金钱无法弥补的历史遗憾。如何避免文物古建筑再次发生类似悲剧，并且为其提供强有力的保险支持，成为人们关注的焦点。2019 年 8 月 29 日，某保险企业在西藏布达拉宫推出了一个全新的解决方案，即以事前风险防范服务为主的"古建筑服务+保险"创新方案。

据悉，该方案得到了西藏自治区文物局、西藏自治区消防总队等单位的悉心指导与支持，积极推进了全国文物古建筑保护工作，以"事前风险防范服务"和"保险保障托底"双核心驱动、最大限度地减小事故的发生概率及影响，是提高我国文物古建筑保护水平的一种有力尝试。创新风险防范科技以及综合金融的解决办法在该方案中被积极应用，将为我国从事文物古建筑保护的管理者们提供有益的借鉴。

近年来，全球范围内的古建筑火灾事故频发，除 2019 年 4 月的巴黎圣母院大火之外，2018 年巴西国家博物馆大火，2018 年 3 月韩国首尔"第一号国宝"崇礼门毁灭性大火、2015 年云南南诏镇 600 年历史的古建筑拱辰楼因电线短路被烧毁等。这些事故都给人类历史文化遗产造成了巨大损失。我国古建筑以木结构及砖木结构为主，火灾事故的发生概率大、严重程度高，面临着较高的损失风险，且国内目前为止还没有完善的古建筑全过程的保障体系，保险公司作为社会管理的重要力量，应积极承担社会责任，建立古建筑全过程保险风险保障机制。

该保险企业从古建筑面临的事故风险分析，结合近几年古建筑损失数据以及古建筑的实际保险需求，为古建筑量身打造了"风控服务+保险保障"方案。从保险角度看，古建筑面临着外在风险、内在风险以及经营风险，应为古建筑提供一揽子保险保障方案，为古建筑提供全面的保险保障。

此外，针对古建筑电气故障，该保险企业还引入了物联网智慧用电系统、红外热像电气检测技术；针对古建筑消防，该保险企业与合作伙伴开发了水喷雾灭火系统、消防物联网火灾探测器、灭火瓶等创新消防产品，可以快速处理初期火灾。针对古建筑综合管理，该保险企业开发了智慧巡检系统并建立了专属古建筑风险实验室等。

该保险企业发挥在综合金融方面的独特优势，有效地解决了古建筑领域客户在风险管理与资金投入方面的实际困难，模式的创新将会为古建筑领域带来一次变革。从注重事后补偿向事前防控的重大转变，该保险企业一直践行保险风险防控服务的庄严承诺，标志着风险防控已成为保险行业的主流趋势。

案例评述：

该保险企业将物联网技术运用到古建筑保护中，通过各种科技设备实现了灾前预警和事故应急处理的及时性。例如，利用智能传感器、监控摄像头等设备对古建筑进行实时监测，一旦发现火灾、水灾等灾害风险，系统将立即发出预警信息，使相关部门和人员能够及时采取行动。同时，该保险企业还利用物联网技术搭建了古建筑保护的数字化平台，实现了对古建筑状态的远程监控和管理，为保护古建筑提供了全方位、全天候的保障。

除灾前预警外，物联网技术还使得事故发生时的应急处理更加高效。通过智能设备的实时监测和数据反馈，保险公司可以迅速了解事故发生的情况，并协助古建筑管理单位进行应急处置，减少损失和影响。例如，当火灾或其他灾害发生时，智能系统可以自动启动灭火装置或紧急通风系统，同时向相关部门和人员发送警报信息，以便及时救援和处置。

通过"保险+物联网"的新模式，该保险企业不仅实现了古建筑的事前预防和事中处理，还提供了事后理赔的多重保障。一旦发生灾害，保险公司将迅速启动理赔程序，为古建筑管理单位提供资金支持和技术指导，帮助其尽快恢复古建筑原貌，减轻损失和重建压力。同时，通过物联网技术的数据记录和分析，保险公司可以更准确地评估损失，为古建筑提供更快速、更精准的理赔服务从而提高保障效率和客户满意度。

案例来源：

何倩楠，潘雨洁. 文物古建 平安相伴：PA 产险古建筑"服务+保险"创新解决方案全国首发［EB/OL］.（2017 - 12 - 11）［2024 - 07 - 01］. https://www.sohu.com/a/343616341_363891.

8.4　课程思政案例

案例题目：

央视新闻联播头条：点赞各地绿色发展创新举措，深圳智慧环责险服务平台位列其中

案例内容：

2021 年 8 月 3 日，央视《新闻联播》栏目头条播出专题"增减之间，绿色成为高质量发展新底色"，点赞全国各地绿色发展创新举措。深圳在绿色经济金融、生态建设领域推行的创新实践，如"智慧环责险服务平台"，也位列其中。

该平台由某头部保险平台打造，旨在以数字化手段助推鹏城绿色高质量发展。这也是该公司近一年半以来，第 9 次获得《新闻联播》关注。

《新闻联播》指出，"十四五"开局之年，中国加快生态文明建设步伐，在着力提高生态系统自我修复能力的同时，以减碳为抓手，加快促进社会经济全面绿色转型。作为中国特色社会主义先行示范区，深圳今年以来，已先后出台多项改革措施，扎实推进相关政策落地，迈出"双碳"新步伐。而由该平台打造的"智慧环责险服务平台"，便是深圳本次创新推动绿色高质量发展的重要助力之一。

为提高社会各界对立法改革后环境污染强制责任保险（以下简称"环强险"）的

认识，促进下一步的市场推广和普及活动，2021 年 7 月 28 日，深圳市生态环境局、原银保监局联合某头部保险企业召开深圳市环境污染强制责任保险启动发布会。

发布会重点介绍了深圳开展环强险制度立法改革推进情况，其中包括《深圳经济特区绿色金融条例》《深圳市环境污染强制责任保险实施办法》解读，环强险目的与意义、保险产品及费率、保险服务要求、实施计划等内容介绍。

同期，由某头部保险平台助力打造的智慧环责险服务平台成为深圳推行环强险服务的重要数字化平台，深圳将携手该公司共促生态文明建设，实现碳达峰、碳中和的目标。在发布会上，各参会领导代表、受邀嘉宾共同见证了深圳首批环强险保单的正式签约。这将是深圳以环强险实施推动绿色金融发展，以标准化、市场化的措施推动生态文明建设的重要跨越。

该公司以"金融+科技""金融+生态"双轮驱动战略为指引，全面构建数字化建设与赋能服务体系。在深圳正式启动环强险的重要阶段，智慧环责险服务平台应势而生，以数字化、平台化、市场化的理念创新业务模式、服务模式，推动企业经营者、保险公司、监管部门、环保服务机构等多方联动、协同，共建生态文明，实现碳达峰、碳中和。

据了解，智慧环责险服务平台可根据企业环境风险物质，通过物联网技术智能测算企业最低投保限额范围，根据企业选择的涉费因子测算保费，在保险费率上创新实现"千企千面"的同时，也以完整便捷的线上化投保方式推动投保流程的标准化与规范化。

在平台创新方面，该公司智慧环责险服务平台积极引入更多的商业主体和生态合作伙伴，以打造出更加完善的商业闭环，形成商业价值链。比如，环保管家的引入与服务延伸，一方面企业在投保之后就可以享受到环保专家专业、系统的环境风险管理服务咨询和指导，从而降低企业环境污染事故的发生率和环境保护处理成本，并大幅提升企业环境处理的合规率。这些都要得益于在服务创新方面，智慧环责险服务平台尝试运用物联网技术，推动投保企业接入在线监测设备，设置预警值和接收提醒，通过智慧化的手段对企业生产终端进行改进，为环境风险管理提供基础的"数据收集—分析—处理—监测"服务。

物联网的核心技术包括传感器技术、网络通信技术、云计算和大数据技术、人工智能技术等。通过这些技术的应用，物联网可以将传感器、智能设备等物理对象的信息进行收集、传输、处理和分析，从而实现对物理世界的实时监测和智能化控制。

在大数据的支持下，企业生产流程的环境风险将获得数据化的处理，使得过去难以评估、管理的环保问题有了更加清晰、明确的参考，尽可能让投保企业能从事故预防阶段就做好风险管理，将环境污染阻断在事前。

未来，在智慧环责险服务平台的支持下，一方面，在市场应用层面有利于降低企业投保的业务操作成本，增强企业的环境风险管理意识和对环责险产品的认可度、获得感；对于保险公司而言，可以实现环责险数据资产管理、线上客户管理和服务管理，还能便捷地满足监管部门管理需求。另一方面，数字化、平台化、市场化的创新路径也有利于深圳环强险业务成为全国标杆，扩大环强险业务的影响力和示范效应，为环强险业务的增长提供优质的业务基础及发展土壤。

案例评述：

从高速增长转向高质量发展，是我国经济发展的重大逻辑转换，是党中央基于对新时代我国经济发展内在规律性的科学认识作出的一个重大战略性判断，是新时代我国经济发展的一个重大理论创新和实践创新。

高质量发展要充分体现新发展理念，充分培育经济增长的新动能，充分畅通国民经济的高效循环，充分体现经济结构的高级度和产业体系的安全、韧性，充分体现参与国际经济的新优势和竞争力。

习近平总书记在党的二十大报告中指出，高质量发展是全面建设社会主义现代化国家的首要任务。要坚持以推动高质量发展为主题，把实施扩大内需战略同深化供给侧结构性改革有机结合起来，增强国内大循环内生动力和可靠性，提升国际循环质量和水平，加快建设现代化经济体系，着力提高全要素生产率，着力提升产业链、供应链韧性和安全水平，着力推进城乡融合和区域协调发展，推动经济实现质的有效提升和量的合理增长。这为我们深刻把握高质量发展的重大意义、丰富内涵和实践要求提供了根本遵循。未来乃至今后很长一段时期，我们都必须深刻把握新时代新要求，立足新发展阶段、坚持新发展理念、构建新发展格局，实现高质量发展，加快建设社会主义现代化国家。

以新一代信息通信技术为核心的物联网技术立足信息化与工业化深度融合，被广泛应用于智慧城市、智慧交通、智慧物流、智慧农业、工业互联网、智能制造等各个领域，为未来我国经济的稳定增长夯实了技术基础。如今，物联网技术已从实验室的研发环节，逐步走向政府、企业和居民生活的具体应用场景。如何推动物联网技术发挥自身优势特长，走上企业生产、运营的第一线，实现可持续的商业化应用，赋能我国经济高质量发展，已然成为迫在眉睫的现实问题。

物联网概念基于感知技术和网络通信技术，是通过连接人机物的信息、物理和功能属性，提供信息感知、传输、处理等服务的基础设施。如今，中国加快推进物联网数字经济创新发展，逐步取得了市场规模高速攀升、技术创新持续突破、示范应用陆续开展和产业生态逐步完善等一系列成就。2024 年 7 月在中国北京举行的世界物联网 500 强峰会上，世界物联网大会执委会主席何绪明在致辞中指出，中国今年建设承载物联网网络的 5G 基站有望超过 300 万个，同时，数字新经济 GDP 有望实现 30% 的增长。通过运用物联网技术赋能环责险的发展，可以有效实现污染的防治与防范化解重大风险的目标。通过利用物联网技术对环境污染进行监测与预警，可以及时地在风险发生前做出应对，在事故预防阶段就做好风险管理，将环境污染阻断在事前。

相较于传统的传感技术，物联网依赖多模态技术与智能硬件相互融合，以实现硬件产品的人工智能普惠升级。因此，物联网应用因其具有的高并发访问、多点接入、大规模数据处理等特点使得终端设备、网络通信、平台应用更易受到安全威胁。当前，在运用物联网技术进行环责险开发应用的同时，也应抓紧补齐国内物联网整体安全方案缺失的短板，完善接入控制与归属管理，整体规划物联网设备、模组、网络和系统等多层次密码安全体系，实现感知、传输、存储、分析到应用全方位数据安全保障。

作为数字中国建设中数实融合的重要抓手，物联网将是数字技术服务普罗大众的未来趋势，其良好发展对带动产业转型升级、增加产业附加值、便捷民众生活、实现经济高质量发展都有着不可小觑的积极作用。

案例来源：

深圳市生态环境局. 央视新闻联播头条点赞各地绿色发展创新举措，深圳智慧环责险服务平台位列其中！[EB/OL].（2021-08-04）[2024-07-01]. https://meeb.sz.gov.cn/xxgk/qt/gzdt/content/post_9040119. html#:~:text=.

8

Internet of Things and Insurance

This chapter mainly explains the basic ideas and principles of the integration of the Internet of Things and the insurance industry, and selects relevant domestic and foreign cases to share with students, inspiring them to develop insurance technology application scenarios and related insurance products using the Internet of Things.

8. 1   Basic Theory of the Internet of Things

8. 1. 1   What is the internet of Things?

The concept of the Internet of Things first appeared in Bill Gates's book *The Road to the Future* in 1995. In 1998, the Massachusetts Institute of Technology in the United States creatively proposed the concept of the "Internet of Things", which was then known as the EPC system. In China, the Internet of Things was originally known as the sensor network. The Chinese Academy of Sciences initiated research on the Internet of Things as early as 1999 and achieved some scientific research results. In the same year, the International Conference on Mobile Computing and Networking held in the United States proposed that "sensor networks are another development opportunity facing humanity in the next century".

The Internet of Things (IoT) refers to the interconnection of different objects and the Internet based on communication awareness technology and other media, so as to exchange information and communicate, and realize intelligent identification, management and other functions through the interconnection of all things.

8. 1. 2   Characteristics of the Internet of Things

The emergence of the Internet of Things has broken traditional thinking. In the "Internet of Things" era, reinforced concrete, cable and other equipment will be integrated with the Internet into a unified infrastructure. The essence of the Internet of Things is the fusion of the physical and digital worlds, aimed at breaking spatial limitations and achieving on-demand information acquisition, transmission, storage, fusion, and uses services between things. In summary, the Internet of Things has at least three characteristics.

8. 1. 2. 1 Overall Perception

Overall perception is one of the fundamental characteristics of the Internet of Things. The Internet of Things utilizes various sensing devices to obtain information about objects, including RFID tags, QR code tags, temperature sensors, humidity sensors, etc. Through these devices, the Internet of Things can perceive the real-time state of objects and their environment, and convert this information into data that people can process.

8. 1. 2. 2 Synchronous Transmission

Through the integration of the Internet and wireless network, the information of objects can be transmitted to people in need in real time and accurately for information exchange and sharing. This transmission process requires ensuring the accuracy and security of information to prevent it from being tampered with or stolen during transmission. In order to achieve reliable transmission, the Internet of Things adopts various communication protocols and technologies.

8. 1. 2. 3 Intelligent Processing

The Internet of Things utilizes various intelligent computing technologies such as cloud computing and fuzzy recognition to analyze and process massive data and information, perform real-time intelligent control on objects, and achieve more intelligent monitoring, control, and acquisition of processing information through various devices. This processing process typically involves techniques such as data mining and machine learning, which can process and analyze large amounts of data to extract valuable information.

In summary, the basic characteristics of the Internet of Things include overall perception, synchronous transmission, and intelligent processing. These features collaborate with each other to achieve intelligent management of objects. For example, in smart homes, through holistic perception technology, the Internet of Things can perceive the status and changes of the home environment in real time; through reliable transmission technology, the Internet of Things can transmit perceived data to the cloud for processing; through intelligent processing technology, the Internet of Things can analyze and process the collected data, achieving intelligent home management.

With the continuous development of Internet of Things technology, these features will become more prominent, bringing more convenience and value to people's lives and work.

8. 1. 3 Development Status and Prospects of the Internet of Things |——

Although the Internet of Things originated abroad, China began researching it as early as 1999. In 2009, there was a wave of concentrated research on IoT technology in China, and ever since then, rapid progress has been achieved. In 2010, IoT technology was first included in the government work report. In 2021, the Ministry of Industry and Information Technology and eight other departments jointly issued the "Three Year Action Plan for the Construction of New Infrastructure of the Internet of Things (2021-2023)". The support at the policy level has driven innovation and breakthrough development in the industry. At present, China's Internet of Things technology has initially formed a complete industrial system. In 2022, the overall industrial scale of China's Internet of Things market reached $ 210. 509 billion, with huge market prospects. According to Statista's statistics, the global IoT market size reached $ 970. 22 billion in 2022 (See Figure 8. 1). Development history of China's IoT industry see Figure 8. 2.

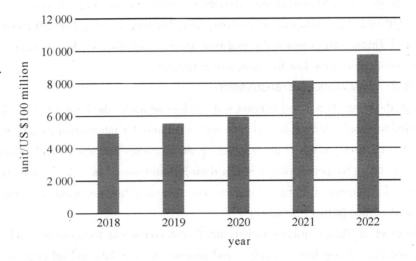

Figure 8. 1   **Global IoT market size trend from** 2018 **to** 2022 （**unit: US $ 100 million**）

Source: Statista Prospective Industry Research Institute.

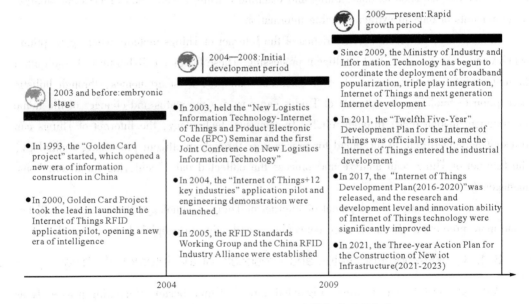

Figure 8. 2   **Development history of China's IoT industry**

Source: Statista Prospective Industry Research Institute.

8. 1. 3. 1   Significant Achievements in the Construction of IoT Infrastructure

The cellular IoT users, represented by smartphones, sensors, industrial equipment, vehicles, etc., have grown rapidly. As of the end of 2023, according to the latest statistical data from the Ministry of Industry and Information Technology, China's cellular IoT users have grown rapidly from January to November. Three basic telecommunications companies have developed 2.312 billion cellular IoT terminal users, a net increase of 467.72 million compared to the end of the preceding year, accounting for 57.3% of the total number of mobile network terminal connections. At the same time, the revenue of IoT business increased by 22.7% year-on-year, becoming a driving force for the growth of the communication industry.

8.1.3.2 The Application of the Internet of Things Promotes the Interconnection of All Things

In developed agricultural areas, sensor facilities are erected in vast fields. Farmers can accurately predict temperature, humidity, and other indicators in the fields without looking at weather forecasts. They can also accurately perceive which areas are affected by diseases and pests. The water level in the rice fields can also be accurately predicted and adjusted at any time.

According to data from the Ministry of Industry and Information Technology, as of the end of August 2023, the scale of IoT terminals applied to public services, the Internet of Vehicles, smart retail, and smart homes has reached 700 million, 440 million, 320 million, and 240 million households, respectively. According to market research firm IoT Analytics, manufacturing/industry accounts for 22% of China's IoT industry applications, ranking first; next is transportation/vehicle networking, accounting for 15%; smart energy, smart retail, smart cities, smart healthcare, and smart logistics account for 14%, 12%, 12%, 9%, and 7% respectively. With the development of the economy and society, and the progress of technological innovation, the empowerment of the Internet of Things has gradually covered various fields of life and production. At present, the Internet of Things has been widely used in industrial manufacturing, agricultural production, transportation, healthcare, power energy, environmental protection and other fields.

8.1.3.3 The Application Innovation of the Internet of Things Continues

In 2023, the China Internet of Things Conference was held in Wuxi. "Innovation and implementation of mobile device biometric identification standards, Wi-Fi networked passive RFID distributed reading and writing systems and applications, home Internet of Things edge intelligent solutions, Spider low orbit satellite Internet constellation and broadband Internet of Things applications, generalized deterministic intelligent identification network systems and core equipment, heterogeneous adaptive edge collaborative intelligent computing technology and applications, near zero power software definition of key technologies and core chips of the Internet of Things" Important technologies in the field of the Internet of Things were widely discussed, and many cutting-edge technologies were gradually being applied. With the new generation of information technology pushing the Internet of Things into a new era of development, the whole society has more expectations for the future of the Internet of Things, and there is still more application space to be developed under the high-speed development.

With the integration of new technologies such as artificial intelligence, big data, and cloud computing, the Internet of Things technology will be applied in more fields and play a greater role. For example, smart home integrates smart devices from household to household, improves the quality of life, and makes home life more efficient, convenient, and comfortable; Intelligent transportation optimizes travel routes and promotes traffic safety through big data. In addition, more fields such as smart healthcare, smart grid, smart logistics, smart agriculture, smart electricity, smart security, and smart cities will see the emergence of IoT technology in the future.

8.1.4 Development Prospects of the Internet of Things

The Internet of Things is one of the key directions for technological innovation in China, and it contains enormous potential for innovation. In recent years, with the continuous breakthroughs and widespread applications of technological innovations such as chips, sensors, RF technology, and cloud computing, the accumulation of innovative elements has promoted the rapid development of the Internet of Things and deepened its application in various practical fields. At present, with the continuous progress of China's economy and society, the demand for high-quality technological innovation is increasing day by day. The new generation of information technology is accelerating the upgrading and transformation of traditional industries, and people are increasingly valuing the role of technological innovation in improving the quality of life. This huge market demand will open up vast space for the development of IoT applications.

8.1.4.1 The Expansion and Deepening of IoT Technology Development

With the continuous development of technological progress, the Internet of Things technology is expected to be applied in a wider range of fields and play a more important role in these areas. For example, smart homes can significantly improve the quality of life by integrating each household's smart devices, making home life more efficient, convenient, and comfortable. Intelligent transportation utilizes big data integration to optimize travel routes and improve traffic safety. In addition, many fields such as smart healthcare, smart grid, smart logistics, smart agriculture, smart electricity, smart security, and smart cities will also witness the widespread application of IoT technology in the future. Overall, the development of the Internet of Things is expected to continue to maintain a high-speed growth trend.

8.1.4.2 Innovation and Integration of IoT Technology with Other Technologies

The development of IoT technology will not be singular. As a product of technological innovation in the information age, the Internet of Things technology is bound to develop together with other scientific and technological advancements, achieving mutual intersection and integration. For example, emerging scientific technologies such as artificial intelligence, big data, and cloud computing make life more convenient and comfortable. In this integration, the Internet of Things will continue to develop and innovate, and ultimately be applied to real life, in order to better serve the public.

8.2 Application of Internet of Things Technology in the Insurance Industry

The Internet of Things combines physical devices with networks, enabling the interconnection of all things on the basis of information transmission. The powerful information exchange capability of the Internet of Things has a disruptive effect on the development of the traditional insurance industry in terms of technology. The European Financial Management Association (EFMA) outlined the development trends of IoT insurance in its report "The Internet of Things: Disrupting Insurance Models". Firstly, the number of IoT devices will increase exponentially: it is expected that by 2035, the number of IoT devices will grow to 1 trillion, and the number of IoT related applications will also reach 100 million. Meanwhile, the report points out that insurance business related to the Internet of Things has been the fastest-growing area in property insurance business in recent years. Insurance companies around the world have launched a large number of insurance products and services based on the Internet of Things in the past year. In addition, the survey also showed that 45% of insurance companies believe that the Internet of Things will be the main driving force for the growth of insurance customers in the next three years. New product service model based on Internet of Things technology See Figure 8.3.

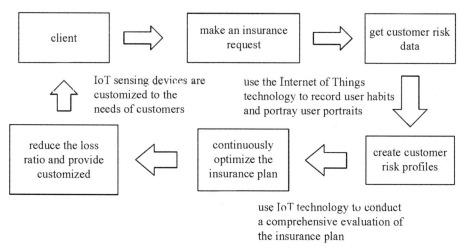

Figure 8.3 **New product service model based on Internet of Things technology**

8.2.1 IoT Technology Empowers Life Insurance and Health Insurance

At the level of insurance underwriting, IoT technology can achieve dynamic underwriting on the basis of traditional manual underwriting. In the field of life and health insurance, the traditional underwriting process mainly relies on past data and medical reports provided by customers, and determines rates based on the life cycle table. Due to information asymmetry, traditional underwriting processes may face unpredictable moral risks. However, the application of IoT technology allows for real-time tracking of policyholders' physical indicators through health monitoring devices, thereby matching customers with the most suitable insurance plans and the most accurate insurance rates. In addition, the Internet of Things can help insurance companies customize a series of big health and medical plans for customers, helping them enjoy a healthy and beautiful life.

8.2.2　IoT Technology Empowers Pension and Medical Insurance

With the intensification of social aging and the introduction of personal pension policies, our country has paid more attention to the medical care and elderly care issues of the elderly. The "silver economy" has become a frequent news focus, and major insurance companies have also launched elderly care products aimed at meeting the needs of elderly customers. At the same time, the rapid development of Internet of Things technology, especially that of relying on smart homes and the Internet of Things technology, has brought a new model of smart elderly care to the lives of the senior citizens. In China, due to the influence of traditional beliefs, the majority of elderly people prefer to live at home for retirement. However, not all children in families have the time and willingness to take care of the elders, coupled with a relative shortage of professional nursing staff in China. The medical care of the aged has therefore received widespread attention from society. The smart elderly care model deploys intelligent products and devices to enable children to monitor the elderly's home status, remind them of medication in real time, detect home safety, monitor vital signs, and even engage in direct dialogue or one click emergency response when necessary, providing high-quality remote health monitoring services.

8.2.3　IoT Technology Empowers Property Insurance, Agricultural Insurance, and Green Insurance

In the future, the role of insurance should not only be limited to compensation after accidents occur, but insurance companies should provide value-added services to customers at every stage of insurance coverage. For example, when a company takes out property insurance, the insurance company can use IoT technology to install intelligent devices for the company, enabling it to monitor safety production and factory dynamics in real time, and issue timely danger warnings. In terms of agricultural insurance, through Internet of Things technology, farmers can real-time understand the humidity, temperature, disease and pest situation of rice fields and fields at home, as well as whether there is an epidemic in livestock, achieving real-time monitoring and accurate prevention and treatment. In the field of environmental liability insurance, the application of IoT technology can deepen the cooperation between insurance companies and environmental monitoring, and efficiently obtain environmental monitoring data. When environmental information is sent to the environmental monitoring center through sensors and wireless transmission devices, insurance institutions can obtain this information, thereby improving their real-time monitoring and rapid response capabilities in terms of risks.

8. 2. 4　IoT Technology Empowers Car Insurance and Enables the Application of IoT Technology

The Internet of Vehicles is a branch of the Internet of Things that utilizes sensing technology to achieve collaborative connectivity between vehicles, between vehicles and people, and between vehicles and roads. By intelligently analyzing, processing, and making decisions on a large amount of collected data, intelligent traffic management can be achieved. Insurance companies analyze the information of vehicles and their drivers to identify common driving habits, in order to match appropriate rates for policyholders, reduce fraudulent behavior, and increase underwriting profits. This approach shifts the handling of insurance accidents from passive acceptance to active management to reduce claims costs. UBI car insurance is a quantitative insurance based on driver behavior and vehicle usage data. It uses OBD in car intelligent terminals to monitor real-time data such as mileage and fuel consumption, evaluate the risk level of car owners, and provide customized policies. Although UBI car insurance is relatively common overseas, it is still in the development stage in China. UBI car insurance achieves differentiated pricing of premiums through differences in driving mileage, but not limited to this. The data from the car sensors and driving recorders, such as actual driving time, location, and specific driving methods, are important factors in calculating insurance premiums. Car owners who engage in safe driving behavior can enjoy discounted rates. At present, the global connected car insurance market is rapidly developing, and UBI car insurance is expected to become an important trend in the development of car insurance in China.

8. 3　Foreign Cases of "Insurance + Internet of Things"

8. 3. 1　The First Case

Case Tile:

Applications for Insurance Companies in the IoT Domain

Case Content:

To provide a sense of the IoT opportunity, we looked at the most common use cases and their characteristics (See Table 8. 1). Predictive maintenance and parametric solutions are among the use cases that take advantage of the greatest numbers of IoT features. Workplace safety is even higher on the list, and its suitability for IoT technology is clearly illustrated by two examples: manufacturing environments and construction sites.

Table 8.1 **Mapping IoT to the property and casualty opportunity**

Seven Internet of Things traits	Workplace safety	Predictive maintenance	Parametric solutions for NDBI	Supply chain disruption	Building management	Catastrophic-event management
Offers an instantaneous view of something that has happened or is about to happen	√		√	√		
Usable for active risk management activities	√	√				√
Accelerates the claims adjudication process	√	√	√	√		√
Ideal for high-frequency, low-severity events	√					
Big installed base of IoT devices today		√			√	
Allows risks that were previously uninsurable to be mitigated			√	√		
Lays a foundation for new, high-value risk mitigation services	√	√	√	√		

Source: BCG analysis.

Manufacturing Environments. IoT clearly has potential in job safety applications. The workers in industrial-manufacturing environments are often exposed to hazardous materials and operate heavy equipment that can cause injuries. A risk engineer visiting such a site would see a lot to be concerned about: barrels where the pressure or heat creates an explosion risk, machine parts prone to shattering when they reach a certain level of use, and so much moving equipment that accidents are an ever-present possibility.

In the past, plant managers had no cost-effective way of mitigating these risks. That could change with IoT and, particularly, with improved analytics capabilities. The tank could be outfitted with a sensor and trigger an automatic shutdown if the pressure or heat got too high. A maintenance light could snap on when a machine part prone to shattering got within 20% of the usage level where breakdowns occur. Workers'safety helmets could be outfitted with sensors that would cause a moving vehicle to automatically stop if a machine-on-machine or machine-on-worker collision were imminent. "P" insurers can play a role in developing these risk prevention services, which would reduce their own exposure and payouts.

Construction Sites. Another promising target for IoT-enabled insurance is the commercial-construction site. Such sites face many risks—involving heavy equipment, unsafe worker practices, and inclement weather. Another type of risk, of something going wrong in the supply chain, can wreak havoc on a construction project's schedule, leading to losses that have nothing to do with physical injuries or equipment damage at the site itself.

The average construction site today may well have some devices and some level of IoT technology. But such sites are unlikely to be producing real-time insights into all the human and machine risks that exist at any given moment. Most things that could go wrong probably aren't tracked by devices, and even if such tracking is happening, the information may not be available to the "P" insurers that are providing insurance for the site. In addition, many "P" carriers are not set up to take advantage of real-time data.

IoT technology can alleviate a number of construction site risks. For instance, wearables can alert site managers to worker fatigue and sound alerts in the case of imminent danger. Computer vision can provide a first notice of loss, and sensors can detect wind levels that make certain kinds of equipment vulnerable. Site managers could get early insight into scheduling issues by arranging for information alerts in the supply chain and could buy parametric insurance contracts to hedge those risks.

Case Comments:

The application of IoT technology in insurance, particularly in industrial-manufacturing environments and construction sites, presents a significant opportunity to enhance risk management and improve safety measures. By leveraging IoT devices and enhanced analytics capabilities, insurers can play a more significant role in developing risk prevention services that not only reduce their own exposure and payouts but also prioritize the safety of workers and mitigate potential hazards. Therefore, the application of IoT technology in insurance not only enables insurers to better assess and mitigate risks but also empowers businesses to manage safety concerns proactivelyand address challenges.

Case Source:

TAGLIONI GB, REBER C, BELLIZIA N, et al. The power of the internet of things in commercial insurance[EB/OL].(2021-10-04)[2024-07-01]. https://www.bcg.com/publications/2021/commercial-insurance-should-start-testing-the-power-of-the-internet-of-things.

8.3.2　The Second Case

Case Tile:

Using IoT Connectivity to Drive Differentiation—The Internet of Things in Insurance

Case Content:

An insurer might use IoT technology to directly augment profitability by transforming the income statement's loss component. IoT-based data, carefully gathered and analyzed, might help insurers evolve from a defensive posture—spreading risk among policyholders and compensating them for losses—to an offensive posture: helping policyholders prevent losses and insurers avoid claims in the first place. And by avoiding claims, insurers could not only reap the rewards of increased profitability, but also reduce premiums and aim to improve customer retention rates. Several examples, both speculative and reallife, include:

(1) Sensors embedded in commercial infrastructure can monitor safety breaches such as smoke, mold, or toxic fumes, allowing for adjustments to the environment to head off or at least mitigate a potentially hazardous event.

(2) Wearable sensors could monitor employee movements in high-risk areas and transmit data to employers in real time to warn the wearer of potential danger as well as decrease fraud related to workplace accidents.

(3) Smart home sensors could detect moisture in a wall from pipe leakage and alert a homeowner to the issue prior to the pipe bursting. This might save the insurer from a large claim and the homeowner from both considerable inconvenience and losing irreplaceable valuables. The same can be said for placing IoT sensors in business properties and commercial machinery, mitigating property damage and injuries to workers and customers, as well as business interruption losses.

(4) Socks and shoes that can alert diabetics early on to potential foot ulcers, odd joint angles, excessive pressure, and how well blood is pumping through capillaries are now entering the market, helping to avoid costly medical and disability claims as well as potentially life-altering amputations.

Telematic sensors in the vehicle monitor an individual's driving to create personalized data collection. The connected car, via in-vehicle telecommunication sensors, has been available in some form for over a decade. The key value for insurers is that sensors can closely monitor individual driving behavior, which directly corresponds to risk, for more accuracy in underwriting and pricing.

Originally, sensor manufacturers made devices available to install on vehicles; today, some carmakers are already integrating sensors into showroom models, available to drivers— and, potentially, their insurers—via smartphone apps. The sensors collect data which, if properly analyzed, might more accurately predict the unique level of risk associated with a specific individual's driving and behavior. Once the data is created, an IoT-based system could quantify and transform it into "personalized" pricing.

Sensors' increasing availability, affordability, and ease of use break what could potentially be a bottleneck at this stage of the Information Value Loop for other IoT capabilities in their early stages.

IoT technology aggregates and communicates information to the carrier to be evaluated. To identify potential correlations and create predictive models that produce reliable underwriting and pricing decisions, auto insurers need massive volumes of statistically and actuarially credible telematics data.

In the hierarchy of auto telematics monitoring, large insurers currently lead the pack when it comes to usage-based insurance market share, given the amount of data they have already accumulated or might potentially amass through their substantial client bases. In contrast, small and midsized insurers—with less comprehensive proprietary sources—will likely need more time to collect sufficient data on their own.

To break this bottleneck, smaller players could pool their telematics data with peers either independently or through a third-party vendor to create and share the broad insights necessary to allow a more level playing field throughout the industry.

Insurers analyze data and use it to encourage drivers to act by improving driver behavior/loss costs. By analyzing the collected data, insurers can now replace or augment proxy variables (age, car type, driving violations, education, gender, and credit score) correlated with the likelihood of having a loss with those factors directly contributing to the probability of loss for an individual driver (braking, acceleration, cornering, and average speed). This is an inherently more equitable method to structure premiums: rather than paying for something that might be true about a risk, a customer pays for what is true based on his own driving performance.

Case Comments:

Insurance companies have developed in a traditional way for decades. However, new technological innovations are providing insurance companies with a new path for development. This innovation not only improves the profits of insurance companies but also strengthens their risk management capabilities. Most importantly, insurance companies have taken on more social responsibilities under the promotion and guidance of Internet of Things technology. New technologies have also helped insurers create a more favorable marketing environment, enhancing consumer experiences. It is foreseeable that the technological trend of insurance will become the main direction of the insurance industry's development in the future.

Case Source:

DELOITTE CENTER. Opting in: Using IoT connectivity to drive differentiation [R]. The Internet of Things in insurance, US, 2016.

9

保险科技监管

本章主要介绍有关保险科技的监管理论，并精选国内外相关案例与学生分享，启发学生主动思考保险科技的监管问题。

9.1 保险科技面临的风险

9.1.1 保险科技面临的风险种类

保险科技的产品及服务主要面临以下六类风险：

9.1.1.1 技术风险

互联网技术是保险科技的重要基础，相关技术风险主要分为两个方面。一是网络本身的脆弱性。网络脆弱性指的是网络中任何构成安全隐患的薄弱环节的特性。二是网络攻击风险，包括网络入侵、破坏网站、拒绝服务攻击、间谍活动和毁灭数据等。

9.1.1.2 操作风险

科技赋能保险之后，给保险业带来了后台网络维护、技术管理等问题，任何客户或员工的操作失误，都可能导致整个业务系统瘫痪，影响保险机构的正常运行。

9.1.1.3 数据风险

保险科技正处于起步阶段，一些技术手段尚未成熟，很容易导致客户数据泄露等问题。一方面，某些保险科技公司的平台软件基本框架来源于第三方，由于公司的技术力量不足和重视程度不够，原有框架内的原生系统漏洞不能被及时修复，该平台极易受到黑客或病毒的攻击，威胁保险数据的安全。另一方面，绝大多数保险产品都需用到客户的各种信息和数据，给客户的数据隐私保护带来了巨大隐患。

9.1.1.4 法规风险

完善的法律法规是保险监管顺利开展的重要前提，保险科技的法规风险主要体现为相关法律和规章制度的不健全、不完善。在金融科技时代，许多资本水平较低的小微保险机构或不受传统保险监管的科技型企业逐步进入保险市场，增加了保险风险的监管难度。特别是在保险科技法律制度和行业规范尚不完善的条件下，保险科技监管容易出现"监管套利"和"监管空白"的问题。

9.1.1.5 歧视风险

歧视风险是保险科技相对于传统保险所出现的新风险。由于科技的加持，某些人群在购买保险科技产品或服务时可能会受到来自保险公司的各种歧视。例如，保险机构可能会拒绝为基因存在某些缺陷的人承保，让投保人无法公正地享受到保险保障服务。

9.1.1.6 偿付风险

偿付能力决定着保险公司的理赔能力。如果偿付能力不达标则会影响到保险公司的正常运营，较之传统保险企业，借助科技力量的保险科技公司更容易发生盲目扩张市场规模的行为，导致偿付风险的加剧。

9.1.2 保险科技相关风险的特征

9.1.2.1 传播速度快

保险科技产品和服务依赖于数字化平台和互联网技术，并且涉及社会的方方面面，这使得保险科技的信息传播速度快、风险波及面广。一旦发生风险暴露，将会产生比传统保险风险更为严重的后果。

9.1.2.2 高度依赖科技成熟度

保险科技建立在各种科技创新基础之上，科技的成熟程度决定着保险科技产品和服务的成熟程度。因此，保险科技的风险在很大程度上依赖于所属科技的成熟度。

9.1.2.3 涉及主体多元化

在传统保险业中，保险的主体通常只有保险企业和投保人。然而，在保险科技时代，科技企业的加入和责任主体的多元化使得保险科技涉及的主体变得更加复杂。

9.2 保险科技监管的基本概念

9.2.1 保险科技监管的定义

保险监管是国家相关监管部门依据法律法规和行业准则对保险机构的市场行为和偿付能力进行监督和管理的总称。传统保险监管的方式有如下三种：

9.2.1.1 公告监管

公告监管是指保险公司自觉地将相关的资产负债，财务信息等内容报与国家金融监督管理总局等监管机构进行备案监管，而非由政府直接参与的强制监管，是一种较为宽松的监管方式。

9.2.1.2 规范监管

规范监管是指通过国家颁布一些相关的法律法规，强制所有保险市场参与主体按照所颁布的规范进行经营的监管，是一种形式上的监管方式。

9.2.1.3 实体监管

实体监管是指国家金融监督管理总局等监管单位按照国家所颁布的有关保险行业经营的法律法规，对参与保险经营活动的市场主体进行全面有效监管的方式。

根据保险科技面临的风险以及对传统保险监管的定义，保险科技监管主要是指国家保险行业监督管理部门依据相关法律法规和行业准则，对保险科技产品和服务以及保险科技企业偿付能力进行的监督和管理，以保护保险科技参与各方的合法权益，并维护保险科技市场的正常秩序。保险科技监管是国家相关部门指导和督促从事保险科技业务的市场主体控制风险的有力手段，也是推动保险科技行业健康发展的必要保障。

按照上述定义，保险科技监管的对象将不再局限于传统保险公司，而是一切提供保险科技产品和服务的市场主体。

9.2.2　保险科技监管的特点

相对于传统保险监管，保险科技监管至少存在如下三个特点，如图9.1所示。

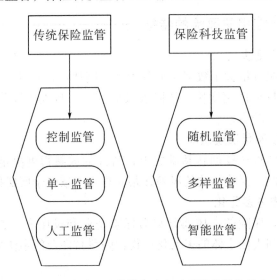

图 9.1　和传统保险监管相比保险科技监管的特点

9.2.2.1　从控制监管到随机监管

传统保险监管通过采取强制性要求和严厉处罚来实现监管保险公司的目的。但控制性监管手段刚性，方法单一。科技型保险监管倡导适应性监管理念，即监管方法、监管目标、监管制度等应根据监管对象和环境等进行适应性调整，迅速适应不同的监管情形。保险作为金融行业，具有金融的高动态性与高风险性，监管规则不可能随时跟上保险科技创新的步伐。传统保险监管的控制性只能作为保险监管一般性的框架，但除此之外还应赋予相关监管者更多的自由度。在面对众多保险科技产品时，科技型保险监管可以快速识别产品潜在风险，叫停违规违约行为，并且根据保险公司的规模、内部结构、风险水平，实施有针对性的监管。

9.2.2.2　从单一监管到多样监管

传统保险监管手段单一，主要采取事后监管模式，即监管机构通过实地监管等传统监管方式发现保险公司存在偿付能力风险时，通常其问题早已存在。随着保险科技产品日趋复杂，事后监管明显力所不足，难以有效应对各种保险科技创新产品。科技型保险监管彰显了多元化的监管路径，在传统监管的基础上，采取多种全新的监管手段。例如，人工智能技术、区块链加密技术、大数据技术等自动化监管。该监管手段具备数据客观、准确，并能对其快速做出自动分析的特点。

9.2.2.3 从人工监管到智能监管

传统保险监管主要依靠人工完成。随着保险科技的发展，仅依靠人工监管无法对保险公司庞大的信息数据进行有效监管。而且人工监管依赖个人职业道德与素养，容易引发道德风险。科技型保险监管作为全新的监管模式，具有智能化特征。第一，监管手段以"技术"为核心，以大数据、云计算等为主要内容的技术使监管效率极大提高，并能有效避免个人因受社会关系影响而做出异常监管行为。第二，数据技术运用造就精准化监管。在多变、复杂且创新频发的时代，通过数据化技术运用，可避免因时间紧迫造成监管者筛选错误的数据并据此监管的局面，从而可以实现保险科技监管的精准化。第三，科技型保险监管的动态性。保险监管者在科技型保险监管中，其数据是基于人工智能、大数据等技术手段收集、提炼、分析而来的，具备随时更新、动态监测、实时有效的特点。

9.2.3 保险科技监管的原则

保险科技日新月异，监管机构需要在鼓励创新和控制风险两方面寻求平衡，既要支持保险科技创新，又要防范保险科技所带来的新风险。保险科技监管至少需要遵循三个基本原则。

9.2.3.1 依法监管

依法监管是所有监管都应遵循的基本原则，对于创新型的保险科技监管也不例外。对于保险业务活动来说，"法无禁止即可为"，但对于监管机构来说应该时刻关注保险业务活动，尤其是保险科技的运用。

9.2.3.2 统一监管

统一监管是对传统型保险和创新型保险进行的统一监管，这是保险科技监管的首要原则。该原则有三个方面的含义：一是创新型的保险科技监管和服务应该被纳入监管范围，不能因为运用了新科技而免于监管；二是相关法律法规对传统保险业务活动的要求不能因为技术手段的创新更迭而降低标准；三是对传统型保险和创新型保险应该采用统一的规则体系。

9.2.3.3 功能监管

所有监管规则的制定都要以充分揭示业务本质为前提，要将保险科技发挥的部分保险核心功能纳入保险监管范畴，对发挥承保、风控、中介的科技创新按照传统规则实施准入管理。同时，保险监管体系要保持一定的弹性，对不断出现的保险科技产品或服务应予以及时的覆盖。

9.2.4 保险科技监管的重点

针对保险科技面临的主要风险，保险科技监管的重点存在于以下六个方面：

9.2.4.1 技术风险监管

科学技术是保险科技发展的基础。关联科技的风险将传导给保险科技产品和服务。监管部门要对应用于保险业的科技手段进行监管，确保低风险的成熟技术应用于保险行业。

9.2.4.2　操作风险监管

根据保险科技产品和服务的特性，保险科技公司将存有大量客户的信息和数据，一旦操作失误将给客户带来不可估量的损失。监管部门必须督促保险科技公司完善操作风险控制，以保障客户的利益。

9.2.4.3　数据风险监管

在保险科技时代，客户信息和数据的安全被摆在了更加突出的位置。有效的数据风险监管可以确保客户隐私不被侵犯和客户的数据不被滥用，提升客户对保险公司的信任度。监管部门可以通过建立健全保险数据安全机制及时发现并处置各种数据风险，推动保险科技的可持续发展。

9.2.4.4　完善相关法规

科技的应用变革了保险业务，传统的保险法规和监管模式很难对保险科技产品进行有效界定和监管，现有的法律框架和行业规范亟待完善。监管部门要顺应保险科技的发展趋势，建立健全相关法律法规，保护保险科技市场各参与方的合法权益，维护保险科技市场的正常秩序。

9.2.4.5　歧视风险监管

如前所述，保险科技的发展可能会对某些特定人群带来保险歧视的风险。为此，监管部门应及时出台相关管理办法，发现并制止保险科技公司滥用科技手段对某些特定人群的保险歧视行为，维护保险市场的公平，确保保险保障能惠及社会的方方面面。

9.2.4.6　偿付风险监管

面对保险科技公司可能存在盲目扩张的行为，监管部门应将保险科技市场的所有主体纳入监管范围，并采取各种手段对偿付能力进行监管，最大限度地防范保险科技公司的偿付风险。

9.2.5　保险科技监管的发展现状和趋势

9.2.5.1　国外现状

当前保险科技正在以势不可挡的趋势向全球发展。世界各国在保险科技监管上达成了一些初步共识：一方面，大数据、人工智能、区块链及物联网等科技的迅速发展为保险业带来机遇的同时也带来了全新的挑战；另一方面，全球保险监管需要进一步与时俱进，以更加先进、高效的监管制度和方法来应对保险科技发展过程中的新风险。

（1）美国

美国在20世纪就开始了保险科技的应用。1995年，很多保险公司建立了自己的专门网站。2001年，美国互联网保费收入突破了10亿美元。2010年，美国互联网保费收入已经占据总保费收入的1/4。然而，互联网保险在带来巨大贡献的同时也拥有不少隐患。例如，计算机网络通信系统本身的缺点导致数据的泄露和被盗而引发的损失风险。对此，美国通过《统一商法典》（1996）、《电子签名法案》（2000）等法规的实施来规范互联网市场，确保互联网保险交易的安全。

（2）英国

英国是最早发展互联网保险的国家，对于保险科技的监管有独到的见解。英国政府对于保险科技监管的理念是在保证监管的前提下，推动保险科技的发展。其中，最具代表性的做法是推行"监管沙盒"制度。该制度为保险初创企业提供类似"新手村"的安全地带，政府对处于安全地带的保险科技产品和服务暂时放松监管，以此加快保险科技类企业的孵化。最终成熟的保险科技产品和服务将被推广。

（3）日本

日本的保险业十分发达，被称作"保险王国"。日本对于保险科技的监管主要体现在法律法规的健全、行业自律水平的提高以及多层准入规则的实施。这些措施都为防范和化解保险科技面临的各种风险带来了保障。

9.2.5.2 国内现状

我国对保险科技发展持积极态度，保险科技监管也在随之而发展。然而，现有的监管模式在应对保险科技所面临的各种风险时仍然存在诸多不足。一是保险科技法律体系及监管政策不完善，存在合规性隐患。二是传统保险监管存在较大滞后性，监管方式创新不足。对于新兴的金融保险业务，我国一直以来采取的是先发展后监管的方式。三是数据失真和算法错误风险隐患加重，网络安全防护能力有待提升。当前我国保险科技监管存在的数据标准化程度低、数据泄露和数据孤岛等问题给专业化监管带来了重重阻碍。四是保险科技人才储备不足，国际交流合作有待加强。现阶段，保险监管机构中既懂技术又懂保险的复合型人才较少，保险科技相较于国际发展速度也较慢。

9.2.5.3 监管科技的发展

监管部门在对保险科技进行监管时，必须要创新自身的监管手段，在科技赋能的条件下大力发展监管科技。监管科技是监管与科技相结合的产物，更是各种科技手段在监管领域的具体应用。在保险科技时代，保险监管面临着现代化转型，科技如何赋能保险监管成为发展保险科技监管不可回避的问题。

保险监管通过区块链、人工智能等新技术的运用，可以开发智能化的监管工具，力求在监管活动中更加准确、更加全面地监管，在提高监管效率的同时降低监管的错误率。只有在监管工作中善于运用新技术，才能进一步提高监管的效率和透明度，真正实现科技赋能保险监管的初衷。

然而，监管科技的发展在带来便利的同时，也不可避免地会带来新问题。对于监管科技的发展过程中出现的数据泄露、技术不成熟等问题则需要监管部门和科技公司群策群力，一起解决。只有解决了现实中存在的问题，监管科技才能得到进一步发展。

9.3　国内案例

9.3.1　国内经典案例之一

案例题目：

监管长护险的黑科技

案例内容：

长期护理保险（以下简称"长护险"）制度，是指以长期处于失能状态的参保人群为保障对象，重点保障重度失能人员基本生活照料和相关医疗护理等所需费用的制度。2016年，国家组织了15个城市启动长护保险试点，目前已经扩大到了49个城市，探索解决"一人失能全家失衡"的问题。

长护险经过七年试点，阶段成效显著，各试点城市长护险基金支付水平大部分达到了70%，减轻了家庭的长期护理负担。截至2022年年底，长护险参保人数达到1.69亿，累计有195万人享受待遇，累计支出基金624亿元，人均年支出1.4万元（如图9.2所示）。试点地区的护理服务体系得到发展，试点地区服务机构总数达到7 600家，是原来的4倍，护理人员数从原来的3万多人增加到33万人。

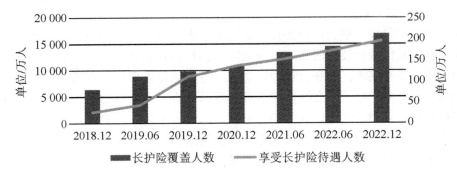

图9.2 我国长护险的发展数据

图片来源：搜狐网.

然而，随着试点的深入推进，长护险独特的特点给监管带来了严峻挑战。长护险服务场所为居家场景，具有人群基数大、分布面广、私密性强等特征。手机App、摄像头、电话随访等常规手段不能满足长护险的监管需求，监管细节漏洞较多，无法精准确认护理时间、护理位置、护理内容、护理对象、护理质量等服务情况。为确保长护险基金用到实处，切实提高失能人员的生活质量，亟须织密长护险服务监管"智能网"，通过科技手段实现服务全流程监管，确保服务质量。

通过部署生物雷达监测仪，利用生物雷达收集数据，可分析被检测人员在床上的细微运动来判断是否在假装卧床。智能设备实时上传患者体征数据，将数据传输到云端后台，通过AI算法分析，能精准检测患者是否离床及在室内的活动轨迹，并清楚了解患者的失能程度。如果被检测对象被认为是假装卧床的人员，系统可以根据事先设定的结果发出警报，通知有关人员到监管中心，以便采取相应的措施。有效杜绝了长护险评估过程中普遍存在的"轻度重评"现象，最大程度地节约医保基金开支，为基金做好"守门员"。

通过专门的"国云智护"设备对护理人员、护理时间、护理位置、护理内容、护理对象、护理质量的合规性实时监测，实现验证何时何地服务人员、服务对象做了什么、做得怎么样、服务对象是否满意等，准确、清晰地还原每一次居家服务。服务有了"记录员"，通过人工智能算法，生物雷达的微波效应，监管角度更加立体、全面，为精准监管、科学决策提供了依据。

智能化监管手段彻底解放了护工双手，规避了护理员服务中出现的不良现象，提高了服务质量。通过人脸识别、精准定位，实现自动打卡，杜绝了代打卡；通过设定电子围栏，自动记录服务时长，杜绝了假服务；通过在系统内置水印相机，护工提供多服务场景照片，进一步验证了服务的真实情况；通过系统可查询护理员服务内容、次数、时长等数据。

ZQGY 数据科技有限公司是"ZQGY 集团"旗下二级公司，主要经营能源大数据和康养大数据业务，公司兼具央企公信力和市场灵活性，充分参与全国数字经济发展、数字社会建设的进程。

历经两年深度研发，投入资金 6 500 余万元，ZQGY 技术团队已成功研发出了具有自主知识产权的"国云智护"系统。它综合了国内 49 个试点城市几乎所有的问题及需求，补齐了市面上现有监管模式的不足及短板，创新性地以人工智能算法、生物雷达技术、软硬件结合的模式从根本上解决了长护险监管的难题，是目前国内技术领先、实用性强、性价比高的行业解决方案。该系统使长护险经办、服务、监管全程智能化，切实为医保监管长护险服务的合规性、真实性、实时性、多样性提供高效率、可追溯的数据。

案例评述：

长护险因为保障对象的特殊性，决定了对其采用传统监管方式的困难。通过部署生物雷达监测仪和采用人工智能算法等科技手段，对长护险的精准监管存在以下重要意义：

（1）从评估入口堵住了"评估注水"现象，防止医保基金被骗；

（2）从服务全流程实现了数字化、可视化监管，相当于全程安排了监督员，提高了监管精准度；

（3）有效提升护理机构运营效率，让护理行业得以更健康发展；

（4）保护了客户隐私的同时让保障对象体验到更好的服务，有更好的幸福感和获得感；

（5）净化行业风气，推动产业发展，长护险护理服务通过以上规范化运作，能最大限度地净化混入行业的"李鬼"，让造假者无处遁形；

总之，科技的加持有效解决了长护险的监管难题，对于提升其他保险科技产品和服务的监管水平具有较强的借鉴意义。

案例来源：

智能居家养老. 长护险监管黑科技，全方位监管服务全过程［EB/OL］.（2023－08－14）［2024－07－01］. http://news.sohu.com/a/711632034_100064556.

9.3.2　国内经典案例之二

案例题目：

广东银保监局监管数字化转型创新实践

案例内容：

广东是我国改革开放的排头兵、先行地、实验区，是《粤港澳大湾区发展规划纲要》落地实施的核心区，金融主体多元、市场交易活跃、创新要素集聚、产业体系完备、人才资本雄厚，有能力、有条件在探索监管科技应用、促进监管数字化转型、以智慧监管引领金融高质量发展等方面贡献更多先行先试经验。

近年来，广东银保监局坚决贯彻执行党中央、国务院的决策部署和原中国银保监会的总体工作安排，围绕建设国际金融枢纽这一总体定位，提高政治站位，深化改革创新，加强多方联动，大力支持银行保险业运用前沿技术促进行业创新，积极研究"智慧监管"实践图谱，稳步推进数字化转型项目落地应用，以科技赋能为建设粤港澳大湾区提供金融支持。

9.3.2.1 立足数据挖掘，实现穿透式监管

通过推动大数据技术和人工智能在监管领域的应用，发挥监管科技的潜能，提高监管者对系统性风险的识别监测和防范能力，为行业行稳致远保驾护航。

实践之一：大数据风险预警系统

为进一步提高数据分析效率，降低建模难度，实现快速跨行分析及资金追踪，广东银保监局以 EAST 系统（中国银保监会检查分析系统，examination and analysis system technology）为基础，开发了"大数据风险预警系统"，实现了高效、快速、便捷的跨行监管数据分析。"大数据风险预警系统"可以根据监管人员的需求，灵活构建各类风险监测和检查分析模型，并通过对多家机构 EAST 数据的关联查询和深度分析，及时、精准、客观地识别风险状况。

截至 2021 年 2 月底，大数据风险预警系统累计采集数据 70 余 T，累计模型总数为 1 959 个，近两年现场协查查询次数近 7.5 万次，流水查询效率提升 50% 以上，800 亿条交易流水记录达到秒级返回查询结果，实现数据概览、可视化建模、流水追踪、专题风险预警等功能，极大地提高了非现场监测分析的精准打击能力。

未来将加强与地方政务数据管理部门、地方金融监管部门合作共享，拓宽数据采集范围，丰富大数据挖掘场景，探索将"大数据风险预警系统"应用在非现场监管、日常监测分析、市场准入、公司治理评估等监管流程。

9.3.2.2 立足监管信息化建设，深化"放管服"改革

通过加强系统建设，提升监管信息化水平，加速内部管理运行，提高监管资源配置效率和监管能力，推进金融监管供给侧结构性改革，放得更活、管得更准、服务更优，让金融监管成为金融高质量发展的强大助推剂。

实践之二：广东银保监局准入备案管理系统（大湾区试用版）

为推进"放管服"改革，进一步规范、简化准入备案流程，广东银保监局运用区块链技术建设了"广东银保监局准入备案管理系统（大湾区试用版）"，实现大湾区辖内银行保险业机构高管和机构备案全流程电子化运行，备案时间为每周 7×24 小时，备案流程最长只需 5 分钟。首笔报告事项于 2021 年 1 月 29 日正式落地，标志着准入管理模式由传统的"线下"进入"线上"时代，准入管理周期由过去的"月度"进入全天候"分秒"时代。

与此同时，系统还具有从业人员处罚信息一键关联、确认回执自动秒达、办理时限智能提醒以及多维度统计查询等功能，为行政许可的准入备案监督管理工作提供了强大支撑。未来将继续强化数据整合、挖掘和分析，并探索将系统适用范围复制推广至全辖区银行业、保险业机构，确保简政放权事项"放下去、接得住、管得好"。

9.3.2.3 立足构建高质量发展新格局，探索跨机构数据安全共享新机制

通过完善监管数据标准和推进数据共享平台建设，引领金融机构强化数据治理，扩展数据渠道，夯实数据基础，发挥数据价值，为金融行业的高质量发展提供新动能。

实践之三：基于区块链的数据共享平台

中小银行因自身发展历程短、客户群底子薄，在风控模型应用中对外部数据需求强烈，但是跨机构及跨行业的数据共享缺乏合理有效的共享机制和安全可控的应用环境。自 2019 年起，广东银保监局组织辖区内 5 家银行机构探索利用区块链技术搭建

"弱中心化"的数据共享平台。

目前，该平台已上线外包风险信息共享模块、银行业从业人员处罚信息共享模块，并正在建设统计信息共享模块，共覆盖全辖区656家银行业金融机构，共享信息两万余条，查询五千余次，为银行业信息共享提供可靠数据渠道，构筑行业信息"过滤网"。

2021年，广东银保监局进一步探索联邦学习在EAST数据跨行共享中的应用，参与各方不需共享数据，仅加密交换模型参数实现联合建模，在数据"可用不可见"的前提下，达到了数据产权保护和数据价值挖掘共享的"不可能双目标"，并以此推动了行业整体风控能力的提升。

未来，广东银保监局将以"共建共治共享"为基本原则，进一步向辖内银行保险机构推广应用工作成果，逐步扩大业务数据类型和范围，开放接纳更多机构接入平台，并进一步采用联邦学习的方式，联合各机构开展跨行建模，并共享模型结果，提升银行保险机构的风险及合规管理水平。

案例评述：

习近平总书记指出，高质量发展不只是一个经济要求，而是对经济社会发展方方面面的总要求。党的十九届五中全会提出，要坚持创新在我国现代化建设全局中的核心地位，深入实施创新驱动发展战略，建设科技强国、数字中国，推进国家治理体系和治理能力现代化。随着实体经济和银行保险业的加速数字化，银行保险业监管的内涵与外延都发生了巨大变化，需要监管由规制监管、经验监管、线下监管等传统监管逐步迈向智慧监管。

智慧监管是金融监管部门在关键核心技术自主可控及网络安全风险有效防御的前提下，运用信息技术和数据驱动监管方式变革，通过积极应用人工智能、区块链、云计算、大数据等科技实现金融监管数字化转型，融合各方数据，挖掘数据价值，实现全方位态势感知、多维度分析评估和实时化预警处置。

案例来源：

慧保天下. 广东银保监局裴光：智慧监管的全境实施路径思考［EB/OL］. (2021-04-23)［2024-07-01］. https://finance.sina.com.cn/money/insurance/bxdt/2021-04-25/doc-ikmyaawc1453230. shtml.

9.4 课程思政案例

案例题目：

保险科技监管助力社会主义法治建设

案例内容：

医疗保障基金是人民群众的"看病钱"，事关人民群众切身利益，事关医疗保障制度健康持续发展，事关国家长治久安。国家历来高度重视医保领域的骗保行为，最高人民法院、最高人民检察院、公安部为依法惩治医保骗保犯罪，维护医疗保障基金安全，维护人民群众合法权益，根据有关规定，于2024年3月联合制定了《关于办理医保骗保刑事案件若干问题的指导意见》。

在此背景下，TXJK"基于医保大数据的精准医保基金监管解决方案"，在行业内首次提出针对医保基金的团伙骗保发现算法模型，以及线上支付事前拦截等方案，解决了传统监管方式依赖人力，成本高、效率低、监管力量不足的问题。

实现路径一是构建画像。精准医保基金监管解决方案的算法模型可以根据时间序列进行参保人之间的构图，利用图算法进行网络挖掘，找到密度不一的大大小小的关系网，主动发现人群异常点，从而快速获取不同类型的作案团伙集合。二是智能分析。算法模型通过多维度分析形成团伙序列，并对团伙行为进行一致性分析，提炼出新规则。通过提炼的新规则和标签传播算法，进行团伙扩散，就可以找到更多的群体行为一致的参保人，从而识别出医保行为异常的重点人群，实现发现精准团伙，为有关部门全面监管、科学决策提供智能解决方案。

精准医保基金监管解决方案有两项核心竞争力。一是依托 TX 大数据能力开发的团伙骗保发现算法模型填补了现有监管系统中只能发现单人、单次就诊违规的空白。二是依托 TX 连接能力构建的医保公共服务体系，打通了"医保局—两定机构—参保单位—参保人"的连接平台，有效拓展了医保服务的广度和深度，有助于法治建设。

案例评述：

法治是社会主义核心价值观的重要内容，更是我国社会长治久安的重要保障。保险监管是维护社会主义法治和社会公平正义的一支重要力量。

用科技赋能保险监管，助力法治建设已经成为防范保险欺诈的重要手段。TXJK 在行业内构建针对医保基金的团伙骗保发现算法模型，通过勾画图像和智能分析，解决了传统监管模式依靠人力，效率低下等"难点""痛点"问题。同时精准医保基金监管解决方案依托大数据能力开发的团伙骗保发现，算法模型和依托 TX 构建的医保公共服务体系有效杜绝了医保领域的骗保行为。

总之，"科技+保险"监管有力地维护了保险行业的法治环境，其能有效遏制保险欺诈等不法行为的发生，进而推进社会主义法治建设。

案例来源：

人民网研究院. 2022 内容科技应用典型案例：腾讯健康"基于医保大数据的精准医保基金监管解决方案"［EB/OL］.（2023－05－26）［2024－07－01］. https://baijiahao. baidu.com/s？id＝17669253212193332335&wfr＝spider&for＝pc.

9

Regulation of InsurTech

This chapter mainly introduces regulatory theories related to InsurTech, and selects relevant domestic and foreign cases to share with students, inspiring them to actively think about regulatory issues in InsurTech.

9. 1　Risks Faced by InsurTech

9. 1. 1　Types of Risks Faced by InsurTech

The products and services of InsurTech mainly face the following types of risks.

9. 1. 1. 1　Technical Risks

Internet technology is an important foundation of InsurTech, and related technical risks can be mainly divided into two aspects. The first is the vulnerability of the network itself. Network vulnerability refers to the characteristics of any weak link in the network that constitutes a security hazard. The second is the risk of cyber attacks. This includes network intrusion, website destruction, denial of service attacks, espionage activities, and data destruction.

9. 1. 1. 2　Operational Risks

After technology empowers insurance, it brings problems such as backend network maintenance and technical management to the insurance industry. Any operational error by customers or employees may lead to the paralysis of the entire business system, affecting the normal operation of insurance institutions.

9. 1. 1. 3　Data Risks

InsurTech is in its early stages, and some technological means are not yet mature, which can easily lead to problems such as customer data leakage. On the one hand, the basic framework of some InsurTech companies' platform software comes from third parties. Due to the insufficient technical strength and importance of the company, native system vulnerabilities within the original framework cannot be repaired in a timely manner, making the platform extremely vulnerable to hackers or virus attacks, threatening the security of insurance data. On the other hand, the vast majority of insurance products require the use of various customer information and data, posing significant risks to customer data privacy protection.

9.1.1.4　Regulatory Risks

Sound laws and regulations are an important prerequisite for the smooth implementation of insurance supervision. The regulatory risks of InsurTech mainly reflect the inadequacy and incompleteness of relevant laws and regulations. In the era of financial technology, many small and micro insurance institutions with lower capital levels or technology-based enterprises that are not subject to traditional insurance supervision gradually enter the insurance market, increasing the difficulty of insurance risk supervision. Especially under the conditions where the legal system and industry norms of InsurTech are not yet perfect, there is a risk of regulatory arbitrage and regulatory gaps in InsurTech regulations.

9.1.1.5　Discrimination Risks

Discrimination risk is a new risk that InsurTech poses compared to traditional insurance. Due to the advancement of technology, certain groups of people may face various forms of discrimination from insurance companies when purchasing InsurTech products or services. For example, insurance institutions may refuse to insure individuals with certain genetic defects, making it difficult for policyholders to fairly enjoy insurance coverage services.

9.1.1.6　Repayment Risks

The solvency determines the claims ability of an insurance company. If the solvency is not up to standard, it will affect the normal operation of insurance companies. Compared to traditional insurance companies, InsurTech companies are more likely to blindly expand their market size with the help of technology, leading to increased solvency risks.

9.1.2　Characteristics of Risks Related to InsurTech

9.1.2.1　Fast propagation Speed

InsurTech products and services rely on digital platforms and Internet technology, and involve all aspects of society, which makes InsurTech information spread faster and risks spread more widely. Once a risk exposure occurs, it will result in more severe consequences than traditional insurance risks.

9.1.2.2　Highly Dependent on Technological Maturity

InsurTech is built on various technological innovations, and the maturity of technology determines the maturity of InsurTech products and services. Therefore, the risk of InsurTech largely depends on the maturity of the technology it belongs to.

9.1.2.3　Involving Subject Diversification

In traditional insurance industry, the main body of insurance is usually only insurance companies and policyholders. However, in the era of InsurTech, the addition of technology enterprises and the diversification of liability subjects have made the subjects involved in InsurTech more complex.

9.2 Basic Concepts of InsurTech Regulation

9.2.1 Definition of InsurTech Regulation ├────────────

Insurance supervision is a general term for the supervision and management of the market behavior and solvency of insurance institutions by relevant national regulatory authorities in accordance with laws, regulations, and industry standards. There are several traditional ways of insurance regulation:

9.2.1.1 Announcement Regulation

Announcement regulation refers to insurance companies voluntarily reporting relevant assets, liabilities, financial information, and other contents to regulatory agencies such as the National Financial Supervision and Administration for filing and supervision, rather than mandatory supervision directly participated by the government. It is a relatively relaxed regulatory approach.

9.2.1.2 Standardized Regulation

Standardized regulation refers to the formal supervision of all insurance market participants to operate in accordance with the regulations issued by the state through the promulgation of relevant laws and regulations.

9.2.1.3 Physical Regulation

Entity supervision refers to the comprehensive and effective supervision of market entities participating in insurance business activities by regulatory units such as the National Financial Supervision and Administration in accordance with the relevant laws and regulations on insurance industry operations issued by the state.

According to the risks faced by InsurTech and the definition of traditional insurance regulation, InsurTech regulation mainly refers to the supervision and management of InsurTech products and services as well as the solvency of InsurTech enterprises by the national insurance industry supervision and management department in accordance with relevant laws, regulations and industry standards, in order to protect the legitimate rights and interests of all parties involved in InsurTech and maintain the normal order of the InsurTech market. InsurTech regulation is a powerful means for relevant national departments to guide and supervise market entities engaged in InsurTech business to control risks, and it is also a necessary guarantee for promoting the healthy development of the InsurTech industry.

According to the above definition, the object of InsurTech regulation will no longer be limited to traditional insurance companies, but all market entities that provide InsurTech products and services.

9.2.2 Characteristics of InsurTech Regulation ├────────────

Compared to traditional insurance regulations, InsurTech regulations have at least the following characteristics (See Figure 9. 1).

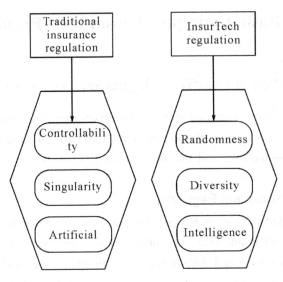

Figure 9. 1   **Charact ristics of InsurTech regulation compared to traditional insurance regulation**

9. 2. 2. 1   From Control Regulation to Random Regulation

Traditional insurance regulation achieves the goal of regulating insurance companies by a-dopting mandatory requirements and severe penalties. But the regulatory measures are rigid and the methods are single. Technology-based insurance regulation advocates the concept of adaptive regulation, which means that regulatory methods, objectives, and systems should be adjusted according to the regulatory objects and environment, and quickly adapt to different regulatory situations. As a financial industry, insurance has high dynamism and high risks in finance, and regulatory rules cannot always keep up with the pace of InsurTech innovation. The controllability of traditional insurance regulation can only serve as a general framework for insurance regulations, and in addition, relevant regulators should be given more freedom. When facing numerous InsurTech products, technology-based insurance supervision can quickly identify potential risks of the products, stop violations and defaults, and implement targeted supervision based on the size, internal structure, and risk level of insurance companies.

9. 2. 2. 2   From Single Regulation to Diverse Regulation

The traditional insurance regulatory methods are single and mainly adopt a post supervision model. When regulatory agencies discover the solvency risk of insurance companies through traditional regulatory methods such as on-site supervision, the problem usually already exists. With the increasing complexity of InsurTech products, post event supervision is clearly inadequate, making it difficult to effectively respond to various innovative InsurTech products. The regulation of technology-based insurance demonstrates a diversified regulatory path, adopting various new regulatory measures on the basis of traditional regulation. For example, artificial intelligence technology, blockchain encryption technology, big data technology, and other automated supervision technologies. This regulatory approach has the characteristics of objective and accurate data, as well as the ability to quickly and automatically analyze it.

9. 2. 2. 3　From Manual Supervision to Intelligent Regulation

Traditional insurance supervision mainly relies on manual work. With the development of InsurTech, relying solely on manual supervision cannot form effective supervision with the vast information data of insurance companies. Moreover, manual supervision relies on individual professional ethics and literacy, which can easily lead to moral risks. As a new regulatory model, technology-based insurance regulation has intelligent characteristics. Firstly, regulatory measures are centered around "technology", with technologies such as big data and cloud computing as the main content, greatly improving regulatory efficiency and effectively avoiding individuals from engaging in abnormal regulatory behavior due to social relationships. Secondly, the application of data technology creates precise supervision. In an era of variability, complexity, and frequent innovation, the application of data-driven technology can avoid the situation where regulators screen incorrect data due to time constraints and rely on it for supervision, thus achieving precision in InsurTech regulation. Thirdly, the dynamism of technology-based insurance regulation. In technology-based insurance supervision, insurance regulators collect, refine, and analyze data based on technical means such as artificial intelligence and big data, which are characterized by real-time updates, dynamic monitoring, and real-time effectiveness.

9. 2. 3　Principles of InsurTech Regulation

InsurTech is advancing rapidly, and regulatory agencies need to seek a balance between encouraging innovation and controlling risks. They need to support InsurTech innovation while also preventing new risks brought about by InsurTech. The regulation of InsurTech needs to follow at least three basic principles.

9. 2. 3. 1　Legal Regulation

Legal supervision is a fundamental principle that all regulations should follow, and innovative InsurTech regulation is no exception. For insurance business activities, it can be done without any prohibition by law, but for regulatory agencies, they should always pay attention to insurance business activities, especially the application of InsurTech.

9. 2. 3. 2　Unified Regulation

Unified supervision is the primary principle of InsurTech regulation, which is the unified regulation of traditional and innovative insurance. This principle has three meanings: firstly, innovative InsurTech regulations and services should be included in the regulatory scope, and cannot be exempted from regulations due to the use of new technologies; secondly, the requirements of relevant laws and regulations for traditional insurance business activities cannot be lowered due to the innovation and replacement of technological means; thirdly, a unified rule system should be adopted for both traditional and innovative insurance.

9. 2. 3. 3　Functional Regulation

The formulation of all regulatory rules should be based on fully revealing the essence of the business, and the part of InsurTech that plays the core function of insurance should be included in the scope of insurance supervision. Access management should be implemented according to traditional rules for technological innovation in underwriting, risk control, and intermediary. At the same time, the insurance regulatory system should maintain a certain degree of flexibility and provide timely coverage for constantly emerging InsurTech products or services.

9.2.4 Key Points of InsurTech Regulation

In response to the main risks faced by InsurTech, there are at least the following key aspects of InsurTech regulations.

9.2.4.1 Technical Risk Regulation

Science and technology are the foundation for the development of InsurTech. The risks of related technologies will be transmitted to InsurTech products and services. Regulatory authorities should regulate the means used for technology in the insurance industry to ensure that low-risk mature technologies are applied to the insurance industry.

9.2.4.2 Operational Risk Regulation

According to the characteristics of InsurTech products and services, InsurTech companies will have a large amount of customer information and data, and any operational errors will bring incalculable losses to customers. Regulatory authorities must urge InsurTech companies to improve operational risk control to protect the interests of customers.

9.2.4.3 Data Risk Regulation

In the era of InsurTech, the security of customer information and data has been placed in a more prominent position. Effective data risk supervision can ensure that customer privacy is not violated and customer data is not abused, enhancing customer trust in insurance companies. Regulatory authorities can timely detect and dispose of various data risks by establishing and improving insurance data security mechanisms, promoting the sustainable development of InsurTech.

9.2.4.4 Improve Relevant Regulation

The application of technology has revolutionized the insurance business, and traditional insurance regulations and regulatory models are difficult to effectively define and regulate InsurTech products. The existing legal framework and industry norms urgently need to be improved. Regulatory authorities should comply with the development trend of InsurTech, establish and improve relevant laws and regulations, protect the legitimate rights and interests of all parties involved in the InsurTech market, and maintain the normal order of the InsurTech market.

9.2.4.5 Discrimination Risk Regulation

As mentioned earlier, the development of InsurTech may bring risks of insurance discrimination to certain specific groups and individuals. In this regard, regulatory authorities should promptly introduce relevant management measures to detect and stop InsurTech companies from abusing technological means to discriminate against certain specific groups of people, maintain fairness in the insurance market, and ensure that insurance protection can benefit all aspects of society.

9.2.4.6 Repayment Risk Regulation

Faced with the potential blind expansion behavior of InsurTech companies, regulatory authorities should include all entities in the InsurTech market in their regulatory scope and take various measures to strengthen their solvency supervision, in order to prevent the solvency risks of InsurTech companies to the greatest extent possible.

9.2.5 Development Status and Trends of InsurTech Regulation ├──

9.2.5.1 International Status Quo

The current InsurTech is developing globally with an unstoppable trend. Countries around the world have reached some preliminary consensus on InsurTech regulations: on the one hand, the rapid development of technologies such as big data, artificial intelligence, blockchain, and the Internet of Things has brought opportunities and new challenges to the insurance industry; on the other hand, global insurance regulation needs to further keep up with the times and respond to new risks in the development of InsurTech with more advanced and efficient regulatory systems and methods.

(1) The United States

The United States began the application of InsurTech in the last century. In 1995, many insurance companies established their own specialized websites. In 2001, the Internet premium income in the United States exceeded $ 1 billion. In 2010, Internet premium income in the United States accounted for a quarter of the total premium income. However, while Internet insurance has brought great contributions, it also has many hidden dangers. For example, the inherent shortcomings of computer network communication systems lead to the risk of data leakage and theft, resulting in losses. In this regard, the United States standardized the Internet market through the implementation of the Uniform Commercial Code (1996), the Electronic Signature Act (2000) and other regulations to ensure the security of Internet insurance transactions [from InsurTech, Zhu Jinyuan, Liu Yong, Wei Li].

(2) The UK

The UK is the first country to develop Internet insurance, and has unique views on the regulation of InsurTech. The UK government's philosophy for regulating InsurTech is to promote the development of InsurTech while ensuring regulations. The most representative approach is to implement a "regulatory sandbox" system. This system provides a safe zone similar to a "novice village" for insurance startups, and the government temporarily relaxes supervision on InsurTech products and services in the safe zone to accelerate the incubation of InsurTech enterprises. The final mature InsurTech products and services will be promoted.

(3) Japan

Japan's insurance industry is very developed and is known as the "insurance kingdom". Japan's regulation of InsurTech is mainly reflected in the sound laws and regulations, the improvement of industry self-discipline, and the implementation of multi-level access rules. These measures provide protection for preventing and resolving various risks faced by InsurTech [source from InsurTech: Zhu Jinyuan, Liu Yong, Wei Li].

9.2.5.2 China

China has a positive attitude towards the development of InsurTech, and InsurTech regulation is also developing accordingly. However, the existing regulatory model still has many short-comings in dealing with various risks faced by InsurTech. One is the imperfect legal system and regulatory policies of InsurTech, which poses compliance risks. Secondly, there is a significant lag in traditional insurance regulation and insufficient innovation in regulatory methods. For emerging financial and insurance businesses, China has always adopted a development followed by regulation approach. Thirdly, the risks of data distortion and algorithm errors are increasing, and the network security protection capabilities need to be improved. The low degree of data standardization, data leakage, and data silos in China's InsurTech supervision currently pose significant obstacles to professional supervision. Fourthly, the reserve of InsurTech talents is insufficient, and international exchange and cooperation need to be strengthened. At present, there are relatively few composite talents in insurance regulatory agencies who understand both technology and insurance, and the development speed of InsurTech is also relatively slow compared to international standards.

9.2.5.3 The Development of Regulatory Technology

When regulating InsurTech, regulatory authorities must improve their own regulatory methods and vigorously develop regulatory technology under the conditions of technology empowerment. Regulatory technology is a product of the combination of regulation and technology, and it is also the specific application of various technological means in the field of regulation. In the era of InsurTech, insurance regulation is facing modernization transformation, and how technology empowers insurance regulation has become an unavoidable issue in the development of InsurTech regulation.

Insurance regulation can develop intelligent regulatory tools through the application of new technologies such as blockchain and artificial intelligence, striving for more accurate and comprehensive insurance regulation in regulatory activities, while improving regulatory efficiency and reducing regulatory error rates. Only by skillfully utilizing new technologies in regulatory work can we further improve the efficiency and transparency of regulation, and truly achieve the original intention of technology empowering insurance regulation.

However, while the development of regulatory technology brings convenience, it inevitably brings new problems. For the problems such as data leakage and immature technology that arise during the development of regulatory technology, it is necessary for regulatory authorities and technology companies to work together to solve them. Only by solving the problems that exist in reality can regulatory technology further develop.

9.3 Foreign Cases of Insurance Regulation and Technology

9.3.1 The First Case

Case Tile:

Network analysis tools for MAS

Case Content：

The Monetary Authority of Singapore (MAS) is developing a network analysis tool to analyse interconnectedness between insurers and reinsurers. The tool will use graph visualisation as well as pattern recognition algorithms. It will aim to identify interconnectedness in terms of risk transfers and exposures between insurers and reinsurers. As such, it will also identify concentration risks within the insurance industry. For example, several insurers may cede risks to the same reinsurer. If the reinsurer fails, this will impact cedent insurers. The tool will be able to identify which insurers and reinsurers are interconnected through these activities. Moreover, it will be able to assess the systemic importance of reinsurers and can inform the design of scenarios for industry-wide stress testing exercises. The tool's analysis will be able to focus on a specific line of business and the type of reinsurer, as well as different cession or recoverable ratios.

Case Comments：

The development of a network analysis tool by the Monetary Authority of Singapore (MAS) has showed the advantages of InsurTech in insurance supervision. By embracing cutting-edge tools for analysis and supervision, regulators can proactively identify and address risks, ultimately contributing to a more secure and resilient insurance sector.

Case Source：

OCAMPO D G, LEHTMETS A, PANDEY M, et al.: Suptech in insurance supervision [EB/OL].(2022-12-01)[2024-07-01] https://www.bis.org/fsi/publ/insights47. pdf.

9.3.2 The Second Case

Case Tile：

EIOPA is developing a Cooperation Platform

Case Content：

EIOPA is developing a Cooperation Platform to enable the use of an efficient notification system, and the exchange of information for the purposes of updating and maintaining the European register of insurance undertakings. The platform aims to promote an efficient and traceable exchange of information between home and host national competent authorities (NCAs), thereby addressing inconsistencies identified in national registers maintained by NCAs and the European register maintained by EIOPA. The inconsistencies, which resulted from the current approach, not only put in question the reliability of the national and European registers, they also expose the NCAs and EIOPA to legal and reputational risks. The platform allows for cross-border notifications and provides an interface to automatically update the EIOPA register based on cross-border information exchanged through the platform. NCAs may also follow the same approach and develop an API to use the information exchanged through the platform to automatically update their own registers. On top of the incremental information exchanges, a periodic full submission to the European register will be requested to allow cross-checking of the data received via incremental exchanges, as well as to capture data not exchanged on the platform, ie mainly undertakings with no cross-border activity. For this full submission, NCAs will be required to send information from a home authority perspective only, to allow for the cross-checking of data received from different NCAs and the European register. If there is a discrepancy, the platform will be used to notify all relevant authorities.

Case Comments:

The Cooperation Platform exemplifies how InsurTech can revolutionize supervision by fostering collaboration and enhancing data accuracy within the insurance industry.

Case Source:

OCAMPO D G, LEHTMETS A, PANDEY M, et al. Suptech in insurance supervision [EB/OL]. (2022-12-01) [2024-07-01] https://www.bis.org/fsi/publ/insights47.pdf.

参考文献

巴曙松，白海峰，2016. 金融科技的发展历程与核心技术应用场景探索 [J]. 清华金融评论（11）：99-103.

陈小平，2021. 人工智能伦理导引 [M]. 合肥：中国科学技术大学出版社.

陈珏，2004. 对我国保险业当前面临困境的思考 [J]. 新疆金融（11）：50-53.

程虹，陈文津，李唐，2018. 机器人在中国：现状、未来与影响：来自中国企业-劳动力匹配调查（CEES）的经验证据 [J]. 宏观质量研究，6（3）：1-21.

仇新红，2020. 区块链技术发展现状及前景探究 [J]. 合作经济与科技（6）：58-60.

窦笑，霍国庆，2024. 机器人发展的三种模式及其政策价值 [J]. 智库理论与实践，9（1）：64-70.

段伟文，2015. 机器人伦理的进路及其内涵 [J]. 科学与社会，5（2）：35-45，54.

封锡盛，2015. 机器人不是人，是机器，但须当人看 [J]. 科学与社会，5（2）：1-9.

郭滕达，2023. 中国区块链发展的现状与思考：基于社会信用体系构建的视角 [J]. 征信，41（7）：43-48.

龚强，班铭媛，张一林，2021. 区块链、企业数字化与供应链金融创新 [J]. 管理世界，37（2）：22-34，3.

胡景谱，陈凡，2024. 文明演进视阈下类人机器的变革图式 [J]. 自然辩证法通讯，46（4）：66-73.

何怀宏，2017. 何以为人 人将何为：人工智能的未来挑战 [J]. 探索与争鸣（10）：28-40.

何蒲，于戈，张岩峰，等，2017. 区块链技术与应用前瞻综述 [J]. 计算机科学，44（4）：1-7，15.

海巍，周霖，2017. 区块链技术视角下的保险运营模式研究 [J]. 保险研究（11）：92-102.

燕志雄，张敬卫，费方域，2016. 代理问题、风险基金性质与中小高科技企业融资

［J］．经济研究，51（9）：132-146.

袁勇，王飞跃，2016. 区块链技术发展现状与展望［J］．自动化学报，42（4）：481-494.

袁勇，倪晓春，曾帅，等，2018. 区块链共识算法的发展现状与展望［J］．自动化学报，44（11）：2011-2022.

金武，洪武，李涛，等，2017. 区块链技术发展现状及其金融应用研究［J］．海南金融（1）：26-30.

刘辛军，于靖军，王国彪，等，2016. 机器人研究进展与科学挑战［J］．中国科学基金，30（5）：425-431.

刘轶，董敏，2022. 区块链赋能下保险欺诈规制的路径优化［J］．江淮论坛（4）：69-74，182.

罗连发，储梦洁，刘俊俊，2019. 机器人的发展：中国与国际的比较［J］．宏观质量研究，7（3）：38-50.

李盾，张恩，王利利，2020. 区块链技术发展现状及前景探究［J］．中国管理信息化，23（20）：181-182.

刘银，2016."保险+基因检测"业务开展的研究［J］．呼伦贝尔学院学报，24（3）：44-49.

李绍芬，2015. 反应工程［M］．北京：化学工业出版社.

梅宏，2020. 大数据：发展现状与未来趋势［EB/OL］．（2019-10-31）［2024-04-25］.szzg.gov.cn/2019/szzg/lljyjl/201911/t20191101_4561019.html.

欧阳丽炜，王帅，袁勇，等，2019. 智能合约：架构及进展［J］．自动化学报，45（3）：445-457.

任晓明，王东浩，2013. 机器人的当代发展及其伦理问题初探［J］．自然辩证法研究，29（6）：113-118.

沈鹏，2023. 数字科技助力保险行业践行 ESG 理念［J］．中国信息界（6）：92-94.

孙毅，范灵俊，洪学海，2018. 区块链技术发展及应用：现状与挑战［J］．中国工程科学，20（2）：27-32.

唐金成，杜先培，2018. 论区块链技术在保险行业的应用［J］．西南金融（9）：58-64.

谭文君，董桂才，张斌儒，2018. 我国工业机器人行业的发展现状及启示［J］．宏观经济管理（4）：42-47.

陶思琦，2023. 人工智能技术的伦理问题及其治理研究［D］．沈阳：沈阳师范大学.

王金鑫，2013. 基因检测技术进步对我国人身保险的影响研究［D］．大连：东北财经大学.

王媛媛，2019. 保险科技如何重塑保险业发展［J］．金融经济学研究，34（6）：29-41.

完颜瑞云，锁凌燕，2019. 保险科技对保险业的影响研究［J］．保险研究（10）：35-46.

完颜瑞云，锁凌燕，陈滔，2022. 保险科技概论 [M]. 北京：高等教育出版社.

王波，2021. 试论我国保险业发展困境与区块链解决方案 [J]. 山西财政税务专科学校学报，23（6）：23-29.

王国军，2021. 保险科技赋能：全方位与全流程 [J]. 中国保险（3）：6-7.

夏后学，谭清美，白俊红，2019. 营商环境、企业寻租与市场创新：来自中国企业营商环境调查的经验证据 [J]. 经济研究，54（4）：84-98.

许闲，2017. 区块链与保险创新：机制、前景与挑战 [J]. 保险研究（5）：43-52.

许闲，2021. 赋能型的保险科技 [J]. 中国保险（3）：26-29.

许闲，2021. 颠覆型保险科技 [J]. 中国保险（6）：21-24.

修永春，2019. 区块链技术推动保险创新的路径研究 [J]. 人民论坛（36）：100-101.

郑嘉颖，2020. 基因信息在人身保险中的使用及其法律规制 [D]. 重庆：西南政法大学.

曾诗钦，霍如，黄韬，等，2020. 区块链技术研究综述：原理、进展与应用 [J]. 通信学报，41（1）：134-151.

朱进元、刘勇，魏丽. 保险科技 [M]. 北京：中信出版社.

周雷，蔡佩瑶，刘婧，2020. 我国保险科技发展现状、问题与对策：基于保险科技赋能高质量发展视角 [J]. 苏州市职业大学学报，31（2）：41-48.

周延礼，2017. 保险科技的应用现状和未来展望 [J]. 清华金融评论（12）：16-18.

A M, 1950. Turing computing machinery and intelligence [J]. Mind：433-460.

FUJITA M, KRUGMAN P, VENABLES A, 1999. The spatial economy：cities, regions, and international trade [M]. Cambridge：MIT Press.

MICHAEL P, 2008. The problem of private under-investment in innovation：a policy mind map [J]. Technovation, 28（8）：518530.

PRINCE AER, UHLMANN WR, SUTER SM, et al., 2021. Genetic testing and insurance implications：surveying the US general population about discrimination concerns and knowledge of the Genetic Information Nondiscrimination Act（GINA）[J]. Risk Manag Insur Rev., 24（4）：341-365.